The Authentic

*a guide to finding and buying traditional, organic
and fine foods direct from the maker and grower*

THE WRITE ANGLE PRESS • LONDON • STOKE

First published in Great Britain in 1998 by The Write Angle Press Limited
79 Pickford Lane, Bexleyheath DA7 4RW, UK

Copyright © 1998 The Write Angle Press Ltd

A catalogue record for this book is available from the British Library

ISBN 0 9520737 8 1

Designed and Typeset by The Write Angle Press
Printed by Crewe Colour Printers, Sandbach, England
Illustrations and cover: Richard Hull
Research: Irene Sheahan

Important Note: The Publishers have collected and printed the information that follows
in good faith and as such cannot accept any liability for loss, financial or otherwise, that
may occur resulting from any error or omission in this work. In addition, the appearance
of a firm's or individual's details in the listings does not imply an endorsement of their
products or imply in any way that the foods are specifically healthy or safe to eat –
in *every* case you, as customers, must satisfy yourself in this respect.

All such foods should be consumed as part of a balanced scheme of nutrition.

The Authentic Food Finder

C O N T E N T S

The Organic Option

Waitrose understands the
importance of the move
towards organic production
and is keen to ensure customers
enjoy the best possible range.
We have been stocking
organic products for 15 years,
and now sell over 250
organic lines with the range
constantly increasing.

WAITROSE
food shops of the John Lewis Partnership

Southern Industrial Area,
Bracknell, Berkshire RG12 8YA
Tel: 01344 424680

I N T R O D U C T I O N

Welcome to this, the first edition of The Authentic Food Finder.

The food scares of recent years have left us all nervous and inquiring as to what is in the food we eat, where it has come from and in the case of food of animal origin what the creature was fed on and what sort of life it lived before it came to our plate. The rise of the organic movement is, in no small part, a healthy response to such concerns.

Buying direct from the farmer, grower or maker of the foods also allows the consumer to satisfy themselves in many of these respects and have their questions and worries answered directly. This book has been designed to promote just such contact between food producers and consumers.

We have spent twelve months compiling this information about the firms – mostly small – from every point of the UK compass who can provide you directly with quality, often handmade foods and organically grown and reared produce for your table and kitchen. Many will serve you via a postal or courier service.

While every care has been taken in compiling these listings, errors can occur. In addition, the level of detail is such that inevitably it will become out of date. Thus we must stress that you should check all material facts directly with the firms concerned, particularly if you are committing money and time to visiting or dealing with them.

Please be sure to read the important note at the foot of page 2. It is repeated on the last page of the book.

ORGANIC CERTIFICATION UK 2

THIS SIGN IS YOUR ASSURANCE THAT THE FOOD YOU ARE BUYING IS

ORGANIC

and has been bred, grown, produced or processed by one of our members to the highest possible standards

Organic Farmers and Growers are certified under UKROFS to inspect and certify all producers and processers of organic produce and are registered under UKAS to carry out inspections under EN45011 Regulations

For more details about membership, inspections or organic produce please contact

Mr C Peers, Views Farm, Great Milton, Oxford, Oxfordshire OX9 7NW
Fax 01844 279362

PLACES

The entries in this book are ordered broadly according to tourist authority regions. England is subdivided into 10 regions. Northern Ireland is treated as a single region. The entries for Scotland all fall into one section, but within this are listed according to the Scottish Tourist Board's eight main regions (some of them combinations). Wales, too, appears as one section, but entries have been placed in North, West/Mid and South Wales.

Within any one area, entries are listed alphabetically by main postal town, which appears in bold type. Where there is more than one entry for a town, then these are listed alphabetically by name of business, these appearing in bold capitals.

BUSINESSES

Businesses that grow, produce and/or process original, traditional and organic foods and foodstuffs form the bulk of the entries throughout the book. Some concerns *only* sell their produce via mail order. These are listed in a single, separate section beginning on page 173. We have also received details from retailers who do not produce or make any foods themselves, but confine their activities to selling. These shops are listed at the end of each section, according to location.

Some main entries were received by us well after the last copy date: these are covered by small Stop Press groups, also printed at the end of the appropriate sections.

HOW TO FIND INFORMATION RAPIDLY

1 If you want to study the spread of products in a particular county/counties in England, turn to the index on page 8. This will guide you to the appropriate section (e.g. for Cornwall, see West Country).

2 If you want to concentrate on particular villages, towns, cities or isles, consult the **Index of Place Names** beginning on page 206. This will give you the exact page number(s) where outlets in those places are featured.

3 If you want to read the entry of a specific business, use the **Index by Business Name** beginning on page 201. It will tell you which page they are on. To help you further, if a business has an initialled name, it will be double-indexed (so, J. Roberts & Son will appear under 'J' and 'R').

4 If you are looking for all suppliers of a particular product, then use the **Index by Food Type** beginning on page 193. In the case of generic types, look first for the group, then the product, both alphabetically (so, for instance, 'Organic' and then 'Eggs' in the organics list). This index gives you every page reference for every product, except those that are so common they appear on every page anyway (examples of these are given at the head of this index).

STRUCTURE OF ENTRIES

Businesses throughout Great Britain and Northern Ireland were questionnaired and the information in this book is based on the forms subsequently submitted. Those listed have had the opportunity to check their entries for accuracy, though not style/format.

Standard entries were all entirely free of charge and we have neither sought nor accepted any payment for their basic inclusion. Some businesses chose to highlight their entry in bold type panels and they have paid for this service.

Inclusion in this book should not be deemed as any recommendation; our aim, as with our other titles, is to be as comprehensive as we can, without comment.

The first part of the entries, comprising name, address, telephone, fax, email, internet and contact name(s) is self explanatory.

As for the remainder, we have chosen not to use a range of symbols according to a legend, but to cover all useful information textually. We have endeavoured to be consistent throughout regarding the location of this detail.

WHERE TO FIND KEY POINTS

Under '**Produce**', the first listed items are those actually grown, made, processed, cooked or otherwise assembled by the company or firm. Any item(s) listed after the comment '**Also stock**' indicates that they originate from somewhere else.   (cont)

References have occasionally been made to certain standards, marques and third party organisations pertinent to the British food scene: explanatory notes on these can be found beginning on page 10.

After the product items, if they are available by mail order, courier or box scheme, it will say so. Any minimum order requirement or special terms will then be noted.

Under **'Prices/Payment'** you may find some sample prices (if relevant). It will also tell you which payment methods are generally acceptable.

Under **'Hours'** you will find the hours that each business is open to the public. Some businesses are not open to the public at all, in which case no hours are listed or it will say so. Others have very ad hoc arrangements and require contacting beforehand, this too being duly noted. *Where practicable, we recommend that you do this anyway.*

'Notes': the first reference will tell you (when appropriate) if there is disabled access. There then follows a list of any other attractions/features actually on site or immediately adjacent.

If the business regularly supplies its produce to outlets which may be closer to you, these are named in this section.

Finally, businesses have been asked to state if they are interested in supplying to hotels, restaurants and the trade (the term 'trade' is used as a shorthand in this respect).

The information given for mail order only establishments and for shops confines itself to relevant details only.

All the information given in this book has been submitted by the businesses and organisations listed and has been accepted in good faith. We cannot under any circumstances accept any liability for loss, financial or otherwise, that may occur from any error, omission or any other aspect of this work.

If you have any queries about specific information, please use the details to contact the company or firm direct... and, please, if you know of any business that you think may be eligible to be listed and which does not appear, let us know about them or ask them to contact us direct, so that they can be considered for inclusion in our next edition.

INDEX OF ENGLISH COUNTIES, METROPOLITAN AREAS & ISLES

The Authentic Food Finder

GOES LIVE

we are now planning an exciting series of road show
events for 1999 where you can meet, see and
sample the wares of the producers, growers
and makers that you'll find in our book

staged at prestigious stately homes, major
equestrian events and agricultural shows around
the UK throughout the summer and autumn season
Authentic Food Finder live shows are for those who know
and need to try the best
join us
for ticket details write to
*Authentic Food Finder Live, 79 Pickford Lane,
Bexleyheath, Kent DA7 4RW*

exhibitors please 'phone 0181 298 0234 for brochure and costs

G L O S S A R Y

We certainly don't wish to be teaching our granny to suck eggs here but the following is a simple glossary of terms and additional explanations of some ideas, movements and concepts that seem to be current in the food industry at present. Most are items that are mentioned in the individual entries for the various producers that we list in the later geographically arranged sections.

Asparagus: This may precipitate an international incident but asparagus has really got to be English. At first sight these frankly stocky spears might suggest that they have remained uncut for too long and thus may prove to be tough when compared with their continental counterparts but don't be fooled, these broad shoots are succulent and full of the most delicate flavour and in our experience never tending to the bitterness which can occur in imported spears. The season is sadly short, perhaps only eight weeks in May to July, as beyond that time subsequent shoots must be allowed to grow out into fern to ensure a vigorous growth in the following year.

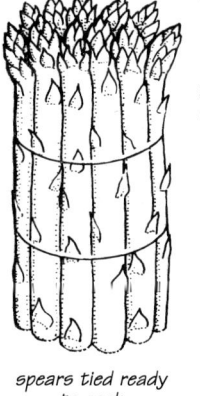

spears tied ready to cook

Biltong: not something out of the Goon Show but a dried beef of South African origin.

Black pudding: A traditional sausage made from pig's blood mixed with oatmeal and lard and stuffed into a casing made from the pig's intestine, mm - nice.

Box schemes: This describes the expanding practice of, mainly organic farmers, distributing their produce by putting together boxes of largely fruit and vegetables for a local circle of customers to whom they deliver. Often prices are set for say a small, medium and large box

and the grower puts together the appropriate produce from what is in season and available. This is done on a weekly basis and delivered often to the customer's home but also to central collection points to which customers go to pick up. For the growers it has the advantage of a known sales base for their produce and builds a close relationship with their buyers. However, careful and time consuming organisation is needed to deal with individual requirements. For customers the advantage is having fresh organic produce direct from the farm (and a farm they know) with consequent economy.

There are however some problems. While it is possible to exclude stuff you don't like, the customer has not always been able to order specific items and indeed you may not know what is going to be in the box and in what quantities until it arrives – making meal planning a bit difficult. In our (perhaps bad) experience box schemes are good as far as they go but choice has been a problem and the box may well need to be supplemented by a run to a supermarket or greengrocer for anything specific or exotic.

Having said this and to be fair, box schemes are developing rapidly and are addressing these problems of choice and variety. Some, as our listings show are now extending themselves to a wide range of non veg and even non food items – most useful in rural areas affected by the disappearance of the village shop. A few careful questions, however, of the scheme organiser in your area should soon reveal which fits in with your life and kitchen style and the level of choice that you feel happy with.

Brack: a tea bread often served with butter and preserves.

Cheese: see rennet

Couverture: The proper name for genuine cocoa butter based chocolate. This will be the basis for high quality hand made chocolates.

Curing: After slaughter the traditional curing of bacon involved the sides or flitches of bacon being rubbed in salt, laid in tubs of brine and periodically turned and resalted. After a month or so they would be hung to dry, probably in the farmhouse kitchen, before being smoked in the chimney over a fire of wood shavings and sawdust. In fact it would have been partly the natural impurities in the salt then used (the nitrites and nitrates) that allowed bacon to be cured in this way to keep for many months – indeed probably right through the winter. When bacon curing left the farm during the last century these salts – saltpetre in particular – were deliberately added in the curing process.

This process is still broadly what happens today with butchers who are producing what is described in our listings as "**home-cure**" or "**dry-cure**" being a parallel process but the meat is not immersed in brine and instead the salts are rubbed into bacon. Bacon may be sold as either "green" or "smoked".

The more modern method of "wet cure" or "**brine cure**" involves the sides of bacon being injected with a brine of the curing salts. This results in a more even level of cure through the meat and it reduces the salting time from a few weeks to just a few days. Of course the "wet-cure" has been favoured by industry for the simple reason that the injection with the water based brine adds to the weight of the consequent joints of bacon, increasing their value. The white specks that appear during the cooking of such bacon are the salts coagulating as the moisture is driven off.

Demeter Standards: Are the standards set out by The Bio-Dynamic Agricultural Association for farms to qualify to become members of this particular organic farming grouping. (See also Organic). Demeter was in fact the Greek Goddess of farming. The philosophy of the association, set up in 1929, is far reaching, seeing the whole earth as a living organism and each farm as a self sustaining, balanced unique individuality within it. These were ideas set out by the Austrian philosopher and scientist Rudolf Steiner in the mid twenties (he also had some interesting theories on education).

In general, a biodynamic farm is a mixed farm aiming for a balance of animals and crops and benign methods of pest and disease control. Such farms are largely self sustaining and depend upon their own resources for manures and feed stuffs. Recycling figures strongly in the process. The aim is then a far reaching and philosophical one of the farm harmonising and benefiting its environment rather than exploiting it.

Such farms are implicitly organic and do not use artificial fertilizers or chemicals in growing or rearing, or preservatives in the processing of their products. Farms can only be certified as operating to Demeter standards after three years of running a bio-dynamic system and they also have to be  inspected on an annual basis to ensure continued compliance. More information can be obtained from: **The Bio-Dynamic Agricultural Association, Rudolf Steiner House, 35 Park Road, London NW1 6XT.**

Eggs: It seems strange that a food item so universally recognizable as the humble egg is in fact so plagued by definitions needed to explain the nature of eggs that have been laid under widely differing circumstances. So even without the hyperbole of the supermarkets and packers we have the following quite different terms: Free Range, Semi-Intensive, Deep Litter, Perchery or Barn Eggs and finally Eggs from Caged Hens. There are minimum production criteria for all of these, defined by regulation EEC1274/91 and implemented by **MAFF**.

A **free range egg** will have been laid by a hen that has continuous daytime access to open air runs that are mainly covered with vegetation. The hens will be kept at a density of no greater than one hen per 10 square metres. A **semi-intensive egg** will however be from a hen where the flock density is not greater than one per 2.5 square metres. **Deep litter hens** are kept indoors only, at an overall density of no greater than 7 hens per square metre with at least one third of the floor space covered with litter material such as straw or wood shavings. The deceptively sounding **perchery or barn Egg**, with its shades of a rural idyll, neverthe-less allows a density of up to 25 birds per square metre in a building with a minimum of 150mm of perch space each. Free range and semi-intensive production also both require built shelter for the birds which would comply with the deep litter or perchery rules. At potentially higher densities there is the production of **eggs from caged hens** where a battery system of cages that may be stacked one on top of the other is permitted.

In addition, the seven grades of egg sizes have changed over the last year and now we have a simpler four-grade system – XL (73 grams and over), L (63 to 72 grams), M (53 to 62 grams) and S (below 53 grams).

Most authentic food seekers will look no further than the free range eggs but here too the situation is not without its minor complications. The RSPCA's **Freedom Food** standards (see also that heading) have a further layer of animal welfare considerations that come into play to qualify for their accolade on the box. In addition, the main Organic Associations are not entirely in agreement as to the exact minimum standards which constitute an organic free range egg. Then, of course, you have a maverick like Martin Pitt (see page 118) who, while he is not registered with Freedom Food and does not have full organic status, has built an excellent reputation for producing fine eggs from the most humane conditions for his hens.

Flour: This may seem to verge on the technical but the wheat grain has three parts – the outside husk or bran, the endosperm in the centre and the kernel or wheat germ that would sprout into the plant. We tell you this because the various tags that get attached to flour relate in large measure to what happens to these parts of the grain in the milling process. In basic terms, the outer bran is an important source of dietary fibre – it probably represents less than 20% of the grain. The wheat germ is about 3% of the grain but it is a concentrated source of minerals and vitamins. The remaining part of the grain, the endosperm, is mainly starch with some protein.

At first there may seem to be a bewilder-ing array of terms associated with flour and the breads made from them. At the simplest level there is a difference between wholemeal and white flour – wholemeal is flour milled to include 100% of the grain with all its fibre, wheat germ and endosperms while white flour is produced from the starchy endosperms only. Obviously wholemeal flour, which will naturally be brown, has the superior nutritional value. Freshly milled white flour will in fact be creamy in colour and manufacturers have for many years bleached it to produce the superfine pearly white flour we find on supermarket shelves. The separation of the vitamin bearing part of the grain has also required fortifying flour with chemically produced vitamins and minerals.

Stoneground flour usually refers to flour prepared in the traditional way of grinding between stones rather than rollers. We list a number of millers who prepare their flour in this way often using wind or water power for their mills. In these cases the flour is of course wholemeal. **Granary flour** is a specific type of wholemeal to which malted wheat or other grains are added back.

Strong flour – or strong white is a particular milling that is high in protein and which will give volume in bread making. **Organic flour** – not surprisingly, a flour produced from a crop of grain organically grown and milled in accordance with the specific procedures set down by one of the Organic bodies (see Organic). **Beremeal** – a wholemeal flour milled from barley. **Peasemeal** – a traditional flour milled from roasted peas and used in Scotland to make a type of porridge.

Freedom Food: In 1994 the RSPCA set up this farm animal welfare monitoring and labelling scheme. Essentially, a set of standards were established which would ensure a minimum level of care for animals reared for food. If a farm, haulier or abattoir meet these standards when they are inspected they can then advertise the fact that they have reached this standard of welfare for stock under their care and display the distinctive blue Freedom Food logo. To carry the logo on a finished food product, all stages of the animal's life (and in the case of meat animals, their eventual slaughter) will have been protected by this welfare code.

Essentially, the five basic areas the standards are directed toward should permit animals to have freedom from: **1**) fear and distress; **2**) pain, injury and disease; **3**) hunger and thirst; **4**) discomfort; as well as **5**) the ability to express their normal behaviour. The launch of the scheme coincided with a time of rising public concern not only about animal welfare itself but the food safety aspects related to it. As a result, an initial membership of around 120 has grown to around 3,500 and the number of participating food stores has grown over ten fold to 4000. More information on Freedom Food can be obtained by 'phoning the **RSPCA** on **01403 223284**.

Gluten free: Gluten is a naturally occurring protein found in varying quantities in cereal products. There are certain medical conditions which result in a sensitivity to gluten in foods – and it is a surprisingly wide range of processed products. While it is possible to eat a healthy gluten free diet, the problem area is with fibre for most of our dietary fibre comes from cereals. Most good health food shops, however, do now carry a range of gluten free foods including even special breads. A gluten free diet does take care but advice can be obtained from **The Coeliac Society at PO Box 220, High Wycombe, Bucks HP11 2HY** or from **The Juvela Nutrition Centre** at **100 Wavetree Boulevard, Liverpool L7 9PT.**

GMOs: or genetically modified organisms; also referred to as a genetically modified food. To add resistance to disease and give increased yields, scientists have for many years been looking at modifying the genetics of plants and now animals. There has indeed been much publicity surrounding the humble soya bean in this respect as genetically modified versions from the USA are being used in processed foods made in the UK. Soya, or its derivatives, are present in approximately 60% of processed foods such as chocolate, bread, baby foods and beer.

The jury is probably still out on whether or not genetically modified foods can be directly harmful to humans. It does seem however that the general public are profoundly suspicious of them and earlier this year the Iceland Group very publicly stole a march on its rivals by announcing that none of their own brand products would contain GMOs. The potential for ecological disruption attached to the introduction of such animals and plants into the food chain does appear to be much more defined and a government moratorium has been proposed on the licensing of GMO technology to allow further investigation of these aspects. Our listings contain a number of companies who tell us that their products are GMO free.

Gnash: a blend of pure chocolate (see Couverture) and cream that is used as a filling – not as a coating or shell – in handmade chocolate making.

Haggis: This famous Scottish delicacy is essentially a sausage. It is round rather than cylindrical however for, historically, the filling is put into the belly or maw of the sheep rather than the intestine. Although MacSweens of Edinburgh have a wonderful variety of fillings – including a vegetarian version – the traditional haggis is filled with a mixture of oatmeal, suet, chopped liver and seasoning.

Haslet: is in the same area being a traditional sausage meat loaf which is wrapped around in a fatty, lacey membrane, a caul, and then roasted.

Hogs pudding: see white pudding.

Hog, Hogg or Hogget: not pork but sheep meat from animals older than lambs but slaughtered before they reach the age to produce wool.

In conversion: a term usually referring to a farm or land which is in the two year period of transition before it can be inspected for final approval as an organic farm. The term has no legal standing but is commonly used by farms who are in exactly that process of converting their farm to full Organic production (see also Organic).

Jerusalem artichoke: Enthusiasts will know, of course, that there are two entirely distinct vegetables which have the same name – but remembering which is which is always the problem. The Globe Artichoke is in fact the flower of a thistle like plant and both its heart and the base of the flower's scale like petals can be eaten. After boiling these great flower heads in water and lemon juice for forty or fifty minutes both parts are delicious served with either a simple Vinaigrette or a Hollandaise Sauce. On the other hand the Jerusalem Artichoke – which incidentally has no connection whatever with Israel – is the tuber of a tall growing plant of the Sunflower family. Indeed, it is more likely that the Italian name for such plants – girasole – has become corrupted into the modern name. The knobbly brown tubers – that look a bit like root ginger – are best cooked in similar ways to potatoes but once again lemon juice is an essential, for when peeled the creamy white flesh discolours rapidly. It has to be said that this innocent looking root vegetable does carry with it a severe flatulence warning: incidentally, a well known gardening text asserts that ...."in summer, a row of Jerusalem Artichokes makes an effective and attractive windbreak...".

Kentish Cobs: are a hybrid of the hazel nut first raised by a Mr Lambert of Goudhurst, Kent in the first quarter of the last century. They appear in the shops in September or October complete with their distinctive leafy covering to the nuts.

Kosher: The dietary laws of the Jewish Faith are both complicated and fascinating. It is of course beyond our remit to attempt to explain them. However, the symbol that is seen (above right) may be encountered, for example on food packaging, where the food contained is suitable for consumption for those following these Kosher rules with regard to their diet. In short, for this logo to be carried, the food producer using it must have been signatory to a lengthy contract which binds them to ingredients, suppliers and making methods approved by the **UK Beth Din** (the Rabbinical

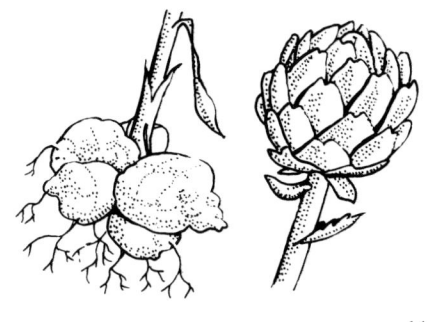

authority in this respect). They will also be subject to periodic Rabbinical inspection. This symbol will guarantee that the food is Kosher.

For more detailed information on Kosher Foods and their availability throughout the UK **The Really Jewish Food Guide** (£6.95) which is available from **United Synagogue Publications, 735 High Road, London N12 0US** is excellent.

Koulibiac: A fish pie of Russian origin eaten on festive occasions, being very colourful when cut open.

Licensed Game Dealer: A quaint piece of legislation – probably aimed originally at combating poaching – The Game Dealers Act of 1831 is still in force in respect of dealers in w*ild* rabbits, hares, partridges, pheasants, grouse and the like. Today the Licensing Department of Local Authorities actually deal with such matters, although with reference to aspects of environmental health rather than the honesty or otherwise of the applicants as might once have been the case.

Lyegrano: a strong flavoured hard cheese which is being described as the English Parmesan.

Macrobiotic: A diet followed for philosophical reasons which aims to maintain a balance between foods – the Yin (positive) or Yang (negative). For the purist, the diet progresses through ten levels becoming increasingly restrictiñve with the 'higher' levels eliminating even fruits and vegetables until the level of a brown rice diet is reached.

MAFF: Ministry of Agriculture, Fisheries and Food.

Mutton: the young may forget that this is the meat of a sheep – not a lamb but a full grown animal that will also have been shorn. At one time looked down upon – as in the phrase "mutton dressed as lamb"

– mutton has in recent years undergone something of a revival in interest for its stronger and mature flavour. See also Hog, Hogg, Hogget.

Nasturtium flowers: The orange flowers of this common trailing plant are picked for use in salads. Oddly, the plant is related to water-cress.

Organic: While it may appear to be a word that is bandied about with some freedom it does have a very defined meaning and it is an offence of interest to a Trading Standards Office to name a product as such if it does not meet the appropriate standards. To carry one of the organic symbols that are shown here, which confirms a product as organic, it must have conformed to the standards set down by the **UK Register of Organic Food Standards (UKROFS)** which is part of MAFF, at each step along the line of production – farmer, processer, packer, haulier and retailer.

Various bodies have been approved by government in addition to UKROFS themselves to inspect and annually certify all those stages as complying with the standards – these bodies are **Organic Farmers and Growers, Organic Food Federation, Bio-**

Dynamic Agricultural Association (see page 11 for the Demeter logo of the Bio-Dynamic Agricultural Association), **Scottish Organic Producers Association (SOPA), Irish Organic Farmers and Growers Association (IOFGA)** and the **The Soil Association**. The appearance of these symbols on imported goods will also mean that they too have been produced to organic standards.

In broad terms, Organic farming does not use or rely upon chemical fertilisers or pesticides but instead depends upon the development of an overall system for the farm that builds a healthy, fertile soil and keeps pests in control by nurturing wildlife as natural predators. An interplay of stock and crop rotation is at the core of building this balance of sustainable fertility. Animals are reared without the use of drugs such as antibiotics or preparations for worming. Jonathon Porritt – who is a patron of The Soil Association and noted environmental campaigner – probably best sets out the mission statement for organic farming as follows: "Sustainable agriculture is a form of food production which builds soil fertility, protects biodiversity and provides people with wholesome healthy food for all time".

Interest has slowly been growing in Organic food. The public, particularly over recent years, have become very concerned with the safety of what they are eating not only in the context of big type scares such as BSE and Salmonella but on the smaller scale of chemicals, additives, pesticides, antibiotics, growth promoters and the like that are routinely used in main-stream food production. The concern being that traces of such chemicals appear in the food we eat. One only has to stop to consider the two dozen or so applications of fungicide, herbicide, insecticide et al that waft around the average apple or pear during its life to see that anyone who is worried about this has got a point. While fear might be the big motivater, the eating quality and in particular taste of organic food has got to run it a close second, for the most common remark when people do munch into, say an organic mushroom, is

"Mmm just like they used to be when I was a kid". We think this is so right across a range of organic produce that we have sampled over the last year and in general the standard of organic food – in particular vegetables – is getting better all th time.

For more detailed background, Lynda Brown's book **"The Shopper's Guide to Organic Food"** (Fourth Estate £7.99) is excellent.

Oysters: Most oysters that are now eaten in the UK are of the cultivated Pacific type while the native flat oyster is, due to a combination of recent years of adverse weather and marine pollution, not so commonly found. The Pacific Oyster (below left) needs a little help with breeding as it will not normally reproduce in the cooler waters surrounding the UK and so begins life in a tank where a breeding stock of oysters is brought into a reproductive phase in warm algae-rich water. Once the oysters have spawned, the microscopic larvae are separated off into another tank with the right balance of sperm and eggs. The consequent fertilisation brings forward the 'spat'

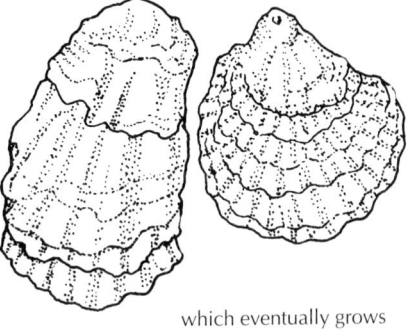

which eventually grows on into being the oyster. The young oysters go through a toughening up process in cooler water before they are transferred to a lagoon-fed nursery and eventually into bags on oyster beds at sea for growing on to maturity – a process that takes upward of three years.

The flat native oyster is gradually making a comeback as seas become cleaner and hatcheries more expert in handling their different breeding pattern. The old adage that you should only eat oysters when there is an 'R' in the month is quite true for the flat oyster as it holds its young inside its shell during the summer months. The native oyster takes about five years to come to market size. **The Seasalter Shellfish (Whitstable) Ltd on 01227 272003** always seem happy to provide information about this fascinating fruit of the sea.

Peel: the long handled flat spade-like implement used by bakers to manoeuvre loaves in and out of the oven.

P Y O: Quite simply "pick your own".

Q The Guild of Q Butchers: was established by the Meat and Livestock Commission as an initiative to establish and raise standards in butchery. The Guild tell us that only those butchers who adhere to a strict set of membership criteria which includes high standards in product quality, hygiene and service and who pass independent and spot checks are able to advertise themselves as members of The Guild of Q Butchers. The Q stands for the word quality.

Rare Breeds: The last fifty years have seen, largely as a result of successive government policies aimed at cheap food, a vast expansion and intensification in agriculture. Measurements of success for very many years have been in terms of more tons per acre in arable, gallons of milk per cow in dairy, eggs per hen in poultry and weight and speed of weight gain in meat production. In the simplest terms more and more, quicker and quicker. In respect of animal husbandry

the holy grail of higher yields has been pursued in two major ways. Firstly through intensive methods of rearing which have concentrated on the type of factory methods which have become the object of growing disgust from the animal lobby – hens in cages, pigs in confined metal pens on slatted floors, calves reared in crates and similar methods all in general depriving the animals of what might be described as their normal pattern of life. Such intensification, with animals in such confined spaces, has brought with it other problems requiring further physical manipulations – the removal of beaks, tails and horns becoming normal practice.

In addition, the incidence of illness in herds kept in these conditions and proximity has increased dramatically the risk of and potential economic loss due to disease. The response to this has been the use of preemptive antibiotics, i.e. dosing stock with such preparations on a routine basis, often within proprietary feeds, with the intention of stopping infection before it is able to take hold. In addition, animals reared for meat have been dosed in feeds with growth promoting hormones – the objective being to bring animals more quickly to slaughter. There has been much public concern in recent times over the possible presence of residues of these various chemicals within both meat and dairy products.

A second way that this objective of 'more, quicker' has been followed has been by the careful selection or rather deselection of breeds of animals used in this intensive process. Selective breeding and cross breeding to bring favourable characteristics into play has produced the hybridised animals that are commonly found on

farms today. It has also to be said that the influence of the buyer from the big supermarkets has also played a part with their demand for uniformity, be it in cuts of meat or egg size and colour.

The breeds of animals that would have been commonly found in our countryside even fifty years ago are now only likely to be encountered in the specialist sections at one of the major agricultural shows or at an exhibit put together by the **Rare Breeds Survival Trust**. This phenomenon of breed disappearance was first addressed in the 1970s by a group of farmers, breeders and other enthusiasts who formed themselves into the Rare Breeds Survival Trust with the objective of halting this decline. Their motivations were at one and the same time emotional – wishing to see old breeds live on in our landscape – but also hard headed and economic for these breeds also represented a varied pool of genetic material upon which future generations might need to draw as economic or even climatic conditions change.

While regarded as eccentric twenty-five years ago, the rare breed movement has of more recent times come increasingly into its own. Public distress with the excesses of commercial animal husbandry came very much to a head in the publicity surrounding the BSE crisis and has resulted in a demand for both meat and dairy produce from animals that have not been intensively reared, not treated with growth promoters or antibiotics and which, in the public perception, have had a 'natural' existence. An increasing level of media attention has made many aware that products from such non-intensive rearing taste better. Farms that have been working with rare breed herds in this way have, we are told, been all but besieged by butchers looking for Tamworth or Middle White bacon, Park White or Red Poll beef and Soay or Balwen lamb to satisfy customer requests. While there may seem to be a contradiction here, the Rare Breeds Survival Trust welcome this interest for they see the continued survival of endangered breeds in the long run as being largely dependent on them becoming commercially successful once again rather than upon dwindling numbers in zoos and recreational farms.

Rennet: Milk, if not used promptly, will curdle and break down into curds (the semi-solid bit) and whey (the fluid). The curd is the part that is used to make cheese. In a dairy, cheese making is more structured and the milk is broken down to its solid by the addition of rennin. Rennin is an enzyme often obtained from the fourth stomach of young calves and is employed in a brine type extract more commonly called a rennet.

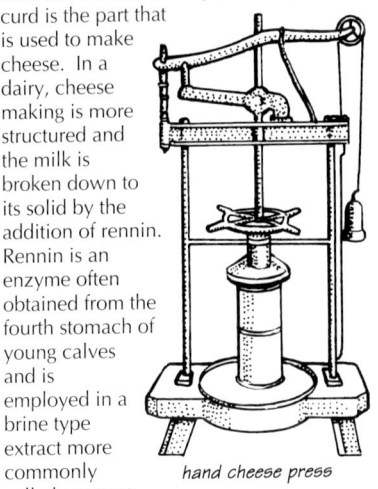

hand cheese press

It is also used in the domestic kitchen to make junket. Non animal based rennet has been available for many years and has been used in the preparation of vegetarian cheese. The requirements for the production of certified organic cheese in this country means that similar rennets have to be used for these cheeses so organic cheese will also be suitable for vegetarians.

Rheas: The generic term for Ostrich · breeds. Interest in Ostrich meat has also grown in recent years and aside from some bad publicity connected with investment in Ostrich farms, the meat has claims to be low in fat and of excellent flavour.

Smoking: The public taste for smoked foods is another growth area. Over perhaps the last five years a much wider range of foods than the traditional kippers and smoked salmon has become readily available – cheeses, butter, poultry, game, meats of all types and even nuts.

Smoking was originally a method of curing and preserving food and so smoked foods have also become, as our listings will testify, the favourite of mail order food concerns. The taste has developed to such a degree that ovens for do it yourself home smoking are often advertised in foodie magazines.

Fish smoking however predominates. When the fish have been filleted, gutted or split they are placed in brine or rubbed with salt after and afterwards hung up to dry before being smoked over a smouldering mixture of wood chips and sawdust. The majority of fish smoked in the UK are "cold smoked" meaning that the temperature does not go above 85°F and the meat of the fish remains raw although becoming flavoured and impregnated with the smoke while it dries out. Smoked Salmon is probably the most famous of today's cold smoked fishes but Kippers and Finnan Haddock are also from this process.

By contrast, "hot smoking" allows the temperature to rise by another 100°F with the result that the fish are actually cooked as well being flavoured with the smoke. Arbroath Smokies are the best known example of hot smoking – starting their life as haddock. Eel is also produced by this process being one of the most expensive of the smoked fishes but with much of it going for export – the Dutch have apparently acquired a strong taste for it.

The wood chips and sawdust that are used to form the smoking mixture are best if they are hardwoods like beech, oak or fruit woods while hickory is an American favourite. Soft woods are too resinous, giving a bitter flavour and depositing a film of tar upon the food. Not authentic are the artificial smoked flavours produced by the use of dips and coatings applied to the food without the use of any smoke at all.

Tablet: A type of Scottish toffee.

Tracklements: A general term referring to mustards, sauces, pickles and jellies.

Turkeys: While supermarkets have been fighting it out on the single battleground of price during December, others have been looking more closely at the quality and taste that these often ridiculously cheap price levels have brought with them. The frozen mass market offerings have certainly been found wanting in the taste and texture department. Food writers have for some while now been extolling the virtues of the fresh, free range turkey and in particular the qualities of old breeds of the bird such as the **Bronze** and the **Norfolk Black**. These, when allowed to grow slowly to maturity, do not produce birds of great size in comparison with those favoured by intensive rearing operations but do produce meat of excellent eating quality.

This quality end of the market is represented by the **Traditional Farmfresh Turkey Association** and thus the description "**Farmfresh**" when applied to a turkey does have a very specific meaning. The TFTA has set down its own welfare and rearing code to which its members must comply to sell produce under their banner. Essentially this code results in slow matured birds, raised without growth promoters or antibiotics that are farm slaughtered, dry

a bronze

plucked and hung for a minimum of seven days before onward movement to the customer. Most mass market turkeys are wet plucked after slaughter, ie: dipped into hot water to allow the easy removal of the feathers by machine without the tearing of what is on these birds fairly young flesh. Dry plucking is generally thought to be the superior and more hygienic method.

Vegetarian: We were kindly provided with this definition by the Vegetarian Society – "A vegetarian is someone living on a diet of grains, pulses, nuts, seeds, vegetables and fruits with or without the use of dairy products and eggs. A vegetarian does not eat any meat, poultry, game, fish, shellfish or crustacea or slaughter by-products such as gelatine, or animal fats". A Vegan does not eat dairy products, eggs or indeed eat or use any other animal product. A fruitarian diet consists mainly of raw fruit, grains and nuts as they believe that only foods that can be harvested without killing the plant should be eaten. The Vegetarian Society endorse food products that conform to their definitions, including those that contain eggs if those eggs come from a guaranteed free range source.

Vegetarian approved animal foods: At first sight it appears to be an anomaly for meat producers, for example, that we list to draw attention to the fact that their stock has been raised on a feed approved by the Vegetarian Society. Why should this be a concern to their customers if the animals are going for meat products in any case ? Essentially these feeds contain no products whatever of animal origin. Fears in this respect were, of course, brought into focus during the BSE crisis when it came widely to public understanding that animal feeds often did contain "recycled animals" – a practice which has now been banned. Animal feeds approved by the Vegetarian Society however are in addition not permitted to contain any fats of animal origin or vitamin additions in gelatine coatings and, from next year, any products that have been genetically modified.

White pudding: similar to a black pudding but without the blood. These are usually produced in a ring but are light brown in colour and while recipes vary the basis is oatmeal, pork fat plus some minced pork and plenty of pepper. Hogs pudding – a traditional West Country dish – is similar but appears as a monster straight sausage.

Zucchini Flowers: The bright yellow flowers of the courgette or marrow plant that are picked and used as a colourful addition to salads – and of course give a 'Z' to make a colourful finish to this glossary.

THORNBY MOOR DAIRY
Crofton Hall
Thursby
Carlisle
CA5 6QB
Tel: 016973 45555
Fax: 016973 45555
Contact: Carolyn & Leonie Fairbairn
Produce: Traditionally made hard, ripening and soft cheeses. Made using unpasteurised goat's and shorthorn cow's milk. They source their milk from single herds (one goat, one cow) within two miles of the dairy. Every effort is made to employ traditional practices including maturing all the cheeses in cloth. Also stock Rosebud preserves, Cumberland mustard, local honey, apple juices, Cartmel Village Shop sticky toffee sauce. Cheese boards/ knives. Also available are Thornby Moor's own free range eggs (hen, duck and goose). Mail Order available. No min. order charge.
Prices/Payment: Cumberland (cow's) farmhouse from £4.10 per lb. Allerdale (goat's), from £4.40 per lb. Cash and cheques only.
Hours: Mon-Fri, 9am-5.30pm. Sat, 10am-5.15pm.
Notes: Disabled access. Cheese making area is visible through a window. Customers are encouraged to sample prior to purchase. All shop staff are trained cheesemakers. Thornby Moor Dairy supply to; Low Sizergh Barn Shop, J & J Grahams, Cheese Shop (Chester) and Oxford Cheese Co. (covered market Oxford).

THE GINGERBREAD SHOP
Grasmere
LA22 9SW
Tel: 01539 435428
Fax: 01539 435155
Contact: G Wilson
Produce: Grasmere gingerbread, prepared and baked to 130 years old recipe. Baked freshly each day. A specialist confectionery made and sold only on the premises. Cumberland rum butter, made to an old traditional recipe, originally made as a spread for christening teas. Baking takes place every day. Also stock preserves, lemon cheese, honey, mint cake, home-made truffles and fudge. Mail Order available. Min order half a pound.
Prices/Payment: Cash and cheques only.
Hours: Mon-Sat, 9.15am-5.30pm. Sun, 12.30pm-5.30pm.
Notes: Disabled access is possible.

ENGLISH ICE CREAM
Gipsy Well
The Banks
Staveley
Kendal
LA8 9NE
Tel: 01539 821562
Contact: Colin English
Produce: Real ice creams and sorbets, using the proper ingredients, i.e. fresh eggs, whole fresh milk, cane sugar, fresh fruits, etc.
Prices/Payment: Average price £5.80, per 2 ltrs champagne, pink champagne £8.50 per 2 ltrs. Cash and cheques only.
Hours: Seven days a week, 9am-5pm. Please always 'phone in advance.
Notes: Most of English Ice Cream's business is to hotels and restaurants, much made to order.

LOW SIZERGH BARN FARMSHOP
Sizergh
Kendal
LA8 8AE
Tel: 015395 60426
Fax: 015395 61475
Contact: Alison Park
Produce: Milk and cream pasteurised and bottled from their own dairy herd; free range eggs (dairy herd and hens certified by RSPCA Freedom Foods). PYO and ready picked strawberries in season; strawberry

jam, damson jam and seville orange marmalade. Traditional home-baked cakes, Borrowdale Tea Bread, carrot cake, lemon cake and Victoria sandwich cake. Also stock farmhouse and traditional cheese, local meat & game, vegetables, preserves and specialist foods. Organic box scheme available. Mail Order available for hampers and cheese on request. No min order charge.
Prices/Payment: Mastercard, Visa, Solo and Switch taken.
Hours: Daily 9am-5.30pm. Jan-Easter 9.30am-5pm. Closed on Monday.
Notes: No disabled access. Tea room, with viewing window to watch the milking every afternoon.

BRYSON'S OF KESWICK
42 Main Street
Keswick
CA12 5JD
Tel: 017687 72257
Fax: 017687 75456
Contact. Paul Carter
Produce: A craft bakery producing bread, cakes and confectionery, using traditional methods and no artificial preservatives. Rich English fruit cakes including fruit, fruit & nut, Simnel, Dundee, cherry slab, Madeira slab and Christmas cake. Mail Order available. Telephone, fax or freepost.
Prices/Payment: All major credit cards. No Switch.
Hours: Easter to December, 8.30am-5.30pm seven days a week. Rest of year, six days.
Notes: Disabled access to retail shop; the attached tearoom has stairs. Other shops in Cockermouth and Ambleside. Bryson's supply locally to the trade.

RICHARD WOODALL
Lane End
Waberthwaite
Millom
LA19 5YJ
Tel: 01229 717237/386
Fax: 01229 717007

Contact: Richard or Colin Woodall
Produce: High quality Cumberland sausage (for which they have a Royal Warrant to supply Her Majesty The Queen). Dry cured Cumberland bacon, dry cured Cumberland ham, Cumbria air dried ham, Cumbria mature royal ham. Also stock general groceries, pickles and preserves. Mail Order available. Please 'phone for leaflet. No min order charge.
Prices/Payment: Sausage, £1.90 per lb. Bacon, £2.69 per lb, smoked bacon £2.95 per lb. Whole Cumberland ham approx. 17 lb @ £3.15 per lb. Visa, Mastercard, Eurocard and Access taken. Not Switch.
Hours: Mon-Fri, 8.30am-5.30pm, closed for lunch, 12.15pm-1.15pm. Sat, 8.30am-12pm.
Notes: No disabled access. Richard Woodall supply to numerous outlets; please 'phone for list of stockists. They are interested in supplying more to the trade.

KENNEDYS FINE CHOCOLATES LTD
The Old School
Orton
Penrith
CA10 3RU
Tel: 015396 24781
Fax: 015396 24781
Email:
Kennedys.Chocolates@btinternet.com
Internet: www.btinternet.com/~chocolates
Contact: David Kennedy
Produce: A large selection of chocolates; sixty varieties to choose from including violet creme, champagne truffle and whisky and ginger. Other specialities include Orange Peel Dark (candied orange peel covered in plain chocolate), Florentine Dark (plain chocolate with fruit and nuts) and Turkish Delight both milk and plain. Available by Mail Order by First Class post. Standard or Fancy boxes , enclose

your own greeting card if required. Make your own selection and choose delivery date. Min order 4oz. Also stock; Thursday Cottage (jams) Wiltshire Tracklements, The Toffee Shop (fudge & toffee), The Best of Taste Co. (fruit compotes), Cumberland Mustard, Duskin Farm apple juice.
Prices/Payment: From £6.50 per 4oz to £105 per 6 lb box. Visa, Delta and Mastercard taken.
Hours: Mon-Sat, 9am-5.30pm. Sun and Public Holidays 11am-5pm. (Closed Xmas Day, Boxing Day and New Years Day).
Notes: Disabled access. Coffee house and ice cream parlour.

LITTLE SALKELD WATERMILL
Little Salkeld
Penrith
CA10 1NN
Tel: 01768 881523
Email: njbj@aol.com
Internet: www.cumbria.com/watermill/
Contact: Nick or Ana Jones
Produce: Organic stoneground flours. Organic cereal products. Organic flour milled from English wheat grown to Soil Association. standard in the traditional way by watermill. They also stock organic pasta, dried goods, teas, coffee, herb teas. There is a Mail Order list available; please 'phone for full details.
Prices/Payment: From 78p per 500g for 100% wholewheat flour to £21.75 per 25kg of special blend flour.
Hours: Shop, Mon-Fri 10am-5pm. Mill and tearoom March to end Oct., Mon, Tues, Thurs, 10.30am-5pm.
Notes: Disabled access. Tearoom (all wholefood, organic, vegetarian), tours of 18th century watermill and bread demonstrations by arrangement. Little Salkeld Watermill supplies to numerous outlets and to the trade.

SLACK'S
Newlands Farm
Raisbeck
Orton
PENRITH
CA10 3SG
TEL: 015396 24667
FAX: 015396 24117
CONTACT: Michael Slack
PRODUCE: An extensive range of home cured and air dried bacons and hams. Both green and smoked. Traditional Cumberland sausage and other speciality sausages, and premium quality cooked ham. Mail Order only. Sent overnight in self chilled boxes, or 1st class post on small orders. For orders up to £24.99 in value there is a delivery charge. Over £25 delivery F.O.C.
PRICES/PAYMENT: Cash and cheques only.
HOURS: Mail Order only.
NOTES: Slack's supply to many stockists in the North and South East of England.

THE OLD SMOKEHOUSE/TRUFFLES
Brougham Hall, Brougham
Penrith
CA10 2DE
Tel: 01768 867772
Fax: 01768 867772
Contact: Rona Newsom
Produce: A full range of smoked fish, game, poultry and meats including farm-cured hams and sausages, free from artificial colourings and preservatives. Also stock venison sausage. They make a range of truffles using real alcohol, real cream and real fruit. Mail Order list providing wide choice available from retail shop on site or by request.
Price/Payment: Cash, cheques only.
Hours:10am-5.30pm seven days a week, April to Christmas Eve. 10am-5pm Mon-Fri, Jan to end March.
Notes: Wheel chairs do negotiate the cobbled entrance. Rona Newsom is always looking for more trade outlets.

THE VILLAGE BAKERY MELMERBY LTD

Melmerby

PENRITH

CA10 1HE

TEL: **01768 818515**
FAX: **01768 818848**
CONTACT: **Andrew Whitley**
PRODUCE: **Handmade organic bread and cakes, made in a woodfired brick oven. Christmas cakes and Christmas puddings. Mail Order available. No minimum order.**
PRICES/PAYMENT: **Christmas pudding from £3.50. All major credit cards taken.**
HOURS: **Restaurant open 9am-5pm.**
NOTES: **Disabled access, bread making courses, restaurant open for big breakfast, light lunches and tea. Suppliers to major London stores. Interested in supplying more to trade.**

MUNCASTER WATER MILL

Ravenglass
CA18 1ST
Tel: 01229 717232
Contact: Mrs Pam Priestley
Miller – Mr Ernie Priestley
Produce: Stoneground organic flour. 100% wholemeal - fine, coarse & cracked wheat; unbleached white, fine brown, semolina, natural bran. "Sam Brown" their own blend of "granary" flour. Also ice cream, sweets, local honey and recipe books. Mail Order available. No min. order charge. Postage charged at cost.
Prices/Payment: Cash and cheques only.
Hours: 10am-5pm daily, Easter-October. 11am-4pm Winter weekends.
Notes: Disabled access. Tea shop with home-made scones, cakes and bread. Leat Walk station on Ravenglass & Eskdale Railway. Muncaster Water Mill is interested in supplying to the trade.

ULLSWATER TROUT

Sockbridge Mill Trout Farm, Tirril
Penrith
CA10 2JT
Tel: 01768 865338
Fax: 01768 865338
Email: jac.ullstrout@btinternet.com
Contact: Gillian Claridge
Produce: Fresh trout, hot smoked trout, cold smoked trout, gravadlax, trout roulade, smoked trout pâté, devilled trout pâté, rainbow terrine. Fresh or frozen. Mail Order available. Regular deliveries made to most of the Lake District and weekly deliveries down the M6 corridor as far as Knutsford.
Prices/Payment: Please 'phone for price list. Cash and cheques only.
Hours: 8.30am-6pm every day
Notes: "Catch your own" trout pond. Refreshments. Ullswater Trout supply J & J Graham (Penrith), E H Booths (Knutsford) and are interested in supplying the trade.

FURNESS FISH, POULTRY & GAME SUPPLIES

Stockbridge Lane
off Daltongate
Ulverston
LA12 7BG
Tel: 01229 585037
Fax: 01229 582485
Contact: Clare
Produce: All cuts of venison, smoked salmon, smoked meats (venison, chicken and duck). Producers of Morcambe Bay potted shrimps All types of game. Venison sausage, game sausage, kippers and smoked mackerel fillets. Mail Order available. Please 'phone for details.
Prices/Payment: Visa, Mastercard, Delta and Switch taken.
Hours: Mon-Fri, 8am-5pm. Sat, 8am-12pm.
Notes: Disabled access. Morecambe Bay Potted Shrimps supply to supermarkets, good quality delicatessens and fishmongers.

The following are SHOPS within this region which do not produce but do sell quality or organic foods

CARTMEL VILLAGE SHOP
Parkgate House
The Square
Cartmel
LA11 6QB
Tel: 01539 536201
Produce: Producers of sticky toffee pudding in various sizes. Available also by mail order. Stockist of local produce including Woodalls sausages and bacon, Thornby Moor Dairy Cheeses, Mrs. Kirkhams unpasteurised Lancashire cheeses and Penrith fudge and toffee.
Hours: Mon-Sat, 9am-5.30pm. Sun, 11am-5pm.

THE 1657 CHOCOLATE HOUSE
54 Branthwaite Brow
Kendal
LA9 9XX
Tel: 01539 740702
Produce: Chocolate. Both to eat and drink. Chocolates, chocolate ice cream, chocolate cake, chocolate pancakes.
Hours: Mon-Sat, 9.30am-5pm. Sun, 1pm-5pm.
Notes: Old fashioned chocolate house, restaurant and shop.

BEDFORDSHIRE

THE PURE MEAT COMPANY
Rectory Farm, Upper Stondon
Henlow
SG16 6LJ
Tel: 01462 851561
Fax: 01462 851561
Contact: R. Birchenall
Produce: Organic beef, pork, lamb and poultry, licenced game dealer. Home-made sausages, smoked chicken, turkey, game and trout. Also stock additive-free specialist soup and stocks. Home smoked products. Nationwide delivery service by courier. Min order over ten pounds in weight; over 25 pounds in weight free delivery. Hamper packs available.
Prices/Payment: 'Phone for current price list. All major credit cards and Switch.
Hours: Mon-Fri, 7am-6pm. Mail order. Shops Mon-Sat, 7am-6pm.
Notes: Disabled access to London shop (see London Section). The Pure Meat Company are interested in supplying to the trade.

CAMBRIDGESHIRE

A. WALLER AND SON
15 Victoria Avenue
Cambridge
CB4 1EG
Tel: 01223 350972
Contact: Mr Richard Welton
Produce: Free range pork, Farm beef, hung for a min. of two weeks. Seven varieties of sausage made from free range pork. Most cooked meats are home-made and home cooked. Also stock Wiltshire dry cure bacon. Cottage Delight pickles and chutneys with no preservatives. James Whites single variety apple juices.
Prices/Payment: Sausages £1.70 per lb. Cheese £3 - £9.78 per lb. Cash and cheques only.
Hours: 8am-5pm
Notes: Disabled access.

DAILY BREAD CO-OPERATIVE (CAMBRIDGE) LTD
Unit 3, Kilmaine Close
Kings Hedges
CAMBRIDGE
CB4 2PH
TEL: 01223 423177
Fax: 01223 425858
CONTACT: Helen Chatfield
PRODUCE: A large range of natural wholefoods including; dried fruits, nuts, beans and pulses, flours and grains. Their mixed mueslis, fruit and nut mixes, soup mixes and rice mixes. They are attempting to offer an organic alternative on all their lines. Also stock organic fresh fruit and veg, soya milks, organic pasta and pasta sauces, olive oils, margarines, cooking aids, vinegars, jams, fruit juices, tea and coffee, organic baby foods and Ecover products.
PRICES/PAYMENT: Special muesli £1.19 per kg, mixed herbs 66p for 50g, porridge oats 49p per kg.
Hours: Tues-Fri, 9am-5.30pm. Sat, 9am-4pm.
NOTES: Disabled access. Large car park, staff always ready to help people to the car with heavy items. Coffee shop, wide range of books to look at/buy, up-to-date info on organics, GMO's and speciality diets. Daily Bread Co-operative are a Christian Co-op who believe food is fundamental and should have good nutritional value and be good value for money. They are interested in supplying to the catering trade. See Northampton, under same name.

CHAPLIN FARMS (FULBOURN) LTD
9 Doggett Lane
Fulbourn
Cambridge
CB1 5BT
Tel: 01223 880722
Fax: 01223 516632

Contact: Adrian Chaplin
Produce: Soft fruit, strawberries, raspberries etc. Plus home made bread, cakes and jams. Also stock preserves, marmalade, pickles, cheeses and honey.
Prices/Payment: Cash and cheques only.
Hours: 9am-6pm
Notes: Disabled access. Tea shop, caravan site and golf driving range. Chaplin Farms are interested in supplying to the trade.

FOSTER'S MILL
The Windmill, Swaffham Prior
Cambridge
CB5 0JZ
Tel: 01638 741009
Fax: 0870 0553922
Email: mark@scorteus.demon.co.uk
Contact: Jonathan Cook
Produce: Stoneground flour from organic wheat using only windpower. Muesli mixed by Foster's Mill, porridge oats and associated products. Also stock honey.
Prices/Payment: Cash and cheques only
Hours: Weekends 1pm-5pm. Please 'phone to check whether open.
Notes: No disabled access. Foster's Mill supply to Lane's Bakery (Burwell). Are interested in supplying to the trade.

P CRUICKSHANK & SON
124 Wulfstan Way
Cambridge
CB1 4QJ
Tel: 01223 566054
Contact: Peter Cruickshank
Produce: Accredited butchers to the Rare Breeds Survival Trust. A variety of sausages. Dry cured bacon. Cooked gammons. Beef, pork. Burgers, kebabs etc. Also stock bread, cakes, pork pies, pasties and steak & kidney pies.
Prices/Payment: All major credit cards taken. Cardnet.
Hours: Mon, 8am-1pm. Tues-Thurs, 8am -5.30pm. Fri, 8am-6pm. Sat, 7am-1pm.
Notes: Disabled access. P Cruickshank & Son are interested in supplying to the catering trade.

DOWNFIELD WINDMILL
Fordham Road
Soham
Ely
CB7 5BG
Tel: 01353 720333
Contact: Mrs I Kite or Mr A Kite
Produce: Grinders of organically grown grain: including wheat, rye and oatmeal.
Prices/Payment: Strong wheat flour for bread-making £1.90 per 3kg, 97p per 1.5kg, oatmeal £1.30 per 1.5kg. Cash and cheques only.
Hours: Sunday and Bank Holidays only 11am-5pm.
Notes: Disabled access to ground floor. Books on windmills aimed mainly for children available. Downfield Windmill are interested in supplying to the trade.

PARKINSON OF CROWLAND
6 West Street
Crowland
Peterborough
PE6 0PY
Tel: 01733 210233
Contact: Des Barker
Produce: Gold Medal winning pork sausages in 8 different varieties. Gold medal winning Lincolnshire brawn. Also stock a full range of British meats, pies, jams and curds and plum bread.
Prices/Payment: Brawn £1.74 per lb, Lincolnshire Gold Medal sausage £1.99 per lb. Cash and cheques only.
Hours: Mon, 9am-12pm. Tues, Thurs, Fri, 9am-5.30pm. Wed, 9am-5pm. Sat, 8am-4pm.
Notes: Disabled access. Demonstra-tions and tastings available at all times.

ORGANIC CONNECTIONS INTERNATIONAL LTD
'Riverdale'
Town Street
Upwell
Wisbech
PE14 9AF
Tel: 01945 773374
Fax: 01945 773033

Contact: Karen Broad
Produce: Home-grown organic fruit and vegetables, herbs. Also importers of organic fruit and vegetables and marketers for a local co-op of growers. Also stock eggs, cheese, bread, apple juice. Box scheme – direct to the consumer's door in a closed/banded box. Min order one box.
Prices/Payment: Standard box £13.50, salad box £8, value box £7.50, family box £25, pasta box £15, fruit £13.50. Most credit cards accepted.
Hours: 'Phone for details.
Notes: May be open to the public in the future.

W. NORMAN & SON LTD
Austin Farm
Burrettgate Road
Walsoken
Wisbech
PE14 7BN
Tel: 01945 583130
Fax: 01945 583130
Contact: Sue Leach
Produce: Apples and pears grown on the farm. Pure apple juice, pressed from a blend of apples grown on their farm. Home delivery to a limited area. No min. order charge.
Prices/Payment: £1.75 per bottle. £24 per case (15 bottles). Cash and cheques only.
Hours: Mon-Sat, 8am-6pm. Sun, 10am-6pm.
Notes: Disabled access. W. Norman are interested in supplying to the trade.

ESSEX

HEPBURNS OF MOUNTNESSING
269 Roman Road
Mountnessing
Brentwood
CM15 OUH
Tel: 01277 353289
Fax: 01277 355589
Contact: Mr Gordon Hepburn
Produce: Member of the Q Guild of Butchers. Primary distributor of

Highgrove beef and lamb. Chickens, turkeys and ducks. Geese are available at Christmas. Hams & bacon; honey based cure smoked over beech wood. Award winning selection of sausages. Bacon cured and smoked on the premises. Convenience foods including marinated meats and barbecue fare. Also stock free range eggs, 50 different traditionally made cheeses and fine wines, dry goods – Cottage Delight, Duchy, Wilkins, Elsenham, ice cream, freshly ground coffee. Home delivery service within 25 mile radius (other by arrangement). Min order £50.
Prices/Payment: Visa, Mastercard, Delta, Switch.
Hours: Mon-Thurs, 8am-5.30pm. Fri, 8am-6.30pm. Sat, 8am-4pm.
Notes: No disabled access, but extremely helpful staff. Regular tastings, they have a mailing list to keep customers informed. Hepburns of Mountnessing are interested in supplying to the trade.

KELLY TURKEY FARMS LTD
Springate Farm
Bicknacre Road
Danbury
Chelmsford
CM3 4EP
Tel: 01245 223581
Fax: 01245 226124
Email: info@kelly-turkeys.com
Internet: www.kelly-turkeys.com
Contact: Sales Dept.
Produce: Bronze turkeys. Free range, additive free. Dry plucked. Christmas turkeys and turkey portions. Mail Order for Christmas. Delivered by 16.00 hrs 23 Dec. No minimum. order.
Prices/Payment: All major credit cards taken.
Hours: Please 'phone for Christmas ordering times.
Notes: Not open to public. Christmas booklet with turkey contains tips, recipes and place cards. Suppliers to numerous outlets.

CLAY BARN ORCHARD
Fingringhoe
Colchester
C05 7AR
Tel: 01206 735405
Fax: 01206 735405
Contact: Charles & Shirley Trollope
Produce: Fruit orchard growing a variety of apples, pears and quinces (14 in all). Quinces available by Mail Order. Min. order 10-12 lbs. Also retail stall.
Prices/Payment: Cash and cheques only.
Hours: Daylight.
Notes: Disabled access. Clay Barn Orchard are suppliers of quinces in bulk for processing.

MUNSON'S POULTRY
"Emdon"
Straight Road, Boxted
Colchester
CO4 5QX
Tel: 01206 272637
Fax: 01206 272962
Contact: John Munson
Produce: Corn fed poultry; Norfolk black, bronze and white turkeys, Indian game meat chickens, White Leghorn and Maran laying chickens, Aylesbury meat ducks, Khaki Campbell and Black East Indian Cross laying ducks, flock of down sheep; 140 ewes. Home-made game pie, home-made pork sausages, smoked sweetcure bacon, smoked mild cure bacon, smoked chicken. All bacon from Tamworth or Duroc pigs. Also stock; smoked Scottish salmon, dry cured bacon, brine cured bacon. Xmas cakes, boxed handmade sweets, chutneys, marmalades. Mail Order to U.K. and some of Europe. No min. order.
Prices/Payment: Please 'phone for comprehensive price list. Visa, Mastercard, American Express.
Hours: Only open to the public to collect pre-ordered goods at Christmas.
Notes: No disabled access. Munson's supply to Harrods, Harvey Nichols, Partridges (all in London). Also to Ritz, Savoy, Connaught, Halcyon, Claridges, Waterside, Delia Smith and similar users.

PROCTERS SPECIALITY SAUSAGES
Red Lion Walk
Colchester
CO1 1DA
Tel: 01206 579100
Contact: Patricia Morse
Produce: Traditional, handmade sausages, 20 recipes inc. Cumberland, farmhouse, Lancashire, Cambridge and old english breakfast, venison with apricot, fresh spinach, nutmeg and black pepper. Continental includes toulouse, boerewors, bratwurst, merguez, chorizo, chilli hot cajun. Also stock dry cured hams & bacons, haggis, free range eggs, salami, olives from Provence and Greece, handraised pork pies and locally produced preserves. Mail Order nationwide (overnight). No min. order charge.
Prices/Payment: Old english breakfast sausages £2.20/lb to venison & redcurrant £3.95 /lb. Cash and cheques only.
Hours: Mon-Sat, 8.30am-5.30pm
Notes: No disabled access. Procters supply to the trade.

LAY & ROBSON
150 Swan Street
Sible Hedingham
Halstead
CO9 3PP
Tel: 01787 462617
Fax: 01787 462611
Contact: James Forbes
Produce: Hot and cold smoked products. Smoked salmon trout, eel, cods roe, haddock, kippers, trout, venison, duck breast, pigeon, pheasant, guinea fowl, chicken, quail, pork fillet, hams, smoked bacon, venison sausages, wild boar sausages. Fresh game furred and feathered, quails eggs, sauces and marinades. Hampers available either in insulated boxes or wicker baskets. Mail Order service available to any U.K. address. No min. order.
Prices/Payment: 100g smoked eel, £3.95, Guinea Fowl £7.95 per 2lb fowl. Hampers from £49.50. All major

credit cards, Switch.
Hours: Mon-Fri, 9am-5.30pm; Sat, 9am-1pm.
Notes: Disabled access is not a problem. Lay & Robson supply to the trade.

THE PRIORY FARM SHOP
Priory Farm
Wrabness
Manningtree
CO11 2UE
Tel: 01255 880338
Contact: Mr E Swift or Mrs C Swift
Produce: A full range of summer and winter vegetables grown on the farm. Home-made cakes; rich fruit cake, teabreads, flapjacks, shortbreads, ginger cake and rock cakes. Also stock vegetables, salads and fruit bought locally. Jams, chutneys, pickles, apple juices and ice cream from East Anglian suppliers.
Prices/Payment: Cake prices range from £1.25 - £25. Cash and cheques only.
Hours: Mon-Sat, 9am-5.30pm.
Notes: Disabled access.

HERTFORDSHIRE

EASTWOODS OF BERKHAMSTED
15 Gravel Path
Berkhamsted
HP4 2EF
Tel: 01442 865012
Fax: 01442 875203
Contact: Joe Collier
Produce: Fresh meats, home-made pies, sausages and dry cured bacon. Also stock Cottage Delight, free range eggs and fresh bread. Mail Order and home delivery service available. No min. charge.
Prices/Payment: All major credit cards, cash and cheques.
Hours: 7.30am-5.30pm.
Notes: Disabled access. Outside catering, cutting demonstrations available. Eastwoods are interested in supplying to the trade.

FIELDFARE ORGANICS
Oakcroft
Dudswell Lane
Berkhamsted
HP4 3TQ
Tel: 01442 877363
Fax: 01442 879950
Email:
fieldfareorganics@btinternet.com
Contact: Sandie Calow
Produce: A complete range of organic fresh fruit and vegetables, including some imported produce. Organic milk, bread, butter, eggs and cheese. Also a wide selection of organic wholefoods. Delivery to most of Hertfordshire and surrounding areas. Box scheme available - customer chooses what they have. Min order £7.50 + £1 delivery charge.
Prices/Payment: Cash and cheques only.
Hours: Office hours are; Mon-Thurs, 9am-6pm. Fri, 9am-5.30pm and Sat, 9am-12pm. Answerphone at all other times.
Notes: Home delivery service only. Not open to the public.

SILVER PALATE
3 Vaughan Road
Harpenden
AL5 4HU
Tel: 01582 713722
Fax: 01582 713722
Contact: Mr Paul Elias Loizou
Produce: Fresh pasta, sauces, gourmet family meals, bread, cakes and patisserie. Also stock over 3,000 other items. From 1999 Mail Order will be available. Min order will be £50.
Prices/Payment: Salmon fillets in lobster sauce for 4-6 persons £11.85. 100% chicken breasts in cream and wild mushroom sauce for 4-6 persons, £10.85. All major credit cards taken.
Hours: Mon-Fri, 9am-7pm,.Sat, 9am-5.30pm. Sun, 9.30am-3pm.
Notes: No disabled access due to flood possibility, but help always available. Interested in limited supply to the trade but don't produce enough for whole-salers.

MILL GREEN MUSEUM & MILL
Mill Green
Hatfield
AL9 5PD
Tel: 01707 271362
Fax: 01707 272511
Email: S.Kirby@welhat.gov.uk.
Contact: Carol Rigby
Produce: Organic wholemeal stoneground flour milled in the traditional way.
Prices/Payment: £1.10 per 1.5kg, £2 per 3kg, £4.60 per 7kg, £9 per 15kg, £18.per 30kg. Discount given for bulk buys. Cash and cheques only.
Hours: Tues-Fri, 10am-5pm. Sat, Sun & Bank Holidays, 2pm-5pm.
Notes: Disabled access to ground floor and sales point. Milling takes place on Tues, Wed and Sun; please 'phone for times. Suppliers to local bakers, and interested in other local trade outlets.

D. SANSOM & SONS
Nine Wells Watercress Farm
Whitwell
Hitchin
SG4 8JP
Tel: 01438 871232
Contact: Mrs T.E. Sansom
Produce: Watercress.
Prices/Payment: Cash and cheques only.
Hours: 8am-Dusk
Notes: Disabled access. D. Sansom & Sons are interested in supplying to the trade.

THE PURE MEAT COMPANY
6 Baker Street
Stevenage
SG1 4AL
Tel: 01438 354312
Fax: 01462 851561
Contact: Mick Randall
Produce: Licenced game dealer. Organic beef, pork, lamb and poultry. Home smoked chicken, turkey, game, trout. Eight varieties of home-made sausages. Home produced cooked ham. Good selection of fresh & smoked fish. Fruit & vegetables and wholefoods. Also carry additive free specialist soups & stocks. Delivery service from Rectory Farm.
Prices/Payment: Free delivery 25lb and over, £9.50 delivery 10lb - 25lb
Credit Cards: All majors plus Switch.
Hours: Mon to Sat, 7am-530pm
Notes: No disabled access. Two other branches, plus suppliers to B&M Seafoods. Interested in supplying to the trade.

LINCOLNSHIRE

WHEELBARROW FOODS
3 Thorngarth Lane
Barrow-upon-Humber
DN19 7AW
Tel: 01469 530721
Contact: Andrew Spacey
Produce: Soil Assoc. approved organic fruit and vegetables and herbs. Also buy in organic foodstuffs for sale at farm gate. No chemicals used. Rice, flour, oats and pasta. Non-organic dried fruit & pulses. Box scheme available. Delivery Scunthorpe, Brigg, Grimsby and locally.
Prices/Payment: Cash or cheques only.
Hours: Mon-Sat, 9am-6pm. Sun, 9am-1pm. Also by arrangement.
Notes: Disabled access. Organic garden. Wheelbarrow Foods supply to Keep Yourself Right (Scunthorpe), Grimsby Wholefood Coop (Grimsby), Louth Wholefood Coop (Louth). Interested in supplying to the trade locally.

F.C. PHIPPS
Osborne House, Mareham-le-Fen
Boston
PE22 7RW
Tel: 01507 568235
Contact: Eric or Beth Phipps
Produce: Accredited butcher for the Rare Breeds Survival Trust. Lincoln Red beef, Gloucester Old Spot and Saddleback pork, Wiltshire and Castlemilk lamb. Stuffed chine, Lincolnshire sausages, haslet, pork pies,

home cured ham and bacon. Game pie with venison, pheasant, hare and pigeon. Duck, orange and walnut pie, lamb and redcurrant. Pâtés, home-made casseroles and desserts. Also stock free range eggs, a range of cheese including Lincolnshire Poacher. Biscuits, chocolates, chutneys, pickles and plum bread. Mail order by Interlink; delivery by refrigerated van in local area. No min. order charge.
Prices/Payment: Cash and cheques only.
Hours: Mon, Tues, Thur, Fri, 8am-5pm. Wed, 8am-1pm. Sat, 8am-3pm.
Notes: No disabled access. F.C. Phipps supply to West End Stores (Alford), Old Leake Post Office and Franklin House Bakery (Spilsby). They supply to pubs and restaurants.

MAUD FOSTER WINDMILL
Boston
PE21 9EG
Tel: 01205 352188
Contact: James Waterfield
Produce: Wide range of stoneground organic flours and cereal products. Mail order service. No min. order.
Prices/Payment: Visa, Mastercard.
Hours: Wed, 10am-5.00pm. Sat, 11am-5.00pm. Sun, 1.00pm. - 5.00pm.
Notes: You can visit this working windmill dating from 1819. Vegetarian cafe.

MOUNT PLEASANT WINDMILL
Kirton Lindsey
Gainsborough
DN21 4NH
Tel: 01652 640177
Contact: Pat & Jane White
Produce: Range of organic stoneground, wholemeal & white flours from high quality organic English wheat – using only the power of the wind. Home delivery – approx 70 mile radius. Min. order £10.00. Also stock gifts and luxury foods in shop.
Hours: Sat, Sun & Bank Holidays, 10am-5pm. Fri, 11am-4pm. Open weekdays in August – please ring.

Notes: Disabled access. Mill tea shop, mill shop, craft shop. Working windmill open to visitors, group visits welcome. Also suppliers to: Natural Choice (Ashbourne), The Green House (Harrogate) Roots (Nottingham) and Beanies (Sheffield).

BELVOIR FRUIT FARMS
Belvoir
Grantham
NG32 1PB
Tel: 01476 870286
Fax: 01476 870114
Contact: Peverel Manners or Di Frankland
Produce: Fruit cordials made from home grown elderflowers, strawberries, raspberries; also exotic cordials made only from natural produce i.e. fresh ginger cordial, spiced elderberry cordial, fresh lime and lemon grass cordial. Mail Order service, min. order 3 bottles.
Prices/payment: All major cards including Switch. Also cheques by post.
Notes: Belvoir Fruit Farms supply a London West End store and several other outlets, and are interested in selling more to the trade. Farm not open for direct sales to the public.

ALFRED ENDERBY LTD
Maclure Street
Fish Docks
Grimsby
DN31 3NE
(Visitors to Fish Dock Road Entrance).
Tel: 01472 342984
Fax: 01472 342984
Internet: www.meff.co.uk
Contact: George or Richard Enderby
Produce: Smoked cod, haddock, Scottish salmon. Smoked salmon sold as whole sides or sliced and vacuum packed. Mail Order available. Min. order 2 sides of salmon (3 kg) set; carriage charge of £10.
Prices/Payment: Smoked haddock and cod £5 per kg; smoked salmon from £11 per kg. Cash, cheques only.

Hours: Mon-Fri, 8am-4pm. Some Sat mornings; 'phone for details.
Notes: No disabled access. Alfred Enderby also supply Howard & Son (Norwich), Fish & Fowl (London), R&J Davis (Cromer) and Terry's Fish (Lewes) and are interested in selling more to the trade.

J.W. WELBOURNE & SON
The Bakery
38 High Street, Navenby
Lincoln
LN5 0DZ
Tel: 01522 810239
Contact: Pete or Mary Welbourne
Produce: Fresh bread and cakes made on the premises daily, from raw material to finished product (no re-heated bread). Meat pies, sausage rolls. Special plum bread (a particular favourite); a rich fruit loaf which keeps well. Also stock cheese and dairy products, cooked meats, Boston sausage, Cartmel sticky toffee puddings. Mail Order is available for plum bread. Min. order six loaves.
Prices/Payment: Large special plum bread, £2.75, small plum bread, £2.10, (at shop). Cash and cheques only.
Hours: Mon-Tues, 9am-4.30pm. Thurs-Fri, 9am-5pm, Wed, 9am-12.30pm, Sat, 8.30-2pm. Open at side door at 7.30am for rolls and croissants.
Notes: No disabled access but every assistance given. The bakery also supply; The Bluebird Store (Chelsea, London), The Honeypot (Hawkshead), Traditional Foods (Nottingham), Cooks Pantry (Newark) and Hicksons (Lincoln), and are interested in supplying to the trade.

SPECIAL EDITION CONTINENTAL CHOCOLATE
59 Honeyholes Lane, Dunholme
Lincoln
LN2 3SU
Tel: 01673 860616
Contact: Scotty Scott, Pam Andrews
Produce: Handmade chocolates using Belgian and German couvertures.

Handmade double cream fudge. No artificial ingredients or preservatives. Available by Mail Order. No min. order, but £3 delivery.
Prices/Payment: Chocolates £12 per lb. Boxes from £2 upwards. Fudges 95p per qtr. Cash and cheques only.
Hours: Please 'phone to arrange visit.
Notes: No disabled access. Suppliers to Rollitts (Navenby), Room 11 (Swinfen), Johnson's Farm Shop (Melton Ross). Special Edition Continental Chocolate are interested in supplying to the trade.

JACKSONS BUTCHERS
118 East Gate
Louth
LN11 9AA
Tel: 01507 602797
Email: nigel.wrisdale@virgin.net
Contact: Nigel or Val Wrisdale
Produce: 'Gold Award' Lincolnshire sausage, pork pies, haslet, stuffed chine, and Lincolnshire plum bread. Lincolnshire champions for bacon curing and they smoke their own bacon with hickory wood. They have an extensive range of pastry products, sweet and savoury. All meat is from local farms (members of a local quality scheme covering beef and lamb and concerned with quality and traceability). Also stock Cottage Delight products (jams, chutneys, curds, pâté) and Rick Bestwick frozen exotic meats (ostrich, kangaroo, venison, crocodile and wild boar).
Prices/Payment: All major cards. Switch, JCB, Solo, Maestro, Electron.
Hours: Mon-Fri, 8am-5pm. Sat, 8am-1pm.
Notes: Disabled access.

SWEPSTONES
26/28 High Street, Holbeach
Spalding
PE12 7DY
Tel: 01406 423128/423283
Fax: 01406 425265
Contact: John or Phyllis Swepstone
Produce: Prize winning Lincolnshire

pork sausage, a variety of speciality sausages, including gluten free. Home-made haslets & pies, including a prize winning Cornish Pastie. In Winter only - brawn (pork cheese). Also stock Epicure products, Walkers shortbread biscuits, wide range of cheeses, including Lincolnshire Poacher. Homefarm products, e.g. jams and chutneys, horseradish etc, Symingtons table creams. Gateaux and ice cream. Hampers & gift baskets made to order.
Prices/Payment: Major credit cards taken.
Hours: Mon, Tues, Sat, 7.30am-5pm. Wed, 7.30am-1pm. Fri, 7.30am-6pm.
Notes: Disabled access. Cheese tastings are offered. Swepstones already supply to many local village shops, butchers and cafés, restaurants and pubs. New customers welcomed.

RUTLAND FOODS
72 High Street
Ketton
Stamford
PE9 3TE
Tel: **01780 720226**
Fax: **01780 720226**
Contact: **Martin Downes**
Produce: **High quality snails dressed in garlic and parsley butter in natural or re-usable plastic shells. Also chopped snails in vol-au-vents with different flavours; snail in ginger and lime, tomato and herbs and orange spice sauce. New – mushroom vol-au-vents in different flavours. Available frozen by prearranged delivery. Min. order £30.**
Prices/Payment: **1 doz in natural shells at £3.50. Snail vol-au-vents £3.85 for 15. Cash and cheques only.**
Hours: **Open by appointment. Please 'phone for details.**
Notes: **Disabled access possible in part. Rutland Foods supply to Food for all Seasons. They are interested in supplying more to the trade.**

NORFKOLK

RICHARD & JULIE DAVIES
7 Garden Street
Cromer
NR27 9HU
Tel: 01263 512727
Fax: 01263 514789
Contact: Julie Davies
Produce: Local crabs and lobsters, boiled and dressed. Also stock wet & smoked fish.
Prices: Whole crabs from £1 each; dressed from £1.25 each. No credit cards.
Hours: From March-Oct. seven days. Winter, Tues to Sat. Early closing Wed, afternoon.
Notes: No disabled access. The Davies's supply to 4 local outlets.

NORTH ELMHAM BAKERY
East Gate Street, North Elmham
Dereham
NR20 5HE
Tel: 01362 668577 **Fax:** 01362 668577
Email:
northelmhambakery@btinternet.com
Contact: Norman Olley
Produce: Traditional bread baked in a traditional 3 tier peel oven. Three doughs; white using Canadian flour, 100% wholemeal and Norfolk Crunch (with added grains) are made into 150 different sizes and shapes each with an individual texture and flavour. These include old fashioned cottage, coburg, bloomer, plaits and fluted loaves. Also 30 different types of cakes fresh daily and wedding cakes that are still iced with royal icing. Available from the bakery at North Elmham and Mr Olley's two shops at Dereham and Watton,
Prices/Payment: Cash and cheques only.
Hours: Bakehouse, 7.30am-11.30am. Shops, 8.30am-3.30pm.
Notes: Disabled access. Bakery demonstrations by appointment. Supply to local shops and is interested in supplying more to the trade.

CHANNELL'S NORFOLK PRESERVES
82 Hamilton Road
Great Yarmouth
NR30 4LZ
Tel: 01493 850452
Fax: 01493 330168
Contact: David Channell
Produce: Home-made luxury orange marmalade with brandy or whisky. Tomato chutney and barbecue sauce. Available shortly by Mail Order.
Prices/Payment: £1.95 per jar for marmalade + postage if Mail Order. Cash and cheques only.
Hours: 8.30am-5.30pm.
Notes: No disabled access. Channell's also supply to Fields Delicatessen (Great Yarmouth), Riverside Stores (Stokesby), Seadell Shops (Hemsby), Woodbastwick Beef, Mill Farm Shop (Salhouse), H&M Gartley (Toft Monks) and Fritton Lake Country World (Fritton). Possibly interested in supplying to the trade.

STARSTON FAYRE
Cranes Watering Farm
Rushall Road
Starston
Harleston
IP20 9NE
Tel: 01379 852387
Fax: 01379 852387
Contact: Susan Moore
Produce: Ice cream made from the milk and cream of the farm's herd of Jersey & Guernsey cows. Untreated milk, cream and pasteurised milk and cream. Stock frozen goat's milk and eggs.
Prices/Payment: £2.60 per half litre of ice cream. £1.35 per half pint double cream; untreated milk 80p per two pints. Cash and cheques only.
Hours: Sat, 9am-1pm
Notes: Limited disabled access. Starston Fayre also supply to Humes Butchers (Harleston), Natural Food Store (Diss), Country Kitchen (Halesworth) and Smiths Greengrocers (Southwold).

A C COOKE & SON
"The Crabpot"
High Street, Cley-next-the-Sea
Holt
NR25 7RX
Tel: 01263 740218 **Fax:** 01263 740776
Contact: Norman or Joan Cooke
Produce: Lobsters and crabs caught by their own fishing boat. Boiled and dressed on the premises. Home-made fish pies, fish cakes (cod, salmon or crab). Also stock fresh fish, fruit and vegetables and general groceries. Lobsters can be sent by mail on request. Please 'phone for details. No min order charge.
Prices/Payment: Cash and cheques only.
Hours: Easter - end of Sept. Seven days 8.30am-5pm. Winter half day Sun and Wed.
Notes: No disabled access. They are interested in supplying to the trade.

CAMPHILL COMMUNITIES EAST ANGLIA
Thornage Hall, Thornage
Holt
NR25 7QH
Tel: 01263 860305/861481
Fax: 01263 861754
Contact: A. Pedersen/R. Bintein
Produce: Biodynamic, Demeter organic standard, vegetables, some meat and bread. Flour. Local box scheme.
Prices/Payment: Cash and cheques only.
Hours: By appointment only.
Notes: Disabled access. Camphill Communities are a residential community of 40 people providing sheltered and integrated employment and living opportunities for about half of its workers who may have special needs. They sell produce through Letheringsett Watermill (see below).

LETHERINGSETT WATERMILL
Riverside Road, Letheringsett
Holt
NR25 7YD
Tel: 01263 713153
Contact: Mike Thurlow
Produce: 100% wholewheat

stoneground flour, traditional & organic. All processed from English wheat grown in Norfolk. The organic flour is milled to Demeter standard. Also stock other flour ranges from Marriages. Dried fruit & nuts. Locally produced jams and preserves. Available by Mail Order. No min. order.
Prices/Payment: Traditional stoneground flour, £1 per 1.5kg. Organic £1.15 per 1.5kg
Hours: Mon-Fri, 9am-4pm, Sat, 9am-1pm.
Notes: No disabled access. The mill is open to the public during opening times and there is a running demonstration every afternoon 2pm-4pm. Letheringsett supply to many outlets (list on request). They are willing to supply to as many outlets as possible subject to product availability.

NARBOROUGH TROUT FARM LTD
Narborough
King's Lynn
PE32 1TE
Tel: 01760 338005
Contact: Mr Rodney Skerry
Produce: Fresh trout, smoked whole or fillets of trout. Smoked trout pâté. Also stock jams, marmalades, gifts, snack and fishing tackle.
Prices/Payment: Fresh trout £5.73 per kg, smoked whole £7.93 per kg, smoked fillets £18.73 per kg and smoked trout pâté £5.20 per 450 g.
Hours: Seven days a week. Winter 9am-5pm. Summer 9am-8pm. Chargecards taken.
Notes: Disabled access. Nature walks and fishing lakes. Narborough Trout Farm supply to the trade in the locality.

THE FISH SHED
Main Road
Brancaster Staithe
King's Lynn
PE31 8BY
Tel: 01485 210532
Fax: 01485 210532
Contact: Stephen or Margaret Bocking
Produce: Home smoked salmon, trout,

chickens, ducks, sausages and mussels. Home-made fish cakes, pâtés and pies. Also stock; smoked eel, taramasalata and smoked cod's roe. Mail Order available for kippers etc. Min. order charge £10.
Prices/Payment: Pâté from £1.30 per tub, smoked salmon £9.99 per lb, pies £2.40 each. Cash and cheques only.
Hours: 10am-5pm daily. Close at 4pm Nov-April. Open Sundays.
Notes: Disabled access.

BRYAN PICKERING
30 The Street
Old Costessey
Norwich
NR8 5DB
Tel: 01603 742002
Contact: Bryan Pickering
Produce: Over 40 types of sausages; bacon and hams cured to traditional recipes; no added water. Smoked meats, dried meats, e.g. biltong, prosciutto hams, gluten free sausages/burgers. Available by Mail Order; 'phone for list.
Prices/Payment: Sausages from £2.16 / lb for traditional pork - £2.80/ lb for smoked pork with brandy. All major credit cards accepted .
Hours: Mon-Fri, 8.30am-5.30pm. Sat, 7.30am-5pm.
Notes: Disabled access. Bryan Pickering is interested in supplying to the trade.

MORTON'S TRADITIONAL TASTE
Whitwell Hall Farms
Skeyton
Norwich
NR10 5AY
Tel: 01692 538227
Fax: 01692 538334
Email: Mortons@whitwellhall.co.uk
Contact: Rob Morton
Produce: Organic chickens, turkeys & eggs. Free range turkeys & geese. White, bronze and black turkeys (both free range and organic). Member of the Soil Assoc. Mail Order available, please 'phone for details.

Prices/Payment: Cash and cheques.
Hours: Open by appointment only,
please telephone before arriving.
Notes: No disabled access. Morton's
are interested in supplying to the trade.

TAVERN TASTY MEATS
Old Tavern, Union Road,
Smallburgh
Norwich
NR12 9NH
Tel: 01692 536460
Contact: Roger & Dot Human
Produce: The only Rare Breed accredited butcher in Norfolk. Specialists in
rearing Gloucestershire Old Spot pork
from a free range herd. Sweetcure their
own oak smoked bacon. Handmade
sausages and pork pies; also rare breed
beef that has been well hung. Also
stock free range chicken. Delivery
(local refrigerated on Thur.) No min.
order charge.
Prices/Payment: Sausages £5.39 per
kg. All major cards taken. Switch.
Hours: Thurs & Fri, 8.30am-4pm. Sat,
9am-1pm.
Notes: Disabled access. Free tastings
on Fri and Sat. Visitors welcome to
look around at the livestock. Tavern
Tasty Meats supply to various outlets in
Norfolk and are interested in supplying
more to the trade.

FIONA DICKSON
Didlington Manor, Didlington
Thetford
IP26 5AT
Tel: 01842 878673
Fax: 01842 878671
Contact: Fiona Dickson
Produce: Honey and honey products,
from bees at Richmond Park, Windsor
Great Park, Sandringham Park Estate
and Didlington Park. All award
winning at the National Honey Show.
Prices/Payment: Wholesale, £1.95 per
half pound, £2.95 per pound and
£6.50 per four times one quarter
pound. Mail Order and Retail prices
£2.75, £3.95, £7.95 as above plus
p&p. Cash and cheques only. FOC

delivery London only, min. order £200.
Hours: Not open to the public.
Notes: Fiona Dickson supplies
Lidgates, Vivians, International Cheese
Shop and Olivers Health Shop (all
London).

SUFFOLK

BUTTERWORTH & SON
66 Guildhall Street
Bury St Edmunds
IP33 1QF
Tel: 01284 755410
Fax: 01284 767969
Contact: Mr Butterworth
Produce: "Suffolk Maid" products;
jams, marmalades, chutneys (including
Suffolk Regiment Malabar Chutney).
Butterfinger biscuits, Magic Moment
cakes, tea, coffee and "Old Colonial"
brand of chutneys & spicey bitings.
Also stock; ethnic ingredients, spices,
condiments & ingredients from India,
China, Thailand etc. Mail Order as
required. No min. order charge.
Prices/Payment: Single items vary from
75p - £2.50. Cash and cheques only.
Hours: Mon-Sat, 9am-5.30pm.
Notes: Disabled access. Butterworth &
Son's produce is available all year
throughout East Anglia. They are
interested in supplying to the trade.

LONGWOOD FARM
Tuddenham St. Mary
Bury St Edmunds
IP28 6TB
Tel: 01638 717120
Fax: 01638 717120
Contact: Matthew Unwin
Produce: Organic (Soil Assoc. Standard). Beef, pork, poultry & lamb, from
their own closed herd. Sausages,
gammons. Turkey and geese for
Christmas. Also stock organic dairy
produce, organic fruit and veg, organic
dry goods and groceries. Mail Order
available nationwide. Local deliveries
in Norfolk and Suffolk. No min. order
charge.

Prices/Payment: Minced beef £3.60 per lb. Back bacon £5.80 per lb. Poultry £2.50 per lb. Cash and cheques only.
Hours: Wed & Fri, 8.30am-4.30pm. Sat, 8.30am-2pm.
Notes: No disabled access. Longwood Farm also sell their produce at Porto-bello Road market, Greenwich market and Spitalfields market (See London).

RUMBURGH FARM PRODUCE
Rumburgh Farm, Rumburgh
Halesworth
IP19 0RU
Tel: 01986 781351
Fax: 01986 781351
Contact: Mick or Charlotte Binder
Produce: Farm reared Norfolk Black and Bronze free range turkeys for the Christmas market. Reared to the standards of the the Traditional Farm Fresh Turkey Assn. Also asparagus (May-June).
Prices/Payment: Turkeys average price £1.65 per lb, oven ready. Cash and cheques only.
Hours: Dawn to Dusk.
Notes: No disabled access. Rumburgh Farm also have a B&B enterprise. £36 for a double en-suite room.
They supply to the trade & farm gate sales and welcome new customers.

ALDER CARR FARM
Creeting St Mary
Ipswich
IP6 8LX
Tel: 01449 720820
Email:
hardingham@aldercar.keme.co.uk
Contact: Mr or Mrs Hardingham
Produce: Fruit cream ices made with Alder Carr's fruit, cream and sugar only. Soft fruit PYO or from the farm shop. Strawberries, raspberries, tayberries, etc. Vegetables; asparagus, broad beans, potatoes etc. Also stock locally produced pies, cheeses, cakes and apple juice. Regional delivery for ice cream; organic box scheme available.

Prices/Payment: Cash and cheques only.
Hours: 9am-5pm daily in Summer. Closed Mondays in Winter and open 9am-4pm. Please 'phone for details.
Notes: Disabled access. Alder Carr supply to Orford Supply Stores, Creaseys, Humble Pie and Villandry. New trade customers always welcome.

JAMES WHITE APPLE JUICES
Whites Fruit Farm, Ashbocking
Ipswich
IP6 9JS
Tel: 01473 890111 **Fax:** 01473 890001
Contact: Paul Wilson
Produce: Freshly pressed apple juice; Bramley, Cox, Russet, apple and blackberry, apple & elderflower, apple & cinnamon. Big Tom spicy tomato drink. Fruit coulis; apricot, blackcur-rant, raspberry, strawberry and 3 red fruits. Traditional still ciders and non-alcoholic ginger aperitif. Mail Order to England and Wales by case. (12 bottles, 75cl). Min. order (12 bottles - mixed products).
Prices/Payment: Home delivery by the case from £24. Individual bottles from £1.95. All major credit cards taken.
Hours: Farm Shop 9.30am-5pm.
Notes: Disabled access. Tastings of James White products available. Suppliers to Majestic Wine ware-houses. Also many farm shops, delis and garden centres. James White are interested in supplying to the trade.

MR & MRS J THOROUGHGOOD
Bushy Ley Cottage, Elmsett
Ipswich
IP7 6PQ
Tel: 01473 658671
Contact: Catherine Thoroughgood
Produce: Vegetables grown to Soil Association standards.
Prices/Payment: French beans 50p per lb, leeks 40p per lb, carrots 30p per lb. Cash and cheques only.
Hours: 8am-8pm seven days a week mid-June until Nov.
Notes: Disabled access.

PROCTERS SPECIALITY SAUSAGES
12 The Walk
Ipswich
IP1 1EE
Tel: 01473 281191
Contact: Mark Smy
Produce: Traditional, handmade sausages, 20 recipes inc. Cumberland, farmhouse, Lancashire, Cambridge and old english breakfast, venison with apricot, fresh spinach, nutmeg and black pepper. Continental includes toulouse, boerewors, bratwurst, merguez, chorizo, chilli hot cajun. Also stock dry cured hams & bacons, haggis, free range eggs, salami, olives from Provence and Greece, handraised pork pies and locally produced preserves. Mail Order nationwide (overnight). No min. order.
Prices/Payment: Old english breakfast sausages £2.20/lb to venison & red currant £3.95/lb. Cash and cheques only.
Hours: Mon-Sat, 8.30am-5.30pm
Notes: No disabled access. Procters supply to the trade.

STONHAM HEDGEROW LIMITED
Hemingstone Fruit Farm, Hemingstone
Ipswich
IP6 9RJ
Tel: 01449 760330
Fax: 01449 760330
Contact: Kathy Neuteboom
Produce: Handmade preserves; marmalades, chutney, jellies. Gift baskets, hampers. Fresh fruit in boxes and bags. Mail Order available. No min. order.
Prices/Payment: Cash and cheques only.
Hours: 10am-4.30pm.
Notes: No disabled access. Stonham Hedgerow supplies; Selfridges Food Hall (London), Corncraft, Chatsworth Farm Shop, Hockerton Farm Shop.

THE SUFFOLK PANTRY
9 High Street
Hadleigh
Ipswich
IP1 5AH
Tel: 01473 827568
Fax: 01473 828523
Email: pantry@unforgettable.com
Contact: Annie David & Mark David
Produce: Chutneys, dressings, marinades, pestos, cashew nut butter, chilli oil, rosemary oil, marmalades, flavoured mayonnaise. Also stock Womersley Park jellies and condiments, mustards, jams, indian pickles, Mary Berry dressings.
Prices/Payment: Chutneys £2.20, pesto, £2.95, cashew nut butter £2.20. Visa, Delta taken.
Hours: Variable, usually 9.30am-5.30pm, Mon-Fri, except Wed close 1.30pm. Sat, 9.30am-1.30pm.
Notes: Disabled access. The Suffolk Pantry are caterers for weddings. They supply Anglia Co-op Rainbow/17 stores in Norfolk and Suffolk from Sept (end) 1998. Bruisyard Vineyards.

OTLEY COLLEGE DAIRY
Charity Lane
Otley
IP6 9EY
Tel: 01473 785543
Fax: 01473 785353
Contact: Annette Burton
Produce: Award winning hard & soft goats cheeses from the college's own herd. Liquid milk also available.
Prices/Payment: Semi-hard plain cheese £8.25 per kg, smoked semi-hard cheese £9.35 per kg. Cash and cheques only.
Hours: 9am-3.30pm, Mon-Fri.
Notes: Disabled access. College plant nursery and 'Country Store' florist shop are also on site. The college supplies to some shops in the area.

EMMETT'S STORE
Peasenhall
Saxmundham
IP17 2HJ
Tel: 01728 660250
Fax: 01728 660404
Contact: Mr N.R. Jerrey or Mrs B.J. Jerrey
Produce: Oak smoked (hot) bacon and hams. Pickled ham which is by

Royal Appointment. Also stock locally smoked fish and smoked cheeses. Available by Mail Order. TNT next day delivery and parcel post. No min. order charge.
Prices/Payment: Cash and cheques only.
Hours: Mon-Fri, 8.30am-1pm and 2pm-5.30pm. Sat, 8.30am-1pm and 2pm- 5.30pm. Sun, 8.30am - 12.30pm.
Notes: Disabled access. Emmett's Store supply Horners (Yoxford), Sparrows (Laxfield), Bailey's Delica-tessen (Beccles) and Thomas the Grocer (Bungay). They are interested in supplying more to the trade.

LAUREL FARM HERBS
Main Road
Kelsale
Saxmundham
IP17 2RG
Tel: 01728 668223
Contact: Chris Seagon
Produce: Various large sizes of pot grown herbs. Many for picking right away or for planting in borders/herb gardens.
Prices/Payment: Prices from £1.25. Mail Order available, please 'phone for details. Cash and cheques only.
Hours: March 1st-Oct 31st: 10am-5pm, closed all day Tues. Nov 1st-Feb 28th: 10am-3pm, Wed, Thurs, Fri only. Other times by appointment. Well signposted.
Notes: Disabled access. Herb Gardens.

FIVE WINDS FARM SMOKEHOUSE AND BUTCHERY
The Station
Melton
Woodbridge
IP12 2PS
Tel: 01394 386116
Fax: 01394 461482
Contact: Howell Jenkins
Produce: Dry cured bacon and gammon, home cured ham, smoked bacon, ham, chicken, game and fish.

Gourmet sausage and smoked cheese. Rare Breeds Survival Trust accredited butcher for Suffolk. Fresh meat from old breeds of beef, pork and lamb, wild boar. Home-made pies, full meat turkey and bacon, steak and kidney. Ready meals. Also stock Quickes cheeses, locally produced jams, marmalades and chutney. 'Phone for mail order details.
Prices/Payment: Visa accepted.
Hours: Mon-Sat, 7.30am-5.30pm
Notes: Disabled access. Five Winds Farm are interested in supplying to the trade.

RED POLL MEATS
Cherry Tree House
Hacheston
Woodbridge
IP13 0DR
Tel: 01728 747240
Fax: 01728 746371
Email: redpoll@mcmail.com
Freephone: 0800 0262498
Contact: Sebastian Hall or Pauline Sfendilis
Produce: Free range and organic meat, mainly from rare breeds. Large Black pork, wild boar, Suffolk lamb, Norfolk black and bronze turkeys, chickens. Suffolk (Black) Cure ham made with molasses, dark sugar and locally brewed beer. Debenham Cure, a delicious moist, non-salty cure, lightly smoked in oak or beech chippings. Also stock newspapers and groceries in the shop/post office. Mail Order available, prices on application. Also personal delivery. Min order only on personal delivery; please enquire.
Prices/Payment: Best rib beef, £3.55 per lb. Leg Suffolk Lamb £2.80 per lb. Suffolk (Black) Cure gammon on bone, £2.97 per lb. Cash and cheques only.
Hours: Mon-Fri, 7am-6pm. Sat, 7am-1pm.
Notes: Disabled access. Farm visits by appointment. Red Poll are interested in supplying to the trade.

LATE ENTRY

D.R. EAREY & SON
97 Swan Street
Sible Hedingham
Halstead
Essex
CO9 3HP
Tel: 01787 460278
Fax: 01787 463626
Contact: Mr Paul Earey
Produce: Variety of home-made pork sausages. Home cooked gammon hams. Also Tiptree jams and preserves. Local home delivery. No min. order charge.
Prices/Payment: Cash and cheques only.
Hours: Mon, 8am-3pm. Tues-Fri, 8am-6pm. Sat, 8am-1pm.

The following are SHOPS within this region which do not produce but do sell quality or organic foods

COOK'S DELIGHT
360-364 High Street
Berkhamstead
Hertfordshire
HP4 1HU
Tel: 01442 863584
Fax: 01442 863702
Email: cooksd@globalnet.co.uk
Produce: Certified organic foods and beverages (Soil Assoc. P1563). Everything on sale except meat and fish. Fruit, vegetables, wines, ales, eggs, dried foods, nuts, babyfood, gluten free foods, teas, herbal teas, herbal coffee, jams, sauces, macrobiotic foods. Over 1,000 items. New ones added every week. Home delivery and box scheme available.
Hours: Mon, 7.30am-7pm. Tues, 7.30am-9pm. Wed, 7.30am-7.30pm. Thurs, 8am-7.30pm. Fri & Sat, 8am-6.30pm.
Notes: Disabled access.

SPICE OF LIFE
4 Burghley Centre
Bourne
Lincs
PE10 9EG
Tel: 01778 394735
Fax: 01406 362939
Produce: Wholefoods, cereals, beans, nuts, dried fruit, freshly baked bread including organic. Local produce and free range eggs. Takeaway; fresh made Tofu, fresh ground coffee and fresh olives.
Hours: Mon-Sat, 9am-5.30pm.
Notes: Disabled access. Mail Order and box scheme available. Bulk discounts. Spice of Life is interested in supplying to the trade.

ARTHURS WHOLEFOODS
3A Wellington Road
Dereham
Norfolk
NR19 2BP
Tel: 01362 697750
Produce: Organic muesli, muesli base, mixed fruit, fresh fruit and vegetables, selection of organic grains, seeds, nuts, pulses, dried fruits, flour. Free range eggs, local made preserves, refill service for honey, vinegar, coffee, shampoo, cleaning products, soy sauce, apple juice, unrefined cooking oils. Recycled paper, cleaning products.
Hours: Mon, Tues, Thurs, Fri, 9am-5.30pm. Weds, 9am-1pm. Sat, 9am-4pm.
Notes: Arthurs Wholefoods are also interested in supplying further to the trade.

THE HAPPY CATERPILLAR ORGANIC FOOD STORE
92 Leigh Road
Leigh-on-Sea
Essex
SS9 1BU
Tel: 01702 712982
Fax: 01702 712982
Produce: Certified organic fruit and vegetables, fresh bread, meat, dairy

(inc eggs), dried produce, babyfoods.
Dietary specialities. Box scheme
available.
Hours: Daily, 9am-5.30pm. Wed,
9am-3pm.
Notes: The Happy Caterpillar
Organic Food Store are interested in
supplying to the trade.

RAINBOW WHOLEFOODS
16 Dove Street
Norwich
Norfolk
Tel: 01603 630484
Fax: 01603 664066
Email: rainbow@paston.co.uk
Produce: Wide range of wholefood,
especially organic foods. Retail and
wholesale. Over 4,000 lines.
Hours: Mon-Sat, 9am-5.30pm.
Notes: Disabled access. Treehouse
vegetarian restaurant above shop.

RAFI'S SPICE BOX
15 Gaol Lane
Sudbury
Suffolk
CO10 6JL
Tel: 01787 881992
Fax: 01787 881992
Produce: Authentic curry mixes. Rafi
Fernandez's all inclusive curry pack
requiring only the addition of poultry,
meats, seafood or vegetables. 22
mixes. Pickles, chutneys and all the
ingredients needed for ethnic
cooking.
Hours: Mon-Sat, 9am-5pm.
Notes: No disabled access. World
wide Mail Order. Cookery school and
dining club.

LOAVES AND FISHES
52 Thoroughfare
Woodbridge
Suffolk
IP12 1AL
Tel: 01394 385650
Produce: Organic vegetables. Fresh
and smoked shellfish. Cheese.
Vitamins and minerals. Cosmetics.

Own label products.
Hours: Mon, Tues, Thurs, Fri, Sat,
8am-5.30pm. Wed, 8am-5pm.
Notes: No disabled access.

DERBYSHIRE

MAYFIELD TROUT
Manor Farm
Mayfield
Ashbourne
DE6 2JR
Tel: 01335 342050
Contact: Geoff or Pauline Allen
Produce: Pink fleshed Rainbow trout, grown in the water of the River Dove. Also home oak smoked trout fillets.
Prices/Payment: Cash and cheques only.
Hours: Telephone orders only for collection at a convienient time.
Notes: Suppliers to Chatsworth Farm Shop and Hulmes Fish Shop (Ashbourne). Mayfield Trout already supply restaurants and hotels and are happy to supply more.

MEYNELL LANGLEY ORGANIC FOOD
Lodge Farm
Lodge Lane
Kirk Langley
Ashbourne
DE6 4NX
Tel: 01332 824815
Contact: Helen Meynell/Godfrey Meynell
Produce: Organic beef and lamb, jointed and bagged, sometimes vacuum packed. Individual joints and cuts of frozen lamb or beef available from the farm. Mail order possible soon. Home delivery in the Derby area. Whole, half lambs and mixed boxes of beef delivered fresh locally . Min. order for delivery beef boxes at £60, lamb boxes at £30.
Prices/Payment: Mixed box of beef at £2.75 per lb. Cash and cheques only.
Hours: Fridays only 1pm-6pm but other times please 'phone first to arrange.
Notes: No disabled access. Meynell Langley Organic Food are interested in supplying to the trade.

CHATSWORTH FARM SHOP
Stud Farm, Pilsley
Bakewell
DE45 1UF
Tel: 01246 583392
Fax: 01246 582514
Email: farmshop@chatsworth-house co.uk
Internet: www.chatsworth-house.co.uk
Contact: Sandy Boyd
Produce: Beef, lamb, venison and game birds from the estate. Also pâtés, pies and a wide range of bakery products. A showcase for small British speciality producers. Over 2500 lines sold.
Mail Order service for all products stocked.
Prices/Payment: Mail Order, postage charged at cost. All Majors taken including Switch.
Hours: Mon-Sat, 9am-5pm. Sun, 11am-5pm.
Notes: Disabled access - but courtyard is cobbled. Won BBC Good Food Award 1997 for best speciality retailer.

HOLDSWORTH CHOCOLATES
Units 2 A& B
Station Road
Bakewell
DE45 1GE
Tel: 01629 813573
Fax: 01629 813850
Email: info@chocolat factory.co.uk
Internet: wwwchocolatefactory.co.uk
Contact: Barbara Holdsworth
Produce: High quality handmade chocolates. Made using natural ingredients, organic, additive and GMO free where available. Mail Order available, price list on request. No min order charge.
Prices/Payment: Cash and cheques only.
Hours: Mon-Fri, 8am-5pm. Sat, 9am-1.30pm.
Notes: No disabled access. Holdsworth Chocolates supply to all major department stores.

THE OLD ORIGINAL BAKEWELL PUDDING SHOP

The Square
Bakewell
DE45 1BT
Tel: 01629 812193
Fax: 01629 812260
Internet:
www.bakewellpuddingshop.co.uk
Contact: Gill Salmon
Produce: Original Bakewell puddings made to secret recipe from 1860, all handmade. A vast selection of home-made bread and cakes. Also stock a wide selection of preserves, pickles, chutneys, chocolates. Mail order post-a-pudding, hampers & larder goods; No min.order.
Prices/Payment: 3 sizes of pudding, the largest presented in a presentation box, £0.99, £2.25, £3.25.
Mail Order £6.50. Cash, cheque, Mastercard, Visa, Switch, Delta.
Hours: 7 days per week (closed Christmas Day). Winter: 8.30a -6pm, Summer: 8.30am-9pm
Notes: Disabled access to the shop. 1st floor restaurant. Pre booked groups can have a go at making their own pudding. Already supplying hotels and restaurants the Pudding Shop is interested in supplying more.

JERRY HOWARTH

7 King Street
Belper
DE56 1PW
Tel: 01773 822557
Contact: Mrs M Howarth
Produce: Home cured bacon & gammons. Parma style ham, black pudding (gold medal winner) and 9 varieties of pork sausage. Pork pies; various savoury pastries. Polony. Also stock groceries. Mail Order available. Postage payable by customer. No min order charge.
Prices/Payment: Sausages £1.67 per lb. Pork pies, £1.45. Cash and cheques only.
Hours: Mon and Wed, 8.30am-5pm. Tues, Thurs, Fri, 8.30am-5.30pm. Sat, 8.30am-4pm
Notes: Disabled access.

GEO. STAFFORD LTD

130 Belper Road
Stanley Common
Ilkeston
DE7 6FQ
Tel: 0115 932 5751
Contact: Janice Greaves
Produce: Gold Medal black puddings, home-made pork dripping, diploma award pork sausages, home cooked ham, beef, pork, haslet. Home-made polony and faggots. All goods made with the finest ingredients. Also stock cold meats, meat pies, fruit pies, cakes, bread, some greengroceries. Mail order overnight service for black puddings, min order 10kg (22lbs); smaller orders normal post.
Prices/Payment: £1.58/lb retail, £1.10/lb wholesale sausages, £1.42/lb retail, wholesale £1.10/lb black pudding. Dripping £1.88/lb retail, £1.40 wholesale. Cash and cheques only.
Hours: Open mornings Tues- Sat and some afternoons - please 'phone for specific times.
Notes: No special disabled access to the shop, but access to preparation area. Staffords are always prepared to give demonstrations and tastings if prior notice is given. Suppliers to six outlets in England, Scotland and Wales.

GLOUCESTERSHIRE

THE KITCHEN GARDEN

Oldown Country Park
Tockington
Bristol
BS32 4PG
Tel: 01454 413605
Fax: 01454 413955
Email: odfr@ad.com
Contact: Eric Dyer
Produce: Soft fruit, asparagus, beans, potatoes. Honey, jams, chutneys, cakes, scones, frozen meals, pork and lamb. Also stock sausages, bacon, cream, cheeses, biscuits, fruit juice, ice cream and chocolates.
Prices/Payment: Visa, Mastercard are accepted

Hours: Summer, 10am-6pm. Winter, 10am-4pm. Tues - Sun + Bank Holiday Mondays.
Notes: Other attractions include a licensed restaurant, garden, woodland walks and a children's farm.

SLIPSTREAM ORGANICS

34A Langdon Road
Cheltenham
GL53 7NZ
Tel: 01242 227273
Contact: Nick McCordall
Produce: Certified organic, locally produced fruit, salads, herbs and vegetables by box scheme and also a stall on the premises.
Prices/Payment: From £5 to £15 plus 50p delivery. Cash and cheques only.
Hours: Stall 9am-5pm – Fri only. 24 hour telephone service for placing an order.
Notes: Disabled access to stall areas. Box scheme operates in Cheltenham, Gloucester and Stroud areas. Established in 1994 Slipstream now supplies over 400 customers.

KOLISKO FARM LTD

Wynstones Drive
Brookthorpe
Gloucester
GL4 0UN
Tel: 01452 812322
Fax: 01452 812322
Contact: Adrian or Andie Luyk
Produce: Vegetables, eggs, milk, yoghurt, meat. Also stock fruit, wholefoods, bread, juices, dairy products and meats.
Prices/Payment: Cash & cheques only.
Hours: Tues & Fri, 8.30am-5pm. Sat, 10am-1pm.
Notes: Disabled access possible. Walled garden & farm which is all fully organic. Dairy shorthorn cows, sheep and chickens. Kolisko Farm supply to A. Souter (Global Organics) Stall (Stroud), Ruskin Mill (Nailsworth) and M. Harrison (Local Box Scheme).

SMARTS TRADITIONAL GLOUCESTER CHEESES

Old Ley Court
Chapel Lane
Birdwood
Churcham
Gloucester
GL2 8AR
Tel: 01452 750225
Fax: 01452 750225
Contact: Diana Smart
Produce: Handmade Single and Double Gloucester cheese made from unpasteurised milk from Smart's own herd. Unpasteurised cream and plain yoghurt (no additives). Delivery in the Gloucester area only. Mail Order service available. No min. order.
Prices/Payment: Single Gloucester £3.40 per lb, Double Gloucester £3.30 per lb. Mini cheeses £3.99 each. Cash and cheques only.
Hours: Tues and Thur, 9am-11am and 12pm-5.30pm.
Notes: Disabled access limited to cheesemaking operation. Cheesemaking demonstrations including tastings and sales, Tues and Thurs as above. Smart's supply; Fine Cheese Co (Bath & Cheltenham), Farmhouse (Gloucester), Fortnum and Mason (London) and Neals Yard Dairy (London).

HOBBS HOUSE BAKERY

39 High Street
Chipping Sodbury
BS37 6BA
Tel: 01454 321629
Fax: 01454 329757
Contact: Trevor Herbert
Produce: Full range of white, wholemeal, malted wheat and speciality breads. Home-made confectionery, marmalades and jams. Sandwiches. Mail Order available. No min. order but recommend min 10kg.
Prices/Payment: Cash, cheques only.
Hours: 7.30am-6pm.
Notes: Disabled access. Hobbs House supply to Fine Cheese Co (Bath, Cheltenham), Wild Oats (Bristol) and Spice of Life (Bradford).

MINOLA SMOKED PRODUCTS
Kencot Hill Farmhouse
Filkins
LECHLADE
GL7 3QY
Tel: 07000 646652/476653
EMAIL: salmon@minola.co.uk
INTERNET:www.minola.co.uk
CONTACT: Hugh and Jane Forestier-Walker
PRODUCE: Smoked Scottish salmon, gravadlax, dilled Scottish salmon, fresh Scottish salmon, smoked trout, cod roe, prawns, oysters, kippers, haddock and smoked mackerel, smoked almonds, smoked cashews, smoked Mature English Cheddar, Wedmore, Cheddar with paprika, Caerphilly, goat's cheese, goat's cheese with chive, smoked unsalted butter. Smoked turkey roll, chicken, Barbary Duck and quail. Smoked bacon, gammon, lamb, venison and quail's eggs. Available by Mail Order, up to 2kg 1st Class Post, over 2kg delivery by overnight carrier. No min order charge. Only smoked salmon and gravadlax are available for Mail Order in Dec.
PRICES/PAYMENT: Please 'phone for price list. Major credit cards and Switch.
HOURS: Mon-Fri, 8am-6pm. Sat, 9am- 5pm. Sun, 9am-12.30pm. Other times by arrangement.
NOTES: Disabled access. Minola Smoked Products supply to Mrs Bumbles, Coxeters's, Well's Stores, Nadder Food Co.
They are interested in supplying more to the trade

THE FLOUR BAG
Burford Street
Lechlade
GL7 3AP
Tel: 01367 252322
Fax: 01367 253563
Contact: Maurice Chaplais
Produce: A variety of traditional and speciality breads including an overnight white bread, a granary style bread and organic wholemeal. Also beer bread with oats, sundried tomato,ciabatta, walnut, pecan and apple, sunflower and soda etc. Also a range of of traditional cakes including almond Madeira cake, chocolate truffle and rich fruit cake, lardy cake and bakewell tarts. Also a range of patisserie including pain au chocolat, french apple flan, strawberry tarts, crème brulée etc. Also stock English cheese, pâtés, salamis and about 20 different olive oils, pastas and honey.
Prices/Payment: Cash and cheques only.
Hours: Mon-Sat, 8.30am-6pm.
Notes: Disabled access. The Flour Bag supplies to Eastbrook Farm Organic shop on Tuesdays andFridays.

DRURY'S MORETON-IN-MARSH
The High Street
Moreton-in-Marsh
GL56 0AF
Tel; 01608 650318
Fax: 01608 650318
Contact: Paul Baggott
Produce: Home-made pies; venison, pheasant, wild boar, duck & orange, chicken & leek, beef & stout; also numerous types of pasties etc. A range of up to 40 types of sausages; i.e. lamb & parsley, pork, leek & ginger, venison, wild boar, pork, stilton & hickory etc. Pâtés; chicken liver, smoked salmon, pigeon etc. Also stock cheeses, deli & butchery. Mustards, preserves, pickles, chutneys, pasta, wines & drinks, cream, bread and biscuits. Postal Service available. Christmas hamper service. No min. order.
Prices/Payment: Sausages from £2.30 per lb, large beef & venison pie, £3.99 - small £1.50. Cash and cheques only.
Hours: 7am-5pm most days, close at 4pm Tues, 4.30pm Sat. Closed Sunday.
Notes: Disabled access. Tastings available. Drury's do supply to the trade and are interested in supplying more.

SUNSHINE HEALTH SHOP
25 Church Street
Stroud
GL5 1JL
Tel: 01453 763923
Contact: Andrew Hill
Produce: Organic bread, cakes and
savouries from their own bakery. Also
a range of organic wholefoods and
health foods. Organic vegetables.
Mail Order service countrywide.
Please 'phone for price list and order
form. Local delivery service. No min.
delivery charge for orders of £20 or
over.
Prices/Payment: Mastercard, Visa,
Delta. Switch.
Hours: Mon-Sat, 9am-5.30pm.
Notes: Disabled access. Tastings from
time to time. Specialist nutritional
advisory service. Interested in supplying to the trade if order quantity is
sufficient. Min. £35 for bakery
products.

HEREFORDSHIRE

CHERRY WOOD FARM
Lyston Lane, Orcop Hill
Hereford
HR2 8EW
Tel: 01981 540177
Contact: C. Stockdale
Produce: Organic lamb, beef, bio-
dynamic flour, eggs, potatoes, carrots,
swedes, turnips, spinach, onions etc.
Can deliver locally.
Prices/Payment: Cash and cheques
only.
Hours: 9am-9pm.
Notes: No disabled access. Cherry
Wood Farm are interested in supplying
to the trade.

D & G WALL
Breinton Manor Fruit Farm
Hereford
HR4 7PJ
Tel: 01432 265271
Contact: David Wall
Produce: Eating and cooking apples,

pears and plums. 23 types of cooking
apples, 3 types of pears, 4 types of
plums. Honey and apple juice. Also
stock a small amount of vegetables and
30 tons of potatoes.
Prices/Payment: Cash and cheques
only.
Hours: Daily 10am-5pm. Sundays Sept
-Christmas, 11am-5pm. Closed on
Sundays after Christmas until shop
closes for Summer at Easter.
Notes: Disabled access. Toilets, large
hard car park. Coaches by appointment.

D.R. & S.M. JENKINS
Green Acres, Dinmore
Hereford
HR4 8ED
Tel: 01568 797045
Contact: S.M. Jenkins
Produce: Over 70 varieties of organic
vegetables in season. Also organic
meat. A range of preserves, organic
cider and wine also available.
Prices/Payment: Minimum order £5.00
for local box scheme. Cash and
cheques only.
Hours: Tue-Sat, 9am-5.30pm. Closed
Sun and Mon.
Notes: Green Acres has disabled
acccess. Farm walks by arrangement.
Suppliers to several organic outlets.
Green Acres is interested in supplying
to the trade.

KAREN TIBBETTS
Henclose Cottage
Little Dewchurch
Hereford
HR2 6PP
Tel: 01432 840826
Contact: Karen Tibbetts
Produce: Lamb, pork, kidmeat, bacon,
sausages, goat's milk and seasonal
vegetables.
Prices/Payment: Cash and cheques
only.
Hours: Please 'phone to arrange
collection.
Notes: No special disabled access, but
flat ground so wheelchairs are not a
problem.

PROSPECT ORGANIC GROWERS
Prospect Cottage, Bartestree
Hereford
HR1 4BY
Tel: 01432 851164
Contact: Christine Edwards
Produce: Very wide range of vegetables and salads throughout the year. Also stock meat, wholefoods, bread, dairy, some imported fruit and veg. Nuts, fruit, mustards, chocolate bars, goat's milk, sheep's milk. Olive oil, sunflower oil, cider vinegar.
Prices/Payment: Cash and cheques only
Hours: Tues-Fri, 9am-6pm. Sat, 9am-1pm
Notes: Disabled access. Prospect Organic Growers supply to other outlets through Organic Marketing Co.

SEPTEMBER DAIRY PRODUCTS
Newhouse Farm, Almeley
Hereford
HR3 6LJ
Tel: 01544 327561
Fax: 01544 327561
Contact: Adam Glyn-Jones
Produce: Milk, cream and free range eggs. Also ice cream made from the above. Honey, cider and meat from the farm and from another local organic meat purveyor. Also stock walking sticks and pottery. Newhouse Farm is in organic conversion due to be completed in Sept. 1999.
Prices/Payment: 1 litre ice cream, £3.40. Cash and cheques only.
Hours: Dawn to dusk seven days a week
Notes: Disabled access. Informal demonstrations by appointment. September Dairy Products also supply Georges (Kington), Husseys (Kington), Harvestore (Hereford) and Organic Options (Leominster).

SHEPHERDS ICE CREAM
Cwm Farm
Peterchurch
Hereford
HR2 0TA
Tel: 01981 550716
Contact: Juliet Noble/Martin Orbach
Produce: Ice cream from sheep's milk

using local fruit where possible; 13 flavours - vanilla, chocolate, tayberry, blackcurrant, damson, strawberry, mango, orange & Cointreau, choc mint chip, pistachio, coconut, ginger, coffee & walnut. Available anytime if you ring beforehand.
Prices/Payment: £2 per half litre, £4.50 per 2 litre. Cash and cheques only
Hours: Available at any time if people ring beforehand.
Notes: No disabled access. Suppliers to ten other outlets.

THE DAIRY HOUSE
Whitehill Park
Weobley
Hereford
HR4 8QE
Tel: 01544 318815
Fax: 01544 318815
Contact: Pru Lloyd
Produce: Soft cheeses, créme fraîche, clotted cream, fromage frais, double cream, live yogurt, fresh cheesecakes, greek style yogurt, speciality cheesecake , made to order. Also stock September ice cream.
Prices/Payment: Cash, cheques only.
Hours: Mon-Fri, 8.30am-4pm. Sat,8.30am-1.00pm.
Notes: Disabled access. Demonstrations if organised in advance. The Dairy House supplies to numerous outlets.

MOUSETRAP CHEESE
The Pleck, Monkland
Leominster
HR6 9DB
Tel: 01568 720307
Contact: Karen and Mark Hindle
Produce: Hard farmhouse cheeses called Little Hereford and Herfordshire Sage.
Made to an old family recipe, from unpasteurised cow's milk. Also stock 30-40 other British farmhouse cheeses, locally made apple juice, honey, ice cream etc. Cottage Delight chutneys & preserves, cheese biscuits. Cheese hampers also available.

Prices/payments: Little Hereford £4.40/
lb and Herefordshire Sage £4.65/lb
Cash and cheques only.
Hours: 10am-5.30pm every day.
(Closed Sun & Mon Nov - Easter). 24hr
Mail Order service available.
Notes: There is disabled access to the
Pleck. Cheesemaking demonstrations,
Mon,Wed and Fri (10am - 2.30pm).
The Hindles are interested in supplying
to the trade.

MEADOWLAND MEATS
Model Farm, Hildersley
Ross-on-Wye
HR9 7NN
Tel: 01989 562208
Fax: 01989 769724
Contact: Peter Askwith
Produce: Model Farm raises organic
meats and other produce. Also stock
cheeses, preserves and fruit juices.
Home delivery service.
Prices/Payment– Cash and cheques
only.
Hours: Mon,Tues, Wed,Thurs, & Sat,
9am-5pm. Fri, 9am-6pm.
Notes: Disabled access. Farm animals
to view (working farm). Possible trade
supply.

TEME VALLEY HONEY
Sutton House Farm, Sutton
Tenbury Wells
WR15 8RJ
Tel: 01584 810424
Contact: Dr Carol Field
Produce: Worcestershire honey both
bottled and in the comb. Available by
Mail Order, postage charged at cost.
No min order charge.
Prices/Payment: Bottled honey £1.80
to £2.20 per lb. Comb honey £1.80
per 7oz (retail prices).
Hours: If they are on the farm then
open. If making a special journey
please 'phone first
Notes: Disabled access. Teme Valley
Honey supply to ; Hole in the Wall
(Tenbury), Barber and Manuel
(Leominster), Franklins Cider (Little
Hereford), The Fruit Basket (Ludlow).

LEICESTERSHIRE

GOODNESS FOODS
18 Silver Street
Leicester
LE1 5ET
Tel: 01327 706611
Fax: 01327 300436
Email: info@goodness.co.uk
Internet:
www.goodness.co.uk.goodness
Contact: Alan Carter or Lesley Cutts
Produce: Flapjacks, mueslis and bread.
Also stock many branded organic
foods, vegetarian meals, jams, juices,
baby foods etc, ice cream, juices,
cereals, teas, coffee and snacks. Mail
Order for abroad, or people who
cannot easily access local source. No
min order charge but carriage paid at
cost.
Prices/Payment: Flapjacks organic and
low fat 59p each. Muesli 500g £1.39,
3kg – £4.54, bread– 2lb loaf 89p. All
major credit cards taken. Switch.
Hours: 9am-5pm.
Notes: Disabled access to shop.
Goodness Foods supply to most
independent health food shops in the
U.K. They are interested in supplying
to the trade. For Mail Order see details
in Mail Order section

THE REAL MEAT COMPANY
8 Allandale Road
Stoneygate
Leicester
Tel: 0116 270 3396
(See Main Entry under Warminster,
Wilts.

GROWING CONCERN
Home Farm
Woodhouse Lane
Nanpantan
Loughborough
LE11 3YG
Tel: 01509 239228
Fax: 01509 239228
Contact: Michael/Mary Bell
Produce: Organic meat from rare

breeds, Traditional Hereford cattle, last commercial beef herd in Britain. Large Black pigs, Dorset Down sheep, geese, ducks and chickens. Home cured hams and bacon. Gourmet sausages, game, cheeses, vegetables and eggs. Farm baked pies, sweet & savouries. Wine license applied for. Mail Order available. No min. order charge.
Prices/Payment: Sausage meat, £2.75 per lb, rump steak £7.75 per lb. Whole birds £2.40 per lb. All major credit cards taken.
Hours: Telephone for details.
Notes: Disabled access. Teashop. Farm visits. Growing Concern are interested in supplying to the trade.

HUNGARY LANE FARM
Sutton Bonington
Loughborough
LE12 5NB
Tel: 01509 673897
Fax: 01509 673897
Contact: Mrs Sue Bradley
Produce: Autumn and winter vegetables, potatoes, wheat and rye flour. Freezer packs of beef, lamb and poultry reared on the farm, which is under Biodynamic/organic management with the Demeter symbol. Also stock organic apple juice and other vegetables and fruit.
Prices/Payment: Cash & cheques only.
Hours: Sats. only last weekend Aug. till end of Feb. 9am-5pm.
Notes: No problem with disabled access. Hungary Lane Farm supply to Denis Brewin Quality Foods (Loughborough) and are happy to supply trade customers.

CLAYBROOKE MILL LTD
Frolesworth Lane
Claybrooke Magna
Lutterworth
LE17 5DB
Tel: 01455 202443
Fax: 01455 202553
Contact: David Mountford
Produce: Stoneground organic and traditional flours, flour mixes and

related cereal products - semolina, bran etc. Also stock gluten, nuts, seeds and grains. Mail order service available - no minimum order.
Prices/Payment: Visa, Solo, Switch, Delta, Access.
Notes: Partial disabled access to the mill. Claybrooke Mill flour is available at Natural Choice (Hinckley), The Health Shop (Nuneaton), Currant Affairs (Leicester) and Peppers Whole Foods (Leicester). Mr Mountford is interested in supplying hotels and restaurants and other outlets.

MANOR OVEN BAKERY
40/42 Sherrard Street
Melton Mowbray
LE13 1XJ
Tel: 01664 565920
Contact: Mr Richard Greasley
Produce: Original breads produced by sour dough method with many different flavours and flours. Traditional English cakes and pastries. Mail order available on selected fruit cakes, e.g. Melton Country Gentleman's cake. The bakery also sells Marriages flours, Higgins Teas & Coffees.
Prices/Payment: Speciality breads from £1.10. Mail Order cakes from £7.50. Cash and cheques only
Hours: Mon- Sat, 9am-5pm.
Notes: Coffee shop also sells gifts, salt breads, marzipan figures etc. Willing to supply to trade and would give discounts, but no delivery.

NORTHFIELD FARM LTD
Northfield Farm
Whissendine Lane
Cold Overton
Oakham
LE15 7QF
Tel: 01664 474271
Email: nthfield1@aol.com
Contact: Jan & Tessa McCourt
Produce: Rare breeds butcher. Rearing and selling their own and other small producers' rare breed beef, pork, lamb & bacon. Home-made sausages & burgers. Also organic free range

chicken and free range eggs. Also stock British and Irish farmhouse cheeses, honeys, chutneys, mustards, olive oils, preserves and other complementary products. Full nationwide Mail Order service available. Delivery charged at £8.95, no matter how large or small the order.

Prices/Payment: Most major credit cards accepted, except Amex & Diners. Switch accepted.

Hours: Tues-Sat, 9.30am-5.30pm, other times by appointment.

Notes: Disabled access to yard but not shop. All animals are on view around the farm. Northfield Farm supply to a number of restaurants and pubs.

WHISSENDINE WINDMILL
14A Melton Road
Whissendine
Oakham
LE15 7EU
Tel: 01664 474172
Contact: Nigel Moon
Produce: A range of stoneground organic flours wholemeal, brown, white, ryemeal, barleymeal, oatmeal, maizemeal, spelt. Organic reg. number (P080027 UK2). Mail Order available. No min. order.

Prices/Payment: 1.5kg pastry flour 95p, bread flour 97p. Cash and cheques only.

Hours: Sun, 2pm-5pm. Please 'phone for times of other days.

Notes: Disabled access. Ground floor only. Visitors can see this 19th century mill at work

NORTHAMPTONSHIRE

HILL FARM HERBS
Park Walk
Brigstock
Kettering
NN14 3HH
Tel: 01536 373694
Fax: 01536 373246
Contact: Mrs E. Simpson
Produce: Herb plants, herb vinegars

and traditional chutneys. Also stock cottage garden plants, dried flowers, gifts, essential oils, pots, baskets and pot-pourri.

Prices/Payment: Herb plants (9cm), £1.25, £1.65. Vinegars from £2.35 per 250ml to £12.60 for gift bottles. £1.95-£2.50 for chutneys. Most credit cards taken.

Hours: Easter to end of Sept, every day 10.30am-5.30pm. Rest of year, closed Mon & Tues. Open other days from 10.30am-4.30pm.

Notes: Disabled access. Tea shop and gardens open Easter-end Sept. Plants displayed in the old farm yard. Limited supplies available for wholesale.

DAILY BREAD
CO-OPERATIVE LTD
The Old Laundry
Bedford Road
Northampton
NN4 7AD
Tel: 01604 621531
Fax: 01604 603725
Contact: Ian Campbell
Produce: A large range of natural wholefoods including; dried fruits, nuts, beans and pulses, flours and grains. Own mixed mueslis, fruit and nut mixes, soup mixes and rice. They are attempting to offer an organic alternative on all their lines. Also stock soya milks, organic pasta and pasta sauces, olive oils, margarines, cooking aids, vinegars, jams, fruit juices, tea and coffee, organic baby foods and Ecover products.

Prices/Payment: Special muesli £1.46 per kg, mixed herbs 68p for 50g, porridge oats 55p per kg. Most major credit/debit cards accepted.

Hours: Mon-Fri, 8.30am-5.30pm. Sat, 8.30am-5pm.

Notes: Disabled access. Daily Bread Co-operative are a Christian Co-op who believe food is fundamental and should have good nutritional value and be good value for money. They would like to sell more to the catering trade. See also Cambridge, under same name.

ARK FARM SHEEP DAIRY
Ark Farm, Tiffield
Towcester
NN12 8AB
Tel: 01327 350202
Contact: Sue/Gerald Williams
Produce: Unpasteurised and pasteurised sheepmilk in pints. Sheep's milk yogurt and sheep's milk ice cream. Also stock sheep milk cheeses.
Prices/Payment: Sheep's milk 80p per pint. Ice cream from £2.99 per litre. Cash and cheques only.
Hours: Every afternoon 2.30pm-5pm. All day Sat, 9am-5pm. Other times by appointment.
Notes: Disabled access. Ark Farm already supply to the trade and are interested in supplying more.

NOTTINGHAMSHIRE

THE GINGER PIG
Harwell Manor, Harwell
Everton
Doncaster
DN10 5BU
Tel: 01777 816737
Contact: Anne Wilson
Produce: Traditionally dry-cured bacon. Pork and a good range of sausages produced from free-range Tamworth pigs (fed on Vegetarian Society approved feeds containing no antibiotics). Free range eggs. Also stock locally reared and traditionally hung & butchered beef and lamb. Mail Order available. Small via 1st class post; large via national carrier. No min order charge.
Prices/Payment: Sausages £2.20 per lb. Dry cured bacon £2.65-£3.95 per lb
Hours: Mon-Sat, 9am-5pm.
Notes: Disabled access. Traditional small butcher's shop on the farm. The Ginger Pig supplies to Bawtry Delicatessen, Whitwells Delicatessen (Uppingham), Flores House Delicatessen (Oakham), Canterburys Delicatessen (West Bridgford, Notts) and The DeliStop (Welwyn). They are interested in supplying to the trade.

LIMETREE PANTRY
19 High Street
Edwinstowe
Mansfield
NG21 9QP
Tel: 01623 824790
Fax: 8 Rings on 'phone
Contact: Harry Toms
Produce: Handmade shortcrust pastry; savoury and fruit pies. Available freshly frozen, overnight home delivery. No min order charge.
Prices/Payment: 8" savoury £5.50, 6" £3.50. Fruit pies 8" £3. Cash and cheques only.
Hours: Lime Tree Pantry retail at craft fayres, agricultural shows and steam rallies and covered some 220 shows in 1998. Pie Shoppe to open in 1999 at the above address. Hours will be 11am-2.30pm and 5.30pm-9pm.
Notes: Suppliers to the Royal Sandringham Estate in Norfolk. They are interested in supplying more to the trade.

P.J. ONIONS (FARMS)
Shelton Lodge
Newark
NG23 5JJ
Tel: 01949 850268
Fax: 01949 850714
Contact: P.J. Onions
Produce: Organic chickens all year. Organic turkeys at Christmas.
Prices/Payment: Chicken £1.95 per lb. Cash and cheques only.
Hours: Tues, 3.30pm-5pm.
Notes: Disabled access. Suppliers to Out of this World supermarkets, Sainsbury (London area), Pure Organic Foods, HDRC Garden centre and C.C. Sparkes (Blackheath, London) and others.

THE COUNTRY VICTUALLER
Winkburn Hall
Newark
NG22 8PQ
Tel: 01636 636465
Fax: 01636 636717
Email: anyone@alderton.co.uk

Contact: Richard Craven
Produce: Sole makers of Alderton ham; marmalade glazed. Orange and stout ham, pâtés/terrine; chicken liver pâté with brandy, wild boar pâté with juniper berries, pheasant terrine. Smoked chicken, smoked turkey breasts, smoked duck breasts. Christmas puddings. Mail Order available; overnight delivery service. Min. order charge £50.
Prices/Payment: From £3.20 for 220g pâté to £70 for whole victuallers orange & stout ham. All major credit cards taken plus Amex.
Hours: Orders can be placed during working hours on answerphone.
Notes: No retail premises. The Country Victualler supply four famous London West End stores and are interested in supplying more to the trade.

COLSTON BASSETT & DISTRICT DAIRY LTD
Harby Lane, Colston Bassett
Nottingham
NG12 3FN
Tel: 01949 81322
Fax: 01949 81132
Contact: Susan Levers
Produce: Colston Bassett Blue Stilton, White Stilton and Shropshire Blue cheese. Hand turned and hand rubbed, matured for three months. Mail Order courier service available. Min. order quarter Stilton (2kg).
Prices/Payment: Cash and cheques only
Hours: Mon-Fri, 9am-4pm, closed 12.30pm-1.30pm for lunch. Sat, 9am-11.30am. Closed Sun and Bank Holidays.
Notes: Disabled access. The dairy already supply to shops but trade enquiries welcome.

CROPWELL BISHOP CREAMERY
Nottingham Road
Cropwell Bishop
Nottingham
NG12 3BQ
Tel: 0115 989 2350

Fax: 0115 989 9046
Internet:
www.cropwelllbishopcreamery.co.uk
Produce: Cropwell Bishop Blue Stilton, Cropwell Bishop Blue Shropshire Cheese, Cropwell Bishop Mature Cheddar, all suitable for vegetarians. Mail Order available. No min. order charge.
Prices/Payment: Cash and cheques only.
Hours: Mon-Fri, 9am-4pm
Notes: No disabled access. Cropwell Bishop Creamery supply to wholesalers

THAYMAR DAIRY ICE CREAM
Haughton Park Farm
nr Bothamsall
RETFORD
DN22 8DB
TEL: 01623 860320
FAX: 01623 860320
CONTACT: Thelma Cheetham
PRODUCE: Dairy ice cream made with Jersey milk & double cream. Over 25 flavours using natural flavourings, no artificial colours or preservatives. Suitable for vegetarians. Sorbet and home-made Charlotte Gateaux & Semi Freddi. Also stock jams, preserves, biscuits, Belvoir cordials, James White apple juices, Elizabeth King pork pies and sausages. Ginger Pig products, gourmet dips etc.
PRICES/PAYMENT: All major credit cards. Switch and Delta.
HOURS: 10am-5.30pm 7 days a week in summer. 10am-5pm Wed to Sunday, Jan-Easter.
NOTES: Disabled access. Cottage tearooms open daily. Book for evening group tastings and factory tour. Thaymar Dairy Ice Cream supply to Taylors of Tickhill, Christys Farm Shop, Cambs Farm Shop and Chatsworth Farm Shop. They are looking for more quality outlets.

CHRISTY FINE FOODS

Hockerton Grange, Hockerton
Southwell
NG25 OPJ
Tel: 01636 816472
Fax: 01636 816472
Contact: Tina Gleeson, Simon Christy
Produce: Rare breed meats, game, eighty British cheeses, English wine, cider and beer. Also stock, jams, chutneys, biscuits and cakes. Order by 1pm delivered next day by noon. No min order charge.
Prices/Payment: Visa, Mastercard, Switch.
Hours: 9am-5.30pm seven days a week.
Notes: Disabled access. Cafe seating 80. Christy Fine Foods are interested in supplying to the trade.

SHROPSHIRE

DUKESHILL HAM CO. LTD

Deuxhill
Bridgnorth
WV16 6AF
Tel: 01746 789519
Fax: 01746 789533
Contact: Neale Hollingsworth
Produce: Traditionally dry-cured Yorkshire Hams, traditional Wiltshire cure ham and the unique dry cured Shropshire Black Ham. Also stock sliced air-dried Parma style ham.
Prices/Payment: Half Wiltshire ham £29.00.Whole Shropshire Black £77.00. All major credit cards and Amex accepted.
Hours: Mail order only 24 hours answering.
Notes: Suppliers to famous West End stores.

WOMERTON GOATS

Womerton Farm
All Stretton
Church Stretton
SY6 6LJ
Tel: 01694 751260
Contact: Ruth Lawrence

Produce: Unpasteurised speciality goat's cheese made with vegetarian rennet. Free range pork & lamb available (seasonally at the moment).
Prices/Payment: From £5 per pound. Cash and cheques only.
Hours: 'Please phone for details.
Notes: From approx Easter 1999 there will be a new farm shop on site, with disabled access. Mail Order will be possible.

D.W. WALL & SON

Wilton House, Corvedale Road
Craven Arms
SY7 9NL
Tel: 01588 672308
Contact: Mike Wall or Kevyn Magill
Produce: Accredited retail butcher in Shropshire for Rare Breeds Survival Trust. Sausage including gluten free or additive free. Full ranged of home-cooked meats. Free local delivery.
Prices/Payment: Cash and cheques only.
Hours: Mon,Tues, Thurs, Fri, 7am-5 30pm, Wed, 7am-1pm. Sat, 7am-4.30pm.
Notes: D.W. Wall & Son have another branch at Ludlow. They specialise in supplies to the catering trade.

SHROPSHIRE HILLS ORGANIC PRODUCE SUPPLIES

Bentley House
Clungunford
Craven Arms
SY7 0PN
Tel: 01588 660747
Email: shops.organics@bigfoot.com
Contact: G Lambert
Produce: Organic fruit and vegetables sold via a vegetable box scheme. Weekly delivery of either standard seasonal boxes of veg or fruit, or an "order-your-own" system from weekly order form. Min order £5.
Prices/Payment: Cash and cheques only.
Notes: Deliveries only available to South Shropshire, North Hereford and Welsh Border.

GREENLINK ORGANIC FOODS
16 Corve Street
Ludlow
SY8 1DA
Tel: 01584 872665
Contact: Jane Straker
Produce: Home-grown organic
vegetables. Dairy products: meat &
poultry from Graig Farm, ice cream
dairy and non dairy, wines, beers and
ciders, bread and wholefoods. Also
stocks ecologically sound cleaning
products and paints. Cruelty free
toiletries, recycled stationery.
Greeting cards and newsagency.
Prices/Payment: Cash and cheques
only.
Hours: Mon-Sat, 7am-7pm. Sun,
7.30am-1pm.
Notes: Disabled access. Greenlink
are interested in supplying to the
trade. See also Great Malvern
(Worcs.), under same name.

PIMHILL FARM SHOP
Lea Hall
Harmer Hill
Shrewsbury
SY4 3DY
Tel: 01939 290342/290075
Fax: 01939 291156
Email:
pimhill.organicfarm@btinternet.com
Contact: Nick Billet
Produce: Organically grown; wheat,
oats and potatoes. Soil Assoc number
M16M P600. Wheat is milled into
flour on the farm and sold in the farm
shop and cafe. Specialists in home
baking and a wide range of organic
food. Also stock an extensive range
of organic lines.
Prices/Payment: Carrot cake £1.99,
Hand raised ham & pork pie 200
gram £1.99, hand made quiche
£2.35. All major credit cards taken.
Switch.
Hours: 10am-5pm every day.
Notes: Disabled access. Pimhill have
been an organic farm for over two
generations. Cafe, shire horse,
children's play area. Possible interest
in supplying to the trade.

VILLA FARM ORGANIC PRODUCE
Plealey Villas, Pontesbury
Shrewsbury
SY5 0XT
Tel: 01743 860304
Contact: Robert Hamer
Produce: Main crop organic vegeta-
bles available for sale in the winter
months. Also pork, beef, lamb and
chicken freezer meats. Organic cereals.
Prices/Payments: Cash and cheques
only
Hours: 10am-5pm six days a week.
Notes: Suppliers to "Food For Thought"
shops in Shropshire.

STAFFORDSHIRE

A JOHNSON & SON
(Member of the Q Guild of Butchers)
1 Hadley Street, Yoxall
Burton-on-Trent
DE13 8NB
Tel: 01543 472235
Fax: 01543 472235
Contact: John Bailey
Produce: Locally sourced beef, pork,
lamb and free range chickens and
traditional breed meat, e.g. Gloucester
Old Spot, Saddle Back, Tamworth –
pork; Dexter, White Park, British White
– beef. Ryeland, Portland, Soay, lamb
and one week annually in Aug, North
Ronaldsay lamb (fed exclusively on
seaweed). Own range of handmade
sausages, dry cured bacon and black
pudding. Also stock handmade cakes,
pickles and curry sauces (mainly
additive and preservative free).
Approx. 30 cheeses mainly British.
Delicatessen selling a range of
handmade products including ready
cooked meals, pâtés, terrines and
puddings, all from natural ingredients.
Mail Order available. Home delivery
available within 20 mile radius.
Prices/Payment: Cash and cheques only.
Hours: Tues, Thur, Fri, Sat, 8.30am-
1pm, 2pm-6pm. Wed, 8.30am-1pm.
Closed Mon.
Notes: Disabled access. A Johnson &
Son supply to the trade.

ASPLINS OATCAKES
2 Haywood Street
Leek
ST13 5JX
Tel: 01538 387556
Contact: Mr L Asplin
Produce: Oatcakes and pikelets. From
a generations old recipe. Also stock
pies, sandwiches, cakes and drinks.
Prices/Payment: Oatcakes and
pikelets 10p each. Cash and cheques
only.
Hours: 6am-1pm, Mon-Sat.
Notes: No disabled access. Asplins
Oatcakes supply to AN & JM Bould,
H.Meakin & Sons and E. Ash.
Also catering suppliers.

STAFFORDSHIRE ORGANIC CHEESE
New House Farm
Acton
Newcastle-under-Lyme
ST5 4EE
Tel/Fax: 01782 680366
Contact: M & B Deaville & Son
Produce: Organic cheeses, hard
pressed cow's milk cheese, hard
sheep's milk cheese. Naturally home-
grown, additive free meat and meat
products. Also stock organic wines,
beers, wholefoods etc. Mail Order
available for cheese.
Prices/Payment: Cheques, cash only.
Hours: Fri, 9am-5.30pm for retail
customers, at other times by arrangement , 'phone first. Closed Sun.
Notes: No disabled access, but help
is given. Staffordshire organic cheese
is available from many stockists all
over the country.

HIGH LANE OATCAKES
597/599 High Lane
Burslem
Stoke-on-Trent
ST6 7EP
Tel: 01782 810180
Fax: 01782 522981
Contact: Roy Gavin
Produce: Staffordshire oatcakes,
pikelets (similar to crumpets) and
donuts. Mail Order Service available

for oatcakes. No min. order charge.
Prices/Payment: Pack of 1 doz
oatcakes, £1.24. Pack of six £2.80 by
Mail Order including postage and
packing. Cash and cheques only.
Hours: Tues, 8am–5.30pm, Thurs, and
Sat, 7am–6pm, Fri, 7am–6.30pm, Sun,
7am–12pm. Closed Monday and
Wednesday

OATCAKES & PIKELETS
62 Waterloo Street
Hanley
Stoke-on-Trent
ST1 3PW
Tel: 01782 261883
Contact: Glenn Fowler
Produce: Staffordshire oatcakes,
traditionally made in this last terrace
house bakery, and served through
the front window. Oatcakes are
found on diet sheets for healthy
eating. Available by post at £3.50
per dozen.
Price: 10p each, 50p half dozen, £1
per dozen at window.
Hours: Thur, 6am-5.50pm, Fri, 6am -
6pm, Sat, 6am-2pm, Sun, 6am-12
midday
Notes: Disabled access; no credit
cards. Possibility of some supply to
the trade.

WARWICKSHIRE

BERKSWELL TRADITIONAL FARM-STEAD MEATS
The Farm Shop
Larges Farm
Back Lane
Meriden
Coventry
CV7 7LD
Tel: 01676 522409
Contact: Philip Tuckey
Produce: Accredited Rare Breed
Survival Trust butcher in the Midlands.
Home dry cured bacon from tradi-
tional breed pork. Speciality sausages
and burgers. They also rear and breed
Gloucester Old Spot pigs, also

fattened traditional native breed beef on their own pasture (grass fed). Also stock preserves and pickles. Honey, cakes and local cheeses. Soon to be available by Mail Order.
Prices/Payment: Switch
Hours: Tues to Sat – please 'phone for hours.
Notes: Disabled access. Berkswell Traditional Farmstead Meats are interested in supplying to the trade.

ELMHURST ORGANIC FARM
Bow Lane
Withybrook
Coventry
CV7 9LQ
Tel: 01788 832233
Fax: 01788 832690
Contact: Ann Pattison
Produce: Home grown organic beef, pork, lamb, chicken. Soil Assoc. No G7601. Sausages made from their own beef. Ann has told us her beef is Ministry registered B.S.E. free. Meat available in assorted packs or per lb. No min. order.
Prices/Payment: From £2.50 per lb pork sausages - £7.25 per lb fillet steak. Cash, cheques only.
Hours: Mon to Sat, 9am-5.30pm.
Notes: No disabled access. Woodland walks, access to the farm. Organised walks if requested beforehand.

HENRY DOUBLEDAY RESEARCH ASSOCIATION
Ryton Organic Gardens
Ryton on Dunsmore
Coventry
CV8 3LG
Tel: 01203 308201
Fax: 01203 639229
Email: enquiry@hdra.org.uk
Internet: www.hdra.org.uk
Contact: Steve Prime – Shop Manager
Produce: Ten acres of organic display gardens open to the public throughout the year. Supplying fruit, vegetables, salads for their shop and restaurant. Also stock a full range of organic goods for supplying nationwide. Mail Order and organic food club available, please 'phone for details.
Prices/Payment: Access, Visa, Switch taken.
Hours: Daily 9am-5pm. Closed Christmas Day and Boxing Day.
Notes: Disabled access. The Henry Doubleday Research Association is a registered charity, Patron HRH The Prince of Wales.

TAKE TWO COOKS
Rosello
Harbury
Leamington Spa
CV33 9JD
Tel: 01926 612417
Contact: Caroline Iacaruso
Produce: Continental patisserie. Handmade pies, chicken and ham, pork and apricot. Handmade chocolates. French & Italian wedding cakes. Panforte di Sienna available at Christmas.
Prices/Payment: Cash and cheques only.
Hours: Do supply to the general public but please 'phone for an appointment.
Notes: Take Two Cooks supply to the trade.

J.W.G. DALBY & SONS
Cestersover Farm, Pailton
Rugby
CV23 0QP
Tel: 01788 832188
Fax: 01788 833713
Contact: Brian Dalby
Produce: Ringswood real dairy ice-cream, made only from natural ingredients in 11 flavours.
Prices/payments: Cash and cheques only
Hours: Open all day.
Notes: The Dalbys supply to Ryan's Stores (Bosworth), Lea's Farm Shop (Husbands nr Rugby), Salmons Farm Shop (Banbury) and to Gaia, Leamington Spa. They are interested in supplying to hotels and restaurants.

MEG RIVERS CAKES
Middle Tysoe
Warwick
CV35 0SE
Tel: 01295 688101
Fax: 01295 680799
Contact: Julian Day
Produce: Cakes and biscuits made with only best quality fruit & nut; local free range eggs, English butter, raw untreated sugar and organic flour. No preservatives, colourings or artificial flavourings are added. Also stock honey, jams, wine, cheese. Mail Order worldwide. Min. order £15.50.
Prices/Payment: Rich English fruit cake 1kg £13.50, Almond fruit cake 750g £12.50. All major credit cards plus Switch and Delta.
Hours: Mon-Fri, 10am-4pm. Sat, 10am-1pm.
Notes: Disabled access. Tastings at Fortnum & Mason, cafe at Compton Verney Art Museum and tea shops.

WEST MIDLANDS

ORGANIC ROUNDABOUT
28 Hamstead Road, Hockley
Birmingham
B19 1DB
Tel: 0121 551 1679
Fax: 0121 515 3524
Produce: Fresh organic fruit and vegetables - standard 4.5 kg bags available or customers can make their own selection from around 40 items every week with no maximun or minimum order. Delivery to local pick-up points, please ' phone for details.
Prices/Payment: Cash and cheques only
Hours: Not open to the public.
Notes: Organic Roundabout are interested in supplying to the trade.

THE SMALL GREEN COMPANY
25 Clark Street
Stourbridge
DY8 3UF
Tel: 01384 396384
Email: mhallam4.06@aol.com

Contact: Michael Hallam
Produce: Fresh organic fruit and veg, organic groceries, & wholefoods, bread, eggs and meat. Weekly order/delivery system, telephone only. Direct doorstep delivery or central regional collection points. No min. order but delivery is 90p. In most areas.
Prices/Payment: £7 for a standard fruit or veg box. Cash and cheques only.
Hours: Not open to the public.
Notes: Weekly order/delivery from list and catalogues.

ESSINGTON FRUIT FARM
Bognop Road, Essington
Wolverhampton
WV11 2BA
Tel: 01902 735724
Contact: Richard Simkin
Produce: PYO soft fruits and vegetables. The farm does not supply shops - the best of the crop is available. Also home-made cakes and pies, home cooking. Farm shop also stocks foreign fruit & vegetables and traditional jams and preserves.
Prices/Payments: Cash and cheques only.
Hours: Late June to End August: Shop 9am-9pm. Tearoom 10am-4pm. Tues to Sun out of Season: Shop 9am-5pm (2pm Sun. Jan-Apr). Tearoom 11am-3pm Saturday, Sunday only.
Notes: Disabled access to tearoom/restaurant. Demonstrations by arrangement.

WORCESTERSHIRE

KITE'S NEST FARM
Snowshill Road
Broadway
WR12 7JT
Tel: 01386 853320
Fax: 01386 853621
Contact: Rosamund Young
Produce: Beef retail cuts and processed products from the farm butchers shop. All meat is from animals off the farm,

raised traditionally on land that has received no sprays or fertilisers for 20 years. The owners tell us they have a guaranteed BSE-free closed herd of suckler cows.

Prices/Payment: Topside £4.20 per lb, mince £2.59 per lb. Cash & cheques only

Hours: 11am-5pm but please telephone first.

Notes: No disabled access. Farm tours by prior arrangement.

T.H. CHECKETTS LTD
Worcester Road, Ombersley
Droitwich
WR9 0EW
Tel: 01905 620284
Fax: 01905 620152
Contact: Tony or Phil Checketts
Produce: Beef, lamb, pork and venison processed in Checketts abattoir. Home-made sausages, burgers, kebabs, grillsticks, boerewors, biltong, home-cooked ham, tongue, pies, faggots, andouilles, home cured bacon. Also stock chickens and other poultry, exotic meats e.g. ostrich, crocodile, kangaroo, range of chutneys, mustards, pickles, stuffing etc. Home delivery of freezer/catering goods, min. order £45.00.
Prices/Payment: All major credit cards and Switch, Delta.
Hours: Tues to Thurs, 8am-5.30pm. Fri, 8am-6pm. Sat, 8am-5pm Sat.
Notes: Demonstrations, talks and tastings by prior arrangement. Checketts are interested in supplying to more hotels and restaurants.

GREENLINK ORGANIC FOODS
9-11 Graham Road
Great Malvern
WR14 2HR
Tel: 01684 576266
Contact: Jane Straker
Produce: Home-grown organic vegetables. Fresh salads, quiches and savoury bakes. Dairy products, meat & poultry from Graig Farm, ice cream dairy and non dairy, wines, beers and ciders. Vegetable box scheme. Min

order depends on location.
Prices/Payment: Credit cards and debit cards taken.
Hours: Mon-Fri, 9am-5.30pm. Sat, 9am-5pm.
Notes: Disabled access. Snack Bar. Greenlink are interested in supplying to the trade. See also Ludlow, under same name.

MALVERN COUNTRY MEALS
37 Church Street
MALVERN
WR14 2AA
TEL: 01684 568498
FAX: 01684 567858
CONTACT: Chrys Titshall
PRODUCE: Fresh meat products, burgers, sausages & innovative specialist items. Winners of international, national & local tasting awards. All fresh meat products are made on the premises by hand using only top quality ingredients. They stock Orkney beef, Welsh or English lamb (depending on season). Free range pork & poultry. Also stock locally made cheese, tracklements and marinades. Mail Order available for handmade sausages and specialist bacon. No min. order charge. Free deliveries over £40.
PRICES/PAYMENT: All major credit cards taken. Delta & Switch.
HOURS: 24 hr answer phone/fax for Mail Order. Mon-Thurs, 8.45am-5.45pm. Fri, 8.45am-6pm. Sat, 8.30am-5pm.
NOTES: BBQ's and tastings at local events. Theme weekends etc. Suppliers to local restaurants, hotels, pubs etc.

CRIDLAN & WALKER
23 Abbey Road
Malvern
WR14 3ES
Tel: 01684 573008
Fax: 01684 566017
Contact: Christopher Leyland
Produce: Organic meat, beef, pork,

lamb, chickens, home-made sausages free from additives and colourings. In natural skins. Organic and Herefordshire bacon, traditionally reared and dry cured. Vegetarian, organic quality cheeses. Also stock organic tinned products. Mail Order leaflet sent on request. Min. order 10 lb.
Prices/Payments: All major credit cards taken, cash & cheques.
Hours: Mon, 8am-1pm, Tues-Sat, 8am-5.30pm
Notes: No disabled access. Cridlan & Walker already supply hotels etc. but would like to supply more to the trade.

TEME VALLEY HONEY
Sutton House Farm
Sutton
Tenbury Wells
WR15 8RJ
Tel: 01584 810424
Contact: Dr Carol Field
Produce: Worcestershire honey both bottled and in the comb. Available by Mail Order, postage charged at cost. No min. order charge.
Prices/Payment: Bottled honey £1.80 to £2.20 per lb. Comb honey £1.80 per 7 oz.
Hours: If they are on the farm then open. If making a special journey please 'phone first.
Notes: Disabled access. Teme Valley Honey supply to; Hole in the Wall (Tenbury), Barber and Manuel (Leominster), Franklins Cider (Little Hereford), The Fruit Basket (Ludlow).

ANSTEYS OF WORCESTER
Broomhall Farm
Broomhall
Worcester
WR5 2NT
Tel: 01905 820232
Fax: 01905 820232
Contact: Colin and Alyson Anstey
Produce: Three cheeses from the milk of the Anstey's herd of Holstein Friesian cows. Old Worcester White; a cheddar style cheese, creamy

textured, with a distinctive strong flavour. Worcester Sauce Cheese; speciality cheese which marries together cheddar style cheese and Lea & Perrins Worcestershire Sauce, to create a marbled effect cheese with a great depth of flavour. Double Worcester; a variation on Double Gloucester. A cloth bound cheese with a rich golden colour and a lighter texture than cheddar. All three are handmade using unpasteurised milk and vegetarian rennet. Mail Order; overnight delivery service available. No min. order.
Also stock pickles, chutneys, jams & marmalade, ice cream, biscuits, wafers.
Prices/Payment: Cheeses £3.95 lb from farm shop. All major credit cards taken and Switch/Delta
Hours: Mon to Sat, 9am-5.30pm Closed Sun and Bank Holidays.
Notes: Disabled access. Tours and visits of cheesemaking dairy by arrangement. Ansteys also supply Evertons of Ombersley (Worcester), Malvern Country Meals (Malvern), Quintessence (Pershore), Harrods (London).

CLIVES FRUIT FARM
Upper Hook Road
Upton-upon- Severn
Worcester
WR8 0SA
Tel: 01684 592664
Fax: 01684 592664
Contact: Mrs J Clive
Produce: PYO home grown fruits, gooseberries, strawberries, raspberries, redcurrants, plums (12 varieties), apples (12 varieties), pears (6 varieties). Also vegetables; courgettes, runner beans and pumpkins. They also sell other locally grown vegetables. Free range eggs. Also stock single variety apple juice, farmhouse preserves, locally produced honey and free range chickens.
Prices/Payment: Lower than shop prices. Cash and cheques only.
Hours: Fruit season 9am-5.30pm.

(Closed Sun. afternoons during winter).
Notes: Disabled access. Children's play area, refreshments, picnic area and nature trail. The Clives have written their own cookery book "Let's Get Fruity". Suppliers to various local fruit shops and Nicks Fruiterers (Upton). They are interested in supplying to the trade.

LIGHTWOOD CHEESE
Lower Lightwood Farm, Cotheridge
Worcester
WR6 5LT
Tel: 01905 333468
Fax: 01905 333468
Contact: Philip Rogers
Produce: Traditional handmade cheese, using only milk from the family dairy herd. The range includes semi-skimmed and full fat cheeses, accounting for all tastes. Also stock local goat's cheese. Mail Order available. Min. Order £10.
Prices/Payment: Own cheeses £8.80 per kg, Goats £20 per kg approx. All major credit cards accepted. Delta.
Hours: Mon-Sat, 9am-6pm
Notes: Disabled access. Tour of cheesemaking, store etc. inc. tastings £2.50. Farmhouse B&B and Lightwood Cheese also supply Cheeseboard (Barnard's Green), Tesco (National), G. Willams Farm Shop (Worcs), Ian Narraway Butchers (Worcs), and are interested in selling more to the trade.

LATE ENTRY

TRINITY HALL FARM
Awsworth Lane
Cossall
Notts
NG16 2SA
Tel: 0115 944 2545
Fax: 0115 932 0073
Contact: Lewis Winter
Produce: Organic food growers. Vegetables, meat, eggs. Also stock:

organic fruits, dried goods, organic meat. Box delivery service for vegetables. No min. order charge.
Prices/Payment: All major credit cards
Hours: Mon-Sat, 9am-5pm. Sun, 10am-4pm.
Notes: Disabled access. Animals, plants, growing tunnels.

The following are SHOPS within this region which do not produce but do sell quality or organic foods

ORGANIC ROOTS
Dark Lane, Kings Norton
Birmingham
West Midlands
B38 0BS
Tel: 01564 822294
Produce: Full range of organic vegetables meat, poultry, fish, whole foods (Soil Assoc. No G1880). Milk, bread. Box scheme available.
Hours: Wed-Sat, 10am-5.30pm.
Notes: Disabled access. Also raise plants. Organic Roots are interested in supplying to the trade.

OUT OF THIS WORLD
6-8 Pittville Street
Cheltenham
Gloucestershire
GL52 2LJ
Tel: 01242 518300
Produce: About 4,000 products with a strong emphasis on organic and fair trade. Fresh organic fruit and vegetables, meat, dairy. Pulses, grains, fruits etc. Deli counter. Beer and wine etc. Mail Order catalogue available.
Hours: Every day, 9am-6pm. Thursday 9am-8pm.
Notes: Disabled access.

RYTON ORGANIC GARDENS SHOP
Ryton Organic Gardens
Coventry
Warwickshire
CV8 3LG

Tel: 01203 308201
Fax: 01203 639229
Email: enquiry@hdra.org.uk
Internet: www.hdra.org.uk
Produce: Over 1,200 organic products including fresh bread and bakery items, fruit and vegetables, delicatessen, meat, vegetarian and vegan foods, dairy produce, wines and beers, baby food, fresh, frozen and dried goods. Vegetable box scheme. Organic Wine Club.
Hours: Daily 9am-5pm (6pm Friday).
Notes: Disabled access.

HAY WHOLEFOODS
Lion Street
Hay-on-Wye
Herefordshire
HR3 5DB
Tel: 01497 820708
Produce: General wholefood shop and delicatessen. Wide range of organic goods including general grocery, wine, beer and vegetables. Sheep's milk ice cream sold in cornets during summer. Vegetable box scheme operating.
Hours: 9.30am-5.30pm.
Notes: Disabled access.

FODDER
26-27 Church Street
Hereford
Herefordshire
HR1 2LR
Tel: 01432 358171
Fax: 01432 277861
Produce: A wide variety of natural foods, organic bread, fruit, wine, vegetables, dairy products, wholefoods, local products inc. organic cider.
Hours: Mon-Sat, 9am-5.30pm.
Notes: No disabled access.

GEORGE'S
25 High Street
Kington
Herefordshire
HR5 3AX
Tel: 01544 231400

Produce: Vegetarian pâtés, houmous, coleslaw. Organic bread, cheese, wines and beers. Fruit slices, cakes. Wholefoods. Delivery service for people unable to get to the shop.
Hours: Mon-Fri, 8.30am-5.30pm. Sat, 8.30am-5pm.
Notes: Disabled access. Pavement café weather permitting.

OUT OF THIS WORLD
Unit One, Villa Street, Beeston
Nottingham
NG9 2NY
Tel: 0115 943 1311
Produce: About 4,000 products with a strong emphasis on organic fair trade. Fresh organic fruit and vegetables, meat, dairy. Pulses, grains, fruits etc. Organic gardening. Beer and wine etc. Mail Order catalogue available.
Hours: Every day, 9am-6pm. Thurs and Fri, 9am-8pm.
Notes: Disabled access.

ROOTS NATURAL FOODS
52 Mansfield Road, Sherwood
Nottingham
NG52 2FR
Tel: 0115 960 9014
Produce: Soil Assoc. registered. Organic and natural foods, fair trade products. Environmentally friendly household products, including: Suma, Granovita, Infinity, Ecover, Community, Aqua Oleum, Weleda, Pauls Tofu, Edenfarm. Own packed muesli grains, pulses etc. Home delivery and organic vegetable box scheme available.
Hours: Mon-Fri, 9am-6pm. Sat, 9am-5pm
Notes: Disabled access. Roots Natural Foods are interested in supplying to the trade.

HONEYSUCKLE WHOLEFOOD CO-OPERATIVE LTD
53 Church Street
Oswestry
Shropshire
SY11 2SZ

Tel: 01691 653125
Produce: Traditional wholefood shop established in 1978. Specialising in organic foods including fresh fruit and vegetables. Wide range of dried fruit, nuts, grains, herbs and spices, essential oils. etc.
Hours: Mon-Sat, 9am-5pm.
Notes: Disabled access.

HOUSE OF CHEESE
13 Church Street
Tetbury
Gloucestershire
GL8 8JG
Tel: 01666 502865
Produce: A wide range of British and French cheeses
Hours: Mon-Sat, 9am-5.30pm. (5pm in winter).

THE ORGANIC SHOP (MARKET WHOLEFOODS)
The Shambles
1a Mellor Road
New Mills
Stockport
N. Derbyshire
SK22 4DW
Tel: 01663 747550
Produce: Organic produce (Soil Assoc. no. R1985). Fruit, vegetables, organic and/or free range, additive free products - eggs, bread, dairy produce, wholefoods and meat. Cruelty free toiletries and cleaning products. Ecover rebottling service. Box scheme available.
Hours: Mon-Sat, 9am-5.30pm. Wed, 9am-12.30pm. Close for lunch 1pm-2pm Mon and Sat.
Notes: No disabled access.

COUNTY DURHAM

H.D. & R. BAINBRIDGE
Post Office & Stores
'Home Bakery'
1 Greenbank, Eggleston
Barnard Castle
DL12 0BQ
Tel: 01833 650250
Contact: Mrs Jeanette Morris
Produce: An established range of celebration and farmhouse fruit cakes, bases only 6" to 12" square; also round and hexagon shapes available. Cold tea loaf and ginger loaf a speciality. All baked to traditional recipes.
Prices/Payment: Prices range from £5.60 for The Celebration fruit cake to £1.35 for cold tea loaf. Cash and cheques only.
Hours: Mon, Tues, Wed and Fri, 9am-5.30pm. Thurs and Sat, 9am-1pm.
Notes: No disabled access. Bainbridge are suppliers to Joneva (Masham, N.Yorks) and Country Bake (Richmond, N. Yorks.)

TEESDALE TRENCHERMAN
Startforth Hall
Barnard Castle
DL12 9AG
Tel: 01833 638370
Fax: 01833 631218
Email: orders@trencherman.co.uk
Contact: Johnny Cooke-Hurle
Produce: Smoked game, chicken and duck. Also supply by mail order a phenomenal range of gourmet and unusual foods (chocolate to caviar). Please apply direct for catalogue and also see Mail Order section for further details,
Prices/Payment: Smoked chicken £4.56 per 2lb. All major credit cards.
Hours: Not open to the public.
Notes: Teesdale Trencherman supply Corbridge Larder and Hunters of Helmsley, and locally to the trade.

ZISSLER & SONS LTD
104 Bondgate
Darlington
DL10 5LZ
Tel: 01325 462590
Contact: P.V. Zissler
Produce: Pork purveyors, sausages, dry cured bacon, roast ham, pork pies, stand pies, gala pie. Mail Order available by Interlink Tues-Fri.
Prices/Payment: Gala Pie £1.50 per pound for a 6lb pie. Roast ham sliced or whole £3.80 per lb. Farmhouse pork sausages £1.50 per pound. Please add £9 for p & p. Cheques only.
Hours: Mon-Sat, 8.30am-5pm.
Notes: Disabled access.

NORTHUMBERLAND

NORTH EAST ORGANIC GROWERS LTD
Earth Balance
West Sleeksburn Farm, Bomarsund
Bedlington
NE22 7AD
Tel: 01670 821070
Fax: 01670 821036
Contact: Box scheme co-ordinator
Produce: Soil Assoc certified organic fruit and vegetables. Vegetable box scheme - weekly deliveries in Northumberland and Tyne & Wear. No min order
Prices/Payment: £5 per bag.
Hours: Orders taken 9am-5pm.
Notes: Earth Balance is a sustainable development project open to the public

CHAIN BRIDGE HONEY FARM
Horncliffe
Berwick-upon-Tweed
TD15 2XT
Tel: 01289 386362
Fax: 01289 386763
Contact: W.S. or D.E.A. Robson
Produce: Honey (both liquid in jars and in comb). 3 main varieties - flower honey (called "Tweedside honey"),

heather honey and a flower and heather blend. Also dipped beeswax candles and Mail Order tubs of honey, cosmetics and polish.
Prices/Payments: 1lb jar - wholesale £1.60, retail £2.20. Cash and cheques only
Hours: Weekdays, 10.30am-5pm. Sat, 10am-5pm. Sun, 2 pm-5pm. Open weekdays only during winter.
Notes: Every effort made to help disabled visitors. Display of restored vintage tractor. Suppliers to 350 shops regionally.

OXFORD FARM SHOP
Oxford Farm, Ancroft
Berwick-upon-Tweed
TD15 2TA
Tel: 01289 387253 **Fax:** 01289 387253
Email: oxfordfarmshop@compuserve.com
Contact: Peter and Maureen Brown
Produce: 23 varieties of jams, marmalades and chutneys, made in traditional 6lb boilings, presented in 12oz jars. A full range of home-baking including meringues. Soft fruit including strawberries, raspberries, brambles, gooseberries, blackcurrants. Also stock speciality foods and limited amount of giftware.
Prices/Payment: Preserves trade price £1.20 to retail £1.70 upwards. Meringues trade price £2 to retail £2.75 upwards. Cash, cheques only.
Hours: Summer 10am to 5pm (8pm in fruit season) Tues-Sun.
Winter, Tues-Sat, 10am-5pm
Notes: Limited disabled access, but good helpful staff. Tea room, pet area and in October, marquee to promote christmas fayre. The Browns supply over forty outlets, and are interested in supplying more.

HEXHAM HERBS
Chesters Walled Garden
Chollerford
Hexham
NE46 4BQ
Tel: 01434 681483

Fax: 01434 681483
Contact: Mrs S White
Produce: A wide range of 300 plus different herbs for sale and nearly 900 to view in this herb garden and nursery in an historic walled garden by Hadrian's Wall.
Also local jams and honey.
Prices/Payment: From £1.20 for 7cm. pot to £2.80 for 1 litre pot. Cash and cheques only
Hours: 10am- 5pm daily, end of Mar to end of Oct. Telephone for details of opening times outside main season.
Notes: Beautifully laid out gardens with disabled access.

SWALLOW FISH LTD
2 South Street
Seahouses
NE68 7RB
Tel: 01665 721052
Fax: 01665 721177
Product: Traditionally smoked salmon, kippers, cod, haddock, smokies- no dyes used. Local crabs, lobsters & langoustines boiled and ready to eat. Local oysters. Wild salmon and sea trout in season, plus a wide variety of fish. Also stock marinated herrings, tinned soups etc. Mail Order service for kippers and smoked salmon.
Prices/Payment: Visa, Mastercard, Eurocard.
Hours: May-Sept: Mon-Fri, 9am-5pm. Sat, 9am-4pm. Oct-Apr: Mon,Tues, Thurs, Fri, 9am-4.30pm. Wed, Sat, 9am-1pm.
Notes: No disabled access. A member of the Swallow family will be happy to show the smoke house and explain the processes. Prior arrangement needed for large groups. Suppliers to trade and retail outlets.

The following are SHOPS within this region which do not produce but do sell quality or organic foods

CORBRIDGE LARDER
Hill Street
Corbridge
Northumberland
NE45 5AA
Tel: 01434 632948
Fax: 01434 633250
Produce: Good local food. Home-made cakes and pastries, terrines and pies, preserves, cheeses, breads, honey, bacon and sausages.
Hours: Mon-Sat, 9am-5pm.
Notes: Shop is on two floors.

MOLLY'S WHOLEFOOD STORE
11 Front Street
Framwellgate Moor
Durham
DH1 5EJ
Tel: 0191 386 2216
Fax: 0191 386 2216
Produce: Retail food co-op. Large range of foods, many organic. Bread from the Village Bakery Melmerby. Organic dairy produce, fruit and vegetable box scheme. Loose vegetables sold in shop. Also homeopathic remedies, Bach flower herbal remedies, aromatherapy oils, books, magazines and cards.
Home delivery within 5 mile radius, small charge for petrol.
Hours: Mon, Wed, Thurs, Fri, 9am-6pm. Tues, 9am-7pm. Sat, 9am-5pm.
Notes: Disabled access. Monthly aromatherapy massage evening. Occasional allergy testing days. Molly's Wholefood Store can supply bulk quantities if required. 10% discount on full cases.

OUT OF THIS WORLD
Gosforth Shopping Centre
High Street, Gosforth
Newcastle upon Tyne
Tyne & Wear
NE3 1JZ

Tel: 0191 213 0421
Produce: About 4,000 products with a strong emphasis on organic fair trade. Fresh organic fruit and vegetables, meat, dairy. Pulses, grains, fruits etc. Deli counter. Beer and wine etc.
Mail Order catalogue available.
Hours: Every day, 9am-6pm.
Notes: Disabled access.

CHESHIRE

HOLLY TREE FARM SHOP
Chester Road, Tabley
Knutsford
WA16 0EU
Tel: 01565 651835
Fax: 01565 654522
Email: bailey@hollytree.u-net.com
Contact: Mrs Karol Bailey
Produce: Home-produced naturally fed free range geese, ducks, turkeys, lamb, etc. 40 varieties of specialist hand-made sausages. Dry-cured traditional bacon. Pâtés, pies and bakery including hand raised banquet pies, home-made cakes, jams & chutneys. Also stock; Patchwork pâtés, Taylors mustards, Cheshire apple juice. Mail Order, overnight delivery nationwide by arrangement. Min order £25.
Prices/Payment: Access, Visa and Switch taken.
Hours: Tues to Sat, 9.30am-6pm. Sun,10am-5pm. Thurs till 7pm.
Notes: Disabled access. Open & tasting days in May & Sept, party visits, mini tastings at weekends, farm animals to meet and cuddle. Holly Tree Farm Shop supplies to restaurants etc.

TATTON PARK
Knutsford
WA16 6QN
Tel: 01565 654822
Fax: 01565 650179
Contact: Anne Charmer or Brendan Flanagan
Produce: Prime venison, bacon, pork, pheasant, rabbit. Venison ready meals, e.g. venison stew with Cheshire dumplings, smoked venison, potted venison, sausage. Also stock cheeses, pâté, bread, jams, puddings, pickles, oils, English wines, beers, cider, local water, English fruit juices and cordials, farm made ice cream, biscuits and cakes.
Prices/Payment: Visa/Mastercard. Switch later in 1998.

Hours: April to October: Tues-Sun, 11.30am-5pm. Nov-March: Tues-Sun, 11.30am-4pm.
Notes: Disabled access. Mansion, gardens, parkland, restaurant, gift shop, garden shop etc.

OAKCROFT ORGANIC GARDENS
Cross O' Th' Hill
Malpas
SY14 8DH
Tel: 01948 860213
Contact: Ms M.S. Fardoons
Produce: Wide range of organic fruit and vegetables grown on land that has been organic since 1962. Salad, green vegetables and soft fruits are a speciality. Also stock other organic vegetables to widen range. Breads, cheeses, free range organic eggs and fruits from abroad. Box scheme deliveries to Tarporley, Northwich, Knutsford, Chester and Llangollen; other areas by arrangement. No min order charge. Also Thursday market stall of vegetables and herbs, organic eggs, cheese and breads at Chester Market from 10am-4.30pm.
Prices/Payment: Most credit cards taken.
Hours: 8am till evening but preferably till 4.30pm.
Notes: Disabled access. Possible interest in supplying to the trade.

ISLE OF MAN

GEO. DEVEREAU & SON LTD
33 Castle Street
Douglas
IMI 2EX
Tel: 01624 673257
Fax: 01624 661741
Contact: Miss T. Canipa
Produce: Fishmongers and Manx kippers curers. Available by Mail Order, U.K., Europe, Canada, USA. Min order 1 pair.
Prices/Payment: 1 pair whole

kippers, £2.65, 1 packet kipper fillets, £2.45. Major credit cards. Switch
Hours: 8am-5pm.
Notes: Disabled access. Geo Devereau & Son Ltd supply to Cubbons Fishmongers, Port Erin Food Hall, Maddrell's Fishmongers and the S.L.F (shop) Ronaldsway Airport (all Isle of Man).

LANCASHIRE

RAMSBOTTOM VICTUALLERS CO. LTD
16-18 Market Place
Ramsbottom
Bury
BL0 9HT
Tel:01706 825070
Fax: 01706 822005
Email: rammy.vics@which.net
Contact: Chris Johnson
Produce: Home-made salad dressings, chutneys, preserves, ice cream and air dried beef. Organic shop also sells items from their restaurant kitchens such as soups, casseroles and ready made meal items. They also stock about 2000 lines from hand-made unpasteurised cheeses and charcuterie, to corn fed, antibiotic free chicken and freshly baked bread. Wines, flour, coffee, preserves, pastas, cakes, biscuits, meat and fresh fruits and vegetables. Home delivery service in the near future.
Prices/Payment: Please 'phone for price list. All major credit and debit cards taken.
Hours: Closed Mon. Sun and Tues, 11am-5pm. Wed-Sat, 10am-9.30pm.
Notes: No disabled access, as premises are in a listed building with narrow doorways and staircases. The Village Restaurant opens from Wed-Fri for lunch at 12.45pm, dinner at 8pm. Sat Lunch 12pm & 2pm, dinner at 8pm. Sun lunch two sittings at 1pm and 3pm. Closed Mon-Tues. Special offers and tastings throughout the year in both shop and restaurant.

THE HERB STALL
Ferrocrite Farm, Arkholme
Carnforth
LA6 1AU
Tel: 015242 21965
Fax: 015242 21965
Contact: Jo Fowler
Produce: Organic (Soil Assoc. No PF17N) vegetables, herb plants (sold either cut or in pots). Home-made preserves made with locally grown produce. Also stock other locally grown organic vegetables and fruit. Organic tinned and dried and dairy produce (all organic). Environment friendly household and personal cleaning products. Delivered locally. Min order £20.
Prices/Payment: Lemon cheese £1.50-£1.75, gooseberry and elderflower jam £1.40. Cash and cheques only.
Hours: Every day except Mondays (open Bank Holidays),10am-7pm.
Notes: Disabled access by arrangement (there are no steps). Poly tunnels open to the public. Organic preserves sold to local trade outlets.

CHAMBERHOUSE FARM
Rochdale Road East
Heywood
OL10 1SD
Tel: 01706 648710
Fax: 01706 648710
Contact: Cameron Baines, Manager
Produce: Sheep's milk, cheese, yoghurt, ice cream. All suitable for vegetarians; handmade on premises.
Prices/Payment: Cheese from £5.70 per lb. Cash and cheques only.
Hours: 1pm-4.45pm daily. 11am-4.45pm weekends Easter to October (summer). 1pm-4.45pm October - March (winter).
Notes: Disabled access. Farm open daily to the public and school groups etc. Sheep milking 1.30pm daily May to Oct. Cow milking 3.30pm daily. Special feature days throughout the year. Chamberhouse Farm supplies to Jill's Cheese Pantry (Rochdale Market).

PORT OF LANCASTER SMOKE HOUSE
West Quay, Glasson Dock
Lancaster
LA2 0DB
Tel: 01524 751493
Fax: 01524 752168
Contact: John, Michael and Pat Price
Produce: Smoked salmon, trout,
haddock, smoked chicken breast,
chicken legs, duck breast, ham,
bacon, and various smoked cheeses
and smoked garlic. Also stock fresh
fish and seafoods, mustards, chutneys, preserves, chocolates and
basketware. Range of hampers
suitable for corporate business trade
and individual requirements. Mail
Order service available, both home
and international; 'phone for brochure. No min. order.
Prices/Payment: Major credit cards
Hours: Mon-Fri, 7.30am-5pm. Sat-
Sun, 10am-5pm.
Notes: Disabled access. Demonstrations and tastings throughout the
year. The Prices are interested in
supplying to the trade.

JAMES BAXTER & SON
Thornton Road

MORECAMBE

LA4 5PB
TEL: **01524 410910**
FAX: **01524 833363**
CONTACT: **R.M. Baxter**
PRODUCE: **Potted brown shrimps.
Locally caught. Two sizes available
57g and 200 g. Also stock Scottish
smoked salmon, whole side
trimmed or sliced packs. Available
by Mail Order. Min. order ten 57g
cartons.**
PRICES/PAYMENT: **Price list available.
Mastercard & Visa.**
HOURS: **Mon-Fri, 9am-1pm.**
Notes: **Disabled access. James
Baxter & Son supply to Partridges,
Blagdens Fishmongers (London),
Ramus Seafoods and Bruce's
Fishmongers.**

A D & P E SHORROCK
New House Farm
Ford Lane, Goosnargh
Preston
PR3 2FJ
Tel: 01772 865250
Contact: AD & PE Shorrock
Produce: Traditional farmhouse
Lancashire cheese, made from the
milk of their own Friesian herd.
Made to age old recipes. Garlic
cheese with herbs also available.
Prices/Payment: Cash and cheques only
Hours: Open every day.
Notes: No disabled access. The
Shorrocks also supply to The Cheese
Shop Chester and Spar Longridge.
They are interested in supplying more
to the trade.

EAVES GREEN GAME FARM
Eaves Green Lane, Goosnargh
Preston
PR3 2FE
Tel: 01772 865300
Contact: Mr Ian Banks
Produce: Seasonal game, specialising
in pheasants, wild duck, teal,
partridge, rabbits and hares. Venison
is available on order. Free range
bronze turkeys available at Christmas.
Prices/Payment: Brace of oven ready
pheasant @£5.50. Brace of oven
ready wild duck @ £6.00. Free range
Bronze turkeys £1.85 per lb.
Hours: Mon-Fri, 8am-6pm. Sat, 9am-
12pm. Sun by appointment.
Notes: No disabled access. Eaves
Green Game Farm supply to Brendan
Anderton, Butchers and George Ball
at Chorley Market. Trade welcome.

J J SANDHAM LTD
Rostock Dairy, Garstang Road
Barton
Preston
PR3 5AA
Tel: 01995 640247
Fax: 01995 640994
Email: jjsandham@bigfoot.com
chris.sandham@virgin.net
Contact: Chris Sandham

Produce: Lancashire cheese; mild, tasty crumbly, garlic, smoked. All are vegetarian. Two organic cheeses. Also stock a variety of British and foreign cheese. Mail order available. Min. order 1kg.
Prices/Payment: All Lancashire cheese at £1.79 per lb to public. Organic cheeses at £2.40 per lb to public. Cash and cheques only.
Hours: 7.30am-2pm.
Notes: Disabled access. J J Sandham supply to Booths Supermarkets and Selfridges (London).

PUGH'S PIGLETS
Bowgreave House Farm
Bowgreave, Garstang
Preston
PR3 1YE
Tel: 01995 602571
Fax: 01995 600126
Contact: Gillian Pugh /Clare Hull
Produce: Old English breed suckling pigs; Middle Whites, Gloucester Old Spots, Berkshire and Saddlebacks. Italian style boned and rolled 'porchetta' and gourmet lamb; whole lamb boned and rolled. Mail Order service available via Interlink door-to-door. Only supply whole suckling pig or whole porchetta, either of which can be jointed to customer's requirements.
Prices/Payment: Whole suckling pig from £52.90, porchetta from £7.83 per kilo. Interlink charge £12 per 10 kg. Cash, cheques only.
Hours: Mon-Fri, 10am-4pm. Please 'phone beforehand for instructions.
Notes: No disabled access. Pugh's Piglets already supply to the trade, but are interested in supplying more.

Manchester
M13 0PD
Tel: 0161 224 8884
Fax: 0161 224 8826
Email: HOMEFARM1@aol.com
Contact: Jon Roy
Produce: Organic and free range produce direct from farm to doorstep. Organic vegetables as a box scheme. Also stock organic cheese, bread, milk, yogurt, butter, juices and free range meat and eggs. Home delivery service only. Min. order £7.50 veg, £15 meat.
Prices/Payment: All major cards
Hours: Please 'phone to order.
Notes: Home Farm Deliveries are interested in supplying to restaurants and hotels.

HALBERSTADT
55 Leicester Road
Salford
M7 4AS
Tel: 0161 792 1109
Contact: J Halberstadt
Produce: Kosher only beef, poultry and lamb. All produced on the premises, many with no additives. Home deliveries throughout Greater Manchester and will deliver to London. No min. order charge in town. Out of town they charge carrier's charge direct to customer. Cash and cheques only.
Prices/Payment: Average price sausages £3.10 per lb.
Hours: Tues, Wed, Thurs, 8am-5.45pm. Half day Sun, Mon, Fri.
Notes: Disabled access should be available by beginning of 1999. Halberstadt are always willing to increase their trade.

MANCHESTER

HOME FARM DELIVERIES
Studio 19
Imex Business Park
Hamilton Road
Longsight

MERSEYSIDE

ABBOTTS ORGANICS
45 Glenavon Road
Prenton
Birkenhead
L43 0RB

Tel: 0151 608 4566
Contact: Sandra Maxby
Produce: Free range eggs, organic vegetables, a broad range of indemic field grown vegetables available. Also stock potatoes, tomatoes, fruits and other out of season vegetables not available from their own land. Available by mobile shop. Min. delivery value £6. No set boxes, pre orders welcome.
Prices/Payment: Competitive prices, orders over £6 delivery charge inclusive. Cash sales only.
Hours: Mobile shop operates on Thurs, Fri and Sat.
Notes: Abbotts Organics supply to Ashfield Farm (Neston), Rileys Fruit & Veg (Preston), Pastime Restaurant (Bristol). They are interested in supplying to the trade.

ACORN VENTURE URBAN FARM
Depot Road
Kirkby
Knowsley
Prescot
L33 3AR
Tel: 0151 548 1524
Contact: Fiona Smith
Produce: Free range meat including lamb, beef, pork, bacon, goat, turkey. Free range hen, duck and goose eggs. Goat's milk produce: cheese, ice cream (12 flavours) and milk. Also stocks plants, home produced honey and feed for the animals.
Prices/Payment: From 95p for six large free range eggs to £11 per kg for fillet steak. Cash and cheques only.
Hours: Seven days a week from 10am to 4pm.
Notes: Disabled access. Acorn Venture Urban farm is a registered charity, and has horses, goats, pigs, sheep, rabbits, poultry, pony rides, a cafe, woodland walks, a sensory garden and a children's play area. They are interested in supplying the trade if feasible.

LATE ENTRY

T. A. SINGLETONS DAIRY LTD
Mill Farm, Preston Road
Longridge
Preston
Lancs
PR3 3AN
Tel: 01772 782112
Fax: 01772 785372
Contact: Mrs Carole Hart
Produce: Hard cheese, butter and cream, blended cheese, i.e. cheddar with herbs and garlic. Also stock Stilton, Edam, Brie, Shropshire blue.
Prices/Payment: All major credit cards taken.
Hours: 8am-5pm. Closed for lunch, 12.30pm-1.30pm.
Notes: Disabled access to shop. Experienced in supplying multiples and in exporting cheeses.

The following are SHOPS within this region which do not produce but do sell quality or organic foods

THE CHEESE SHOP
116 Northgate Street
Chester
Cheshire
CH1 2HT
Tel: 01244 346240
Produce: Over 100 British cheeses. Cheshires, Welsh cheeses, fresh goat's cheeses. Also smoked cheese, cheese pâtés and farmhouse butters and chutneys.
Hours: Mon-Sat, 8.30am-5.30pm. Sun, 10am-5pm.

LIMITED RESOURCES
53 Old Birley Street
Hulme
Manchester
Greater Manchester
M15 5RF
Tel: 0161 226 4777

Fax: 0161 226 3777
Email: office@limitedresources.co.uk
Produce: Over 400 different organic
products. Home delivery and box
scheme. Six different sizes of vegetable box and two sizes of fruit box.
Hours: Cafe and Shop: Mon-Fri,
10am-6pm. Sat, 10am-5pm. Home
delivery ordering hours, Mon-Fri,
9am-5pm. Cafe open until 9pm Thurs
Notes: Disabled access. Vegetarian
Cafe. Home deliveries in South
Manchester.

DEMETER
12 Welles Street
Sandbach
Cheshire
CW11 1GT
Tel: 01270 760445
Email:
100255.1220@compuserve.com
Produce: Specialist suppliers of
quality natural food, from Agen
Prunes to Arlequin Walnuts; local
honey to Asafoetida; Black Mission
figs to organic porridge oats. Essential oils, medicinal herbs, Bach
Flower Remedies, vitamin and
mineral dietary supplements.
Hours: Mon-Sat, 9am-5.45pm.
Notes: Disabled access. Also stock
books, art cards and prints. Information service and internet search
capabilities.

KENT

DENNIS OF BEXLEY
1/2 Bourne Parade
Bourne Road, Bexley Village
Bexley
DA5 1LQ
Tel: 01322 522126
Fax: 01322 662753
Contact: Keith Mulford
Produce: 30 varieties of home-made
pies, 20 varieties of home-made
encroûtes all with cooking/heating
instructions. Q Guild butchers II
farmhouse sausage. Aberdeen Angus
beef from the Buccleuch Estate in
Scotland. Also stock chutneys and
jams by Cottage Delight. Mail Order.
Prices/Payment: Individual pie from
£1.20. Indv,encroûte from £1.50.
Mail Order Min. £100.00 anywhere
in the country. All major debit and
credit cards, Amex.
Hours: Mon- Sat, 7.30am-6.00pm.
Sun, 10am-3.00 pm.
Notes: Disabled access; in-store tastings.
Numerous U.K. and European awards.

PICKETTES
53 Pickford Lane
Bexleyheath
DA7 4QU
Tel: 0181 303 4858
Contact: Mr Des Dufty
Produce: Hot & cold eating pies, meat
& vegetarian. Home cured hams, salt
beef, roast beef (Aberdeen Angus), leg
of pork, turkey breast, ox tongue. Extra
meaty sausages with low preservative
content. Moussaka, lasagne, shepherds
pie. Home-made coleslaw. Also stock
cheese, marinades, jams, sauces,
breads, spices, mustards, pickles, oils
etc. Large selection of fruit & vegetables, flowers, plants.
Prices/Payment: All major credit cards
Hours: Mon-Sat, 7.30am-5.30pm.
Notes: Disabled access. Forecourt
B.B.Q. tastings in summer. Pickettes
are interested in supplying to trade.

ORGANIC HEALTH (PERRY COURT)
The Well House
Perry Court Farm, Garlinge Green
Canterbury
CT4 5RU
Tel: 01227 732563
Fax: 01227 732563
Contact: Jackie Garfit
Produce: Specialist organic and
special diet farm shop. Perry Court
Farm organic beef, Eastbrook Farm
organic meats, fruit, vegetables,
dairy, baked goods and over 1,000
organic lines including their own
organic flour. Mail Order for organic
and special diet foods. No min.
order.
Prices/Payment: Cash and cheques
only.
Hours: Thurs, 9am-5pm.Fri, 8.30am-
5pm. Sat, 9am-12pm.
Notes: Disabled access. Perry Court
Farm (not shop) are interested in
selling their organic beef, flour and
vegetables to the trade. Contact
Patrick Brockman on 01227 738449.

WARDS OF ADISHAM
Little Bossington Farmhouse
Adisham
Canterbury
CT3 3LN
Tel: 01227 720596
Fax: 01227 720596
Contact: Ian Ward
Produce: Home-made Kentish
farmhouse fudge. Made to an old
family recipe, using sugar, milk,
butter, golden syrup and vanilla
essence. No glucose syrup used.
Real additives like ginger, Belgian
chocolate and chopped walnuts.
Five different flavours. Mail Order
available, U.K. and Europe; please
'phone for brochure. Gift service.
Min. order, boxes 1 lb and over. U.K.
£10.50, Europe £12.50.
Prices/Payment: 8oz bag from £3.
Decorated gift boxes by mail order
from £10.50 inc. p&p. Cash and
cheques only.

Hours: 9am-6pm by appointment; please 'phone first.

Notes: Wards supply over 35 outlets regularly, including; Penshurst Place, Great Dixter, Chiddingstone Castle (all Kent) and other shops from Dover to Battersea. They are interested in supplying more to the trade.

CRABBLE CORN MILL TRUST

Lower Road, River
Dover
CT17 0UY
Tel: 01304 823292
Fax: 01304 826040
Email: mill@invmed.demon.co.uk
Internet: www.invmed.demon.co.uk/mill
Contact: Head Miller
Produce: Organic stoneground wholemeal flour, milled from local-grown wheat. Produced by an historic (1812) watermill. Sold at the mill or delivered to the Kent area.
Prices: Special 'factory gate' price for customers that collect. Wholesale/retail prices and delivery charges on application. Min order 10 bags1 sack. No credit cards.
Hours: Winter: Sun, 11am-5pm. Sun only (closed Xmas & Jan). Summer: Sat, Sun & Bank Holidays. School Summer holidays also Wed, Thurs, Fri.
Notes: Disabled access to lower two floors out of six. Cafe, gardens, mill tours with or without guides, gallery (local arts & crafts).
Also supply other local outlets and are interested in supplying to the trade. Crabble Corn Mill is a totally volunteer-run trust.

BROGDALE TRUST

Brogdale Road
Faversham
ME13 8XZ
Tel: 01795 535286
Fax: 01795 531710
Internet: www.brogdale.org.uk
Contact: Joy Wade
Produce: Home of the National Fruit Collections. Over 4000 varieties of fruit are grown. They also make and sell single variety apple juices. Also stock ciders, jams, pickles, wines and fruit related products. Mail Order available for fruit, fruit juice and plants. No min. order.
Prices/Payment: Mastercard, Switch and Visa card.
Hours: 9.30am-5.30pm every day except Christmas and Boxing Day.
Notes: Disabled access. Tea shop, plant centre, orchard walks.
Brogdale Trust supply Fortnum and Mason, Selfridges and Bluebird Store (all London). They are interested in supplying to the trade.

LUDDESDOWN ORGANIC FARMS LTD

Court Lodge, Luddesdown
Nr. Cobham
Gravesend
DA13 0XE
Tel: 01474 815044
Fax: 01474 812048
Contact: Jill or Gerry Minister.
Produce: Organic vegetables and organic beef, from the farm. All produced according to the standards of the Soil Association reg no. S38S. Veg. sold by box scheme, weekly delivery to the door. Beef in packs; please 'phone for individual requirements. Sometimes stock organic turkeys and fruit.
Prices/Payment: Beef from £3.26 per lb, mince and burgers from £2.02 per lb. Cash and cheques only.
Hours: Not open to the public. Please 'phone to order.
Notes: Disabled access. Annual open day. The Ministers are interested in supplying to the trade.

OTFORD FARMERS

Sepham Farm
Otford
TN14 5JT
Tel: 01959 522774
Fax: 01959 525040
Contact: Mr Nick Chard

Produce: Home produced strawberries, raspberries, gooseberries, redcurrants, blackcurrants, tayberries, cherries, plums, apples and pears. Also apple, apple and raspberry, apple and blackberry juices. Farm shop also sells Willetts Farm ice cream.
Prices/Payment: Apple juice 750ml £1.20, apple and raspberry, apple and blackcurrant, £1.35. Cash & cheques only.
Hours: Tues-Sun, 9am-5pm. Closed on Bank Holidays.
Notes: Disabled access. Sepham Farm adjoins chalk grassland nature reserve. Otford Farmers will consider selling to the trade.

ALLENS FARM
Allens Lane, Plaxtol
Sevenoaks
TN15 0QZ
Tel: 01732 822904
Fax: 01732 822824
Internet:
www.cobweb.comm.co.uk.\cobnut\
Contact: Mrs Jill Webb
Produce: Kent Cob nuts. A dessert nut similar to a hazel but much larger and very milky, not oily. Some years also stock plums and damsons. Prepared to mail nuts and deliver locally. No min. order.
Prices/Payment: Fluctuates but approx £1.20 per lb picked, 70p per lb PYO Cash and cheques only.
Hours: Mon-Sat, 9am-5pm depending on the weather. Advisable to 'phone first.
Notes: Disabled access. Footpath through the farm. Allens Farm also supply Kelsey Bros. Farm Shop. They are interested in supplying to the trade.

JAYS FISH PRODUCTS
The Smokery
Winkhurst Lane, Ide Hill
Sevenoaks
TN14 6LD
Tel: 01732 750889
Fax: 01732 750588
Contact: Roger Jay

Produce: Totally traditional oak smoked salmon and other fishes. Also stock approx. 80 types of fish & shellfish. Mail Order world-wide, home deliveries locally. Also supplies approx. 80 independent retailers.
Prices/Payment: Cash and cheques only
Hours: Tue, Wed, Fri, 9am-5.30pm. Mon & Thurs, 9 am-3pm. Saturdays, 9.30am- 5pm.
Notes: Disabled access to the shop. Jays are interested in selling to trade.

MERRIMANS
Sandy Lane, Ivy Hatch
Sevenoaks
TN15 0PB
Tel: 01732 810884
Fax: 01732 810884
Email: gill@levity.demon.co.uk
Contact: Gillian Jones
Produce: Kentish cobnuts
Prices/Payment: £1 per lb bag at the gate. Cash and cheques only.
Hours: 9am-5.30pm through-out September.
Notes: Limited disabled access. Merrimans would be happy to supply to the trade. and by mail order.

PLATTINUMS LTD
PO Box 265
Sevenoaks
TN15 8ZX
Tel: 01787 248330
Contact: R. Clark
Produce: Kentish cobnuts and cobnut based products, e.g. Kentish cobnuts in dark chocolate. Mail Order service for chocolates. No min. order charge.
Prices/Payment: Kentish cobnuts in dark chocolate, 115g @ £6.95. Cash and cheques only.
Hours: 9am-5pm weekdays; telephone and postal enquiries only.
Notes: Plattinums is not open to the public. Suppliers to Fortnum & Mason (London), Bluebird (London), Chocolate Shop (Sevenoaks, Kent), Oscars (West Malling, Kent). Plattinums are interested in supplying more to the trade.

SYNDALE VALLEY CHEESEMAKERS
The Old Dairy, Grove End Farm
Tunstall
Sittingbourne
ME9 8DY
Tel: 01795 886218
Contact: Geoff Parker
Produce: Curd cheese, soft fresh cheeses, semi-hard cheese, hard cheese, using pasteurised Friesian cow's milk and vegetarian rennet. Cheese cakes and speciality cheese loaves. Also stock goat's cheese, Somerset cheddar, Staffordshire organic cheeses, duck liver pâté. Mail Order service and courier service. Cheese club about to be set up. Min order £10.
Prices/Payment: 100g soft cheese £1, 275g soft cheese £2. Hard cheese £8.77kg. Cash and cheques only.
Hours: By arrangement usually on cheesemaking days. 4 open days a year. Visits, talks & tastings by appointment.
Notes: Disabled access to some areas. Syndale Valley Cheesemakers supply to Doddington Post Office Stores, Macknade Farm Shop, Super 'M' (Blean) and Lurcocks of Lenham. They are interested in supplying more to the trade.

ASH GREEN ORGANIC FOODS
Little Darman Farm, Darman Lane
Paddock Wood
Tonbridge
TN12 6PW
Tel: 01892 838070
Fax: 01892 838070
Contact: Mark Temple/Lesley Howard
Produce: Bramleys, eating apples, pears and plums. Also stock a wide selection of other fresh and dry goods, locally sourced whenever possible and always from certified suppliers. Home delivery service on any or all of their produce. Min. order £15 though flexible.
Prices/Payment: Cash and cheques only
Hours: Tues-Fri, 9.30am-2.30pm at Little Darman Farm; also at Greenwich Market and Spitalfields Market (see London Section). Tastings of fresh produce are always available.
Notes: Disabled access. Ash Green Organic Foods supply a wholesale basis.

WILLETTS FARM DAIRY ICE CREAM
Willetts Farm
Blackham
Tunbridge Wells
TN3 9TU
Tel: 01892 740320
Fax: 01892 740320
Contact: Robin Ashby
Produce: A real dairy ice cream.
Prices: Cash and cheques only.
Hours: 9am-5pm
Notes: No disabled access. Willetts Farm supply to Kingfisher Farm (Dorking), Cherry Gardens (Groombridge), Full of Beans (Lewes), Hudsons (Eastbourne) and many other outlets in Kent, Sussex & Surrey.

SEASALTER SHELLFISH (WHITSTABLE) LTD
East Quay, The Harbour
WHITSTABLE
CT5 1AB
TEL: 01227 272003
FAX: 01227 264829
EMAIL: seasalter@compuserve.com
CONTACT: Elaine Kirkcaldie
PRODUCE: Whitstable cultivated oysters, Manila clams, cockles. Also stock oyster knives and souvenirs. Mail order courier service available. Min. order 2 doz. oysters £24.
PRICES/PAYMENT: Direct from Whitstable gate price £2.76 per doz. Farmed oysters (23p each). Delivered 50 oysters £23.50 trade price. All major credit cards accepted.
HOURS: Mon-Fri, 9am-5pm.Weekends,10am-4pm.
NOTES: Disabled access to ground floor. Oyster and fishery exhibition with maritime garden and light refreshments. Oysters can be bought from museum at weekends. Seasalter Shellfish supply Network Fisheries and L.G. Wicker (Billingsgate), Asda Supermarkets (London area) and St Augustines Fish (Whitstable).

SURREY

THE REAL MEAT COMPANY
9 Gordon Road
Carshalton Beeches
Tel: 0181 395 8946
(See Main Entry under Warminster)

R. COE & SONS
Kingfisher Farm Shop/Watercress
Abinger Hammer
Dorking
RH5 6QX
Tel: 01306 730703 **Fax:** 01306 731654
Contact: Barrie/Margaret/Marion
Arminson
Produce: Watercress (wholesale). Also
stock, fruit, veg, all dairy produce,
meats, dry goods, jams, pickles,
flowers, plants, growing mediums,
cakes, pies and bread.
Prices/Payment: Visa, Mastercard,
Delta, Visa, Solo, Electron and Switch.
Hours: 9am-6pm daily. 10am-5pm Sun/
Bank Holiday.10am-4pm Winter Sun
Notes: Disabled access. Annual tasting
day, Oct/Nov.

WILLIAMS OF CLAYGATE
19-21 The Parade, Claygate
Esher
KT10 0PD
Tel: 01372 462901
Contact: Martin Williams/Lee Platt
Produce: Home-made sausages, meat
pies, cooked meats, quiches, salads.
Home-made cakes, pizzas, bread,
smoked turkey, own ham on bone,
rotisserie chickens & ducks, beef from
Scotland, lamb, pork. Home-made
jams. Also stock high quality biscuits,
pickles, jams, cakes, approx 50
varieties of cheeses and grocery items.
Prices/Payment: Visa, Mastercard.
Switch.
Hours: Mon-Sat, 8am-5.30pm.
Notes: Disabled access. In-shop
cookery demonstrations, coffee shop.
Williams of Claygate are interested in
supplying to the trade.

HAZELBROW TURKEYS
Hazelbrow Farm, Rad Lane
Peaslake
Guildford
GU5 9PB
Tel: 01306 730313
Fax: 01306 730503
Email: richardson.j@btinternet.com
Contact: J.E. Richardson
Produce: Free range bronze and barn
reared traditional farm fresh turkeys for
Christmas only.
Prices/Payment: Cash and cheques
only
Hours: For 3 days before Christmas
8am-6pm, until noon Christmas Eve.
Notes: Disabled access. The following
butchers stock Hazelbrow turkeys at
Christmas only. C.L. Lewis (Ascot &
Sunningdale), Williams Butchers
(Claygate), Country Produce
(Horsham), J Honour (Old Woking), S
Jenner (Horsell), Chapman & Son
(Tadworth), Little Butchers (Bagshott),
Mr. Humphries (Midhurst).

CYRNEL BAKERY LTD
High Street
Lingfield
RH7 6AA
Tel: 01342 836359
Contact: Helen Harrison
Produce: Bread & pastry goods, some
organic. A wide variety of bread, cakes
and pastries using top quality ingredients - butter, free range eggs, locally
grown flour, all additive free. Lines for
special diets and seasonal goods. Also
stock vegetarian frozen, handmade
pastries from Lillies Pies of Uckfield
Prices/Payment: Bread from 70p, cakes
from 55p, filled rolls from £1.10. Cash
and cheques only.
Hours: 8am-5pm
Notes: Disabled access. This address is
a shop only – Cyrnel have a shop and
bakery in Forest Row. Cyrnel Bakery
supply to The Seasons (Forest Row),
Unwins Food & Wine (East
Grinstead), Corbins (Uckfield), Full of
Beans (Lewes) and Wealden
Wholefoods. They are interested in
supplying more to the trade.

FANNY'S FARM SHOP
Markedge Lane, off Gatton Bottom
Merstham
Redhill
RH1 3AW
Tel: 01737 554444
Contact: Mrs Fanny Maiklem
Produce: Specialised home-made
cakes, marmalade, honey, wine, runner
beans. Also stock chutney, jams,
pickles, eggs. Also china, bric-a-brac,
antiques.
Prices/payment: All majors taken and
Amex.
Hours: 9am - 7pm seven days a week.
Notes: Disabled access, Tea Shop.
Pigs, chickens and ducks to view.
Marmalade tastings.

THE ORIGINAL MAIDS OF HONOUR LTD
288 Kew Road, Kew Gardens
Richmond
TW9 3DU
Tel: 0181 940 2752
Contact: John or Gillian Newens
Produce: Original Maids of Honour
cakes, first baked in King Henry VIII's
reign. Also a large range of home
made cakes, buns and savoury pies.
Also stock Hadleigh made chocolates
from Hadleigh, Essex.
Prices/Payment: Maid of Honour cake
95p each, chicken and ham pie, £4.60
per lb. Macaroon Gateau, £3.95 each.
All major credit cards.
Hours: Tues-Sat,9.30am-5.30pm.
Notes: Disabled access. Tea shop,
restaurant and terrace in summer. Fully
licensed.

TASTE OF THE PAST
74 The Broadway, Tolworth
Surbiton
KT6 7SB
Tel: 0181 399 4916
Contact: Lee South
Produce: Traditional breed meat, sold
as is and further processed e.g. cured
Tamworth pork (ham, bacon, etc.),
Berkshire pig pork sausages. Pies with
traditional breed fillings, e.g (Soay)

lamb pie. Also stock cheese, bacon,
bread, grocery products. Mail Order
catalogue on request, please 'phone for
details. Min order charge £35 plus
p&p.
Prices/Payment: Rich Soay lamb pie,
99p per 7oz. Traditional breed
sausages from £1.99 per lb. Highland
Beef rump steak £5.99 per lb. All
major credit cards, not Switch.
Hours: Mon-Sat, 9am-5pm.
Notes: Disabled access not a problem.
Some tastings available. Taste of the
Past wish to sell to the trade.

THE ROYAL HORTICULTURAL SOCIETY
The R.H.S. Garden, Wisley
Woking
GU23 6QB
Tel: 01483 224234
Fax: 01483 212343
Contact: Jim Arbury, Fruit Department
Superintendent
Produce: A very wide range of soft and
top fruits are grown at Wisley & sold
with many unusual cultivars, incl.
strawberries, raspberries, gooseberries,
red, white and black currants, blueber-
ries, apples, pears, plums, cherries and
some vegetables are also sold.
Prices/Payment: Prices vary according
to season. Cash and cheques only.
Hours: Open subject to availability of
fruit, as fruit supply allows. Mon-
Fri,12.15pm-4pm (during soft fruit
season June to Aug). Sept-Dec every
day, 12.15pm-4pm.
Notes: Disabled access. Wisley
Gardens is an extensive and diverse
public garden with a gift/book shop,
plant centre & restaurant.

EAST SUSSEX

ASHURST ORGANICS
The Orchard
Ashurst Farm
Plumpton
Lewes
BN7 3AP

Tel: 01273 891219
Contact: Collette/Peter
Produce: Over 30 different types of organic vegetables sold through an organic veg box scheme to local area. Also bread, eggs and honey.
Prices/Payment: Two box sizes £6.50 & £9.50. Cash and cheques only
Hours: Telephone anytime to order. Box scheme operates to drop-off points for collection. Ashurst Organics also supply Boathouse Farm Shop, West Chiltington P.O. Stores and Worth Eating, No direct sales at farm gate, although occasional open days. Some limited possibility of small trade supply.

SCRAGOAK FARM
Brightling Road
Robertsbridge
TN32 5EY
Tel: 01424 838454
Fax: 01424 838420
Contact: Michelle, Louise or Jerry.
Produce: Organic box scheme deliveries throughout the South East and South London. Farm shop also sells own produce plus imported produce, all organic. Also stocks organic meat, dairy products, fish, wholefoods and groceries. Large or small box scheme. Vegetables and fruit delivered via coordinators. Please 'phone for list.
Prices/Payment: All major credit cards taken.
Hours: Wed, Thurs, Fri, Sat, 9.30am-5pm
Notes: Disabled access. Ramp and double doors. Customers are free to look around the farm.

JUST DESSERTS OF RYE
Unit 7
65-81 Winchelsea Road
Rye
TN31 7EL
Tel: 01797 224708
Fax: 01424 713231
Email: jdratrye@aol.com
Contact: Mr Dominique Moyse
Produce: Pies, tarts, gateaux, quiches, meat pies, meringues; individual, 4

portion or 12 portion. Delivery service available for orders above £30. Please order 72 hours in advance.
Prices/Payment: Fruit pies from £3.25 per 4 portions, £8.60 per 12 portions. Cheesecakes from £5.75 per 6 portions, £9.85 per 12 portions. Cash and cheques only.
Hours: 9am-5pm.
Notes: Disabled access. Just Desserts also supply to Weald Smokery Farm Shop and Syon Park Farm Shop. They are interested in supplying more to the trade.

OLD SPOT FARM SHOP
Piltdown
Uckfield
TN22 3XN
Tel: 01825 722894
Fax: 01825 723623
Contact: Ray Gould
Produce: Home cured & smoked bacon, gammons and hams. Over 20 varieties of handmade sausages. Home-made quiches. Home grown organic vegetables, organic beef, additive free pork and chicken. Free range organic veal (in conversion) and wild venison. Also stock over 60 cheeses, preserves, organic wines, milk, cream, eggs, bread, cakes and biscuits. Overnight carrier nationwide. Local delivery. Min. order charge £25.
Prices/Payment: Visa, Delta, Mastercard, Switch.
Hours: Tues-Sun, 9am-5.30pm. Closed Mon.
Notes: Disabled access. Tastings invited. Old Spot Farm Shop supply to Tulleys Farm Shop and Durleigh Marsh Farm Shop.

SUSSEX HIGH WEALD DAIRY PRODUCTS
Putlands Farm Shop
Duddleswell
Uckfield
TN22 3BJ
Tel: 01825 712647
Fax: 01825 712474
Contact: Mark Hardy

Produce: A range of cheese, yogurt and fromage frais made from both sheep's milk and organic cow's milk. Inc. Duddleswell, Sussex Slipcote and Ashdown Foresters. Also stock apple juice and other locally made produce. Mail Order for cheese, please ring for catalogue. No min. order.
Prices/Payment: Cheese from £6 per kg, Yogurts at 70p for 200g (sheep's milk). Cash and cheques only.
Hours: Mon-Sat, 9am-5pm. Closed Sunday from 1pm.
Notes: Disabled access. Visitors can see the farm animals and cheesemaking demonstrations by appointment. Sussex High Weald Dairy Products supply, Planet Organic (London), Garson Farm Shop (Esher), The Seasons (Forest Row) and Infinity Foods (Brighton). They also supply to catering outlets throughout London and the South East.

WILLOWDOWN DAIRY GOATS
Humphreys Farm, Nutley
Uckfield
TN22 3LS
Tel: 01825 712432
Contact: M Willcock
Produce: Unpasteurised goat's milk. Goat's milk yoghurt and soft and hard cheese.
Prices/Payment: Milk £1.08 per 2 pts. Yoghurt 69p per 10oz carton. Soft cheese £1.06 per 4 oz and hard cheese £1.16 per 4oz. Cash and cheques only.
Hours: 9am-5pm.
Notes: Reasonable disabled access. Possible interest in supplying to the trade.

THE WEALD SMOKERY
Mount Farm, Flimwell
Wadhurst
TN5 7QL
Tel: 01580 879601
Fax: 01580 879564
Contact: Andrew Wickham
Produce: Smoked meats, hand prepared and smoked over oak log fires and oak chippings, using brick kilns. All free from artificial colours and flavours. Range includes, chicken, duck breasts. Toulouse sausages, venison, air dried ham, dry cure smoked streaky bacon, Bresaola, kassela, smoked turkey breast. Full range of smoked fish salmon, trout, kippers and eels, haddock etc. Also stock farmhouse cheese, quality wine, gourmet foods and deli items. Mail order service available with colour brochure.
Prices/Payment: £4.75 two smoked chicken breasts, £4.55 lb smoked trout, £4.75 for 115g sliced smoked duck. Mastercard, Visa, Amex.
Hours: Mon-Sat, 9am-5.30pm. Sun (in summer) 11-5.30pm.
Notes: Disabled access. The Weald Smokery supplies four local outlets, and hotels & restaurants.

MAYNARDS
Windmill Hill, Ticehurst
Wadhurst
TN5 7HQ
Tel: 01580 200619
Fax: 01580 200394
Contact: D. Maynard
Produce: PYO fruit. Strawberries, gooseberries, raspberries, red & blackcurrants, sweet cherries. Logan & tayberries, cobnuts, damsons, apples & plums. Many unusual varieties.
Prices/Payment: Strawberries 80p per lb. Morrello cherries £1 per lb and cobnuts 80p per lb. Cash and cheques only.
Hours: 9am-dusk. Only during harvest season.
Notes: Disabled access.

WEST SUSSEX

C.R. UPTON
The Lodge
4 Top Road
Slindon
Arundel

BN18 0RP
Tel: 01243 814219
Contact: Mr C. Upton
Produce: Well known pumpkins and squashes. Large selection of varieties, in an eye catching display. All produce for collection from Slindon address
Prices/Payment: From 20p to £10. Cash and cheques only.
Hours: Seven days a week, 10am until dusk. Season Aug-Nov.
Notes: Limited driveway for disabled access.

WILLOW NURSERY

44 Hill Lane
Barnham
Bognor Regis
PO22 0BL
Tel: 01243 552852
Fax: 01243 552852
Contact: D. Wheeler
Produce: Organically grown vegetables and salad crops. Box scheme available. Please 'phone for full details. Min. order £5.
Prices/Payment: Cash and cheques only.
Hours: By appointment only.
Notes: No disabled access. Willow Nursery are interested in supplying to the trade.

JETHRO'S MARINADES

1 Sheddingdean Business Centre
Burgess Hill
RH15 8QY
Tel: 01444 244311
Fax: 01444 248700
Contact: Adrienne Palmer
Produce: Marinades for all meats, fish. Stir fry sauces, ginger & lime and ginger lime hot dressings. Salad vinaigrettes. Mail order on all products, min. order 6 bottles.
Prices/Payment: £2.10 per 250ml bottle & £7.00 per 4 pack. Cash and cheques only
Hours: 9am-4pm
Notes: Disabled access. Supply small independent shops across U.K.

O'HAGAN'S SAUSAGES & SMOKERY

Delling Lane, Bosham

CHICHESTER

PO18 8NN
TEL: 01243 574833
FAX: 01243 576733
CONTACT: Bill O'Hagan
PRODUCE: Over 40 varieties of fresh sausage including hi-fibre pork sausages in 16 varieties, beef and game sausages, Morrocan lamb, lamb & mint, lamb & rosemary, lamb & coriander sausage, 11 flavours of gluten free sausage, 4 flavours of poultry sausage, 4 smoked British sausages, salmon, trout, eel, their dry cure bacon and hams, poultry and game and when available biltong. Available by Mail Order. Min order £30 includes p&p.
PRICES/PAYMENT: Please 'phone for price list. All major credit cards taken.
HOURS: Mon-Sat, normal shop hours.
NOTES: Disabled access. O'Hagan's have other shops at The Butter Market, North Street, Chichester (Tel: 01243 532833) and at Greenwich (See London Section).

CYRNEL BAKERY LTD

Lower Road
Forest Row
East Grinstead
RH18 5HE
Tel: 01342 836359
Contact: Helen Harrison
Produce: Bread & pastry goods, some organic. A wide variety of bread, cakes and pastries using top quality ingredients - butter, free range eggs, locally grown flour, all additive free. Lines for special diets and seasonal goods. Also stock a few vegetarian frozen pastries, pies from Lillies Pies of Uckfield, handmade.

Prices/Payment: Bread from 70p, cakes from 55p, filled rolls from £1.10. Cash and cheques only.
Hours: 8am-5pm
Notes: Disabled access. Cyrnel Bakery have a shop in Lingfield and also supply to The Seasons (Forest Row), Unwins Food & Wine (East Grinstead), Corbins (Uckfield), Full of Beans (Lewes) and Wealden Wholefoods. They are interested in supplying more to the trade.

OLD PLAW HATCH FARM LTD
Sharpthorne
East Grinstead
RH19 4JL
Tel: 01342 810652/01342 810201
Fax: 01342 811478
Contact: Jayne Thomas
Produce: An extensive range of produce all of which meet the Demeter standards. Raw green top milk, unpasteurised cream, hard cheese yoghurts, eggs, meats, salads, vegetables and soft fruit.
Hours: Farm shop: Mon-Sat, 9am-6.30pm. Sun, 10am-5pm.
Notes: Disabled access. Old Plaw Hatch Farm supply Planet Organic, Bumblebee, Wild Oats (all London) and Infinity Foods (Brighton). They are interested in supplying more to the trade.

ALAN WOODWARD
Butchers
High Street
Henfield
BN5 9DA
Tel: 01273 492814
Contact: Alan Woodward
Produce: High quality meats and prize winning sausages. (Twice Great Britain's champion of champions sausage maker). All are made with local pork, scotch beef and local lamb. Flavours include cider and apple, gaucho hots, hop and ale, Italian herb, Sussex Village (with juniper and a hint of gin) and Toulouse. Also stock Quinns

Preserves, Gordons mustards and Cornerweighs herbs and spices.
Prices/Payment: Sausages from £2.40 per lb. Cash and cheques only.
Hours: Tues, Thurs and Fri, 8am-5.30pm. Closed 1pm-2pm. Sat, 8am-5pm. Closed all day Mon.
Notes: Disabled access.

SPRINGS SMOKED SALMON
Edburton
Henfield
BN5 9LN
Tel: 01273 857338
Fax: 01273 857228
Contact: Sales Office
Produce: A range of traditionally smoked fish and poultry using only salt and oak wood; no colours or preservatives used in the process. Also stock; 200 lines of frozen shellfish and fish products, 300 delicatessen lines all available in their shops. Available by Mail Order. Please 'phone 01903 815066. Home delivery Brighton, Hove and Worthing. Min. order £5.
Prices/Payment: Smoked Scotch salmon from £7.80 per lb. Pacific smoked salmon from £6 per lb. Cash or cheques only.
Hours: Mon-Fri, 8.30am -5pm. Sun for lunch 1.30pm-2pm. Sat, 8am-12pm only.
Notes: Disabled access. Springs Smoked Salmon are 20% retail and 80% wholesale and are interested in supplying more to the trade.

QUINNS PRESERVES
103 Howard Road
Sompting
Lancing
BN15 0LP
Tel: 01903 521668
Fax: 01903 521668
Contact: Jackie Quinn/Kim Patton
Produce: Specialist producers of fine home-made jams including; blueberry, fruits of the forest, kiwi & passionfruit, melon and ginger. Marmalades including; grapefruit and

brandy, three fruit ginger and whiskey seville. Chutneys including; hot mango, hot Indian, lemon and mustard seed and pear. Jellies, including; port and blackcurrant, grape and cranberry and apple.
Prices/Payment: Jam 227g £1.95, marmalade, 227g £1.75. Cash and cheques only.
Notes: Available from; 60 outlets around the South East of England. Please 'phone for list. Quinns Preserves are interested in supplying to the trade.

The following are SHOPS within this region which do not produce but do sell quality or organic foods

CANTERBURY WHOLEFOODS
10 The Borough
Canterbury
Kent
CT10 3DN
Tel: 01227 464623
Fax: 01227 764838
Produce: Wholefoods, delicatessen and ethnic foods. Organic fruit and vegetables, organic wines and beers. Macrobiotic foods, cheese and olive counter, fresh bread daily, ethnic cuisines, convenience foods, water filters etc. Home Delivery service. Min order £30 Canterbury area, £60 outside area.
Hours: Mon-Sat, 9am-6pm.
Notes: Disabled access. Canterbury Wholefoods supports the LETS scheme. If you are a member of the scheme and want to buy organic foods they will accept 20% payment in Tales.

MICHAEL HUMPHRIES
The Long Road
Rowledge
Farnham
Surrey
GU10 4DQ
Tel: 01252 792204

Produce: Butchers selling well hung meat. Home-made pies, pâtés, meats en croûte. Dry cure bacon. Hams and potted game.
Hours: Mon, 7am-1pm. Tues-Fri, 7am-5pm. Sat, 7am-2pm.
Notes: Also at West Street, Midhurst, West Sussex. Tel: 01730 813135.

CORNERWEIGHS
1 Elm Lodge, Caudle Street
Henfield
West Sussex
BN5 9DQ
Tel: 01273 492794
Fax: 01273 492794
Produce: 700 lines of natural foods, 40% of which are organic. Also some products from "Taste of the South East", Solgar vitamins and minerals, Natural Science (Dead Sea Products), Australian Bodycare, Ecover, Meridian, Green & Blacks, Provamel, Biona, Granose and Fair Trade products.
Hours: Mon, Tues, Thurs, Fri, 9am-5.30pm. Wed, 9am-1.30pm. Sat, 9.30am-5pm. Closed 1pm-2pm for lunch.
Notes: Try before you buy on any loose products. Special days, tastings, demonstrations.

OLIVERS WHOLEFOOD STORE
5 Station Approach, Kew Gardens
Richmond
Surrey
TW9 3QB
Tel: 0181 948 3990
Fax: 0181 948 3991
Produce: Large organic green grocers and health food shop. Everything organic from Champagne to chocolate. Yogurt ice machine in summer. You choose the fruit, they mix it with yogurt. Organic meat can be ordered in advance. Home delivery and Mail Order on any items stocked. Min. order £30.
Hours: Mon-Sat, 9am-7pm. Sun, 10am-6pm.
Notes: Disabled access.

THE ORGANIC STORE
8 Staines Road
Twickenham
Middlesex
TW2 5AH
Tel: 0181 893 3310
Fax: 0181 404 1129
Email: organika@compuserve.com
Produce: Fruit and vegetables, dairy, dry goods, meat, wine and beers, baby foods, grains, pulses and breads. Home delivery catalogue available.
Hours: Mon-Fri, 8.30am-7pm. Closed 2pm on Wed. Sat, 8.30am-5pm. Sun, 12pm-4pm.
Notes: No disabled access. Wine tastings.

BERKSHIRE

COPAS BROTHERS (TURKEYS)
Lower Mount Farm, Long Lane
Cookham
SL6 9EE
Tel: 01628 529595
Fax: 01628 529512
Contact: Tanya Copas
Produce: Traditional farmfresh
Christmas turkeys. Available in barn-reared White or free range Bronze.
Slow-growing specialist breeds. Dry plucked and hung in a traditional manner to develop flavour and texture. Oven-ready and packed in a presentation box with cooking instructions. Also stock Hebridean smoked salmon, cranberry sauce, stuffings etc.
Prices/Payment: Christmas 1998 prices; Barn reared White Turkey £5.50 per kg; crowns £7.65 per kg. Free range Bronze £6.10 per kg; crowns £8.40 per kg. Credit cards taken.
Hours: Orders taken from late Oct. for collection 23rd Dec.
Notes: Disabled access. Copas Bros supply to high quality butchers & farmshops throughout the U.K. including; R.A. Byford & Sons Ltd (Rayleigh), Edwards Butchers (Conwy), Jennings Butchers (Hurst), Charles McHardy Butchers (Stonehaven) and Dennis of Bexley. Full list of stockists on request. Copas Bros are happy to supply to the trade.

DOVES FARM FOODS
Salisbury Road
Hungerford
RG17 0RF
Tel: 01488 684880
Fax: 01488 685235
Contact: Clare Marriage
Produce: A large range of speciality flours and organic foods, including; biscuits, cookies, crackers and breakfast cereals. Mail Order

available - please send S.A.E. for info. No min order but the more you order the cheaper delivery becomes.
Prices/Payment: Cash and cheques only.
Hours: Mon-Fri, 9am-5pm for mill shop; only end of runs and bulk sales available.
Notes: No disabled access. Doves Farm Foods supply to independent health food stores nationwide.

LONG LANE FARM
Touchen End
Maidenhead
SL6 3LG
Tel: 01628 637567
Fax: 01628 632546
Email: Joannasbeef@compuserve.com
Contact: Joanna Wheatley
Produce: Organic beef sold in freezer packs at the farm gate. Min order 10kg.
Prices/Payment: 10kg pack of assorted cuts, £65. Larger packs available. Cash and cheques only.
Hours: 9am-5pm.

WALTHAM PLACE FARM SHOP
Church Hill, White Waltham
Maidenhead
SL6 3JH
Tel: 01628 829154
Fax: 01628 825045
Contact: Vicky Robinson
Produce: Organic vegetables, meats, dairy produce. Jams, chutneys, breads using home-grown organic ingredients. Also stock organic tea, coffee & cordials, free range eggs. Delivery up to 10 miles.
Prices/Payment: Delivery charges over £20 free. Under £20 charge £3.50. Cash, cheques only.
Hours: Fri, 1.30pm-5pm.
Sat, 10am-1.00pm
Notes: Limited disabled access. Gardens: Wed, 2pm-5pm April-Oct. Limited produce, but hotels, restaurants welcome to contact.

GARLANDS FARM SHOP
Gardeners Lane
Upper Basildon
Reading
RG8 8NP
Tel: 01491 671556
Fax: 01491 671556
Contact: Gabriel Hutchings/Denise
Ingrem
Produce: Organic fruit and vegeta-
bles, certified as retailers and growers
of organic food by the Soil Associa-
tion. Also stock a comprehensive
range of organic groceries, dairy,
cheese, beer, wine, wholefoods, ice
cream, special diets catered for.
Home delivery over 3 counties,
Berks, S. Oxfordshire and E. Wilts.
Min order £10. Veg bags delivered
for only £7.
Prices/Payment: Please 'phone for
price list. Cash and cheques only.
Hours: Tues-Sat, 9am-4pm.
Notes: Disabled access. Organic
garden.

KULIKA TRUST
Warren Farm
Rectory Road
Streatley
Reading
RG8 9QE
Tel: 01491 872149
Fax: 01491 873719
Email:
106623.165@compuserve.com
Contact: Alastair Taylor
Produce: Organic fresh seasonal
vegetables, home-made jams and
pickles. Organic meat; beef, lamb
and pork (check availability).
Sausages, bacon and free range eggs.
Also stock a selection of prepacked
organic and fairly traded goods. Box
scheme into local villages or collect
on Fri, Sat from the farm.
Prices/Payment: Set box of £5 then
people can add on top. Cash and
cheques only.
Hours: Daily, 8am-6pm.
Notes: Disabled access. Warren Farm
is a training centre for African
farmers. Suppliers to Londis Stores

(Goring) during the summer and to
Garlands Farm Shop. They are
interested in selling their summer
excess to the trade.

SALLY LUNN'S
11 Peascod Street
Windsor
SL4 1DT
Tel: 01753 862627
Contact: Julian Abraham
Produce: Sally Lunn's bakes and
serves the world famous and historic
Sally Lunn bun. The bun is a rich
round and generous brioche style
bread created by Sally Lunn in the
1680's. The refreshment rooms are
open all day serving Sally Lunn's buns
which can be eaten with sweet or
savoury accompaniments.
Prices/Payment: Buns to take away
are £1.08, sweet treats in the refreshment rooms start from around £3 with
meals/snacks from £4. All major
credit cards taken No Amex, Diners
JCB & Switch,
Hours: Mon-Sun: 10.am-6pm evening
meals from 6pm.
Notes: Disabled access is good
throughout. Coffee also roasted on
the premises. Sally Lunn's has a
policy not to sell their products
through any other suppliers. See also
entry for Bath

B A McLEISH (Butchers)
73 Rances Lane
Wokingham
RG40 2LQ
Tel: 01189 786258
Contact: Brian McLeish/Steven Ball
Produce: Producers of handmade
sausages and burgers. Also make their
own pies.
Prices/Payment: Pie prices start from
95p each. Sausages from £1.99 per
lb. Cash and cheques only.
Hours: Tues-Fri, 7.30am-5.30pm.
Closed for lunch from 1pm-2pm. Sat,
7am-4pm.
Notes: B A McLeish are interested in
supplying to the trade.

BUCKINGHAMSHIRE

SOPHIE'S CHOCOLATES
3/4 The Gatehouse
Elgiva Lane
Chesham
HP5 2JD
Tel: 01494 782999
Contact: Sophie Webb
Produce: Chocolates freshly made on the premises. Over 25 different types; seasonal lines including personalised Easter eggs, Valentine hearts, Christmas Truffle Treats. Gift boxes, plus a variety of chocolate figures. Also make wedding & celebration cakes, a traditional rich fruit cake, vanilla sponge or special chocolate cake all decorated to your choice. Also stock Turkish Delight from Turkey, Italian silver and gold sugared almonds. Cornish fudge. Mail Order service available, (popular for weddings). No min. order.
Prices/Payment: Chocolates from £16.50 per lb. Wedding cakes (including handmade sugar flowers) from £8.50 for an 8" single cake to £240 for a 4-tier 12" cake. Cash and cheques only.
Hours: Mon-Fri, 10am-5pm. Sat, 9.30am-5pm.
Notes: No disabled access. Sophie's Chocolates are interested in supplying to the trade.

G STEVENS & SONS
Warrington House Farm Shop
Warrington
Olney
MK46 4HN
Tel: 01234 711464
Contact: Robert Stevens
Produce: Asparagus, raspberries, strawberries, black & red currants and tayberries. Also stock P Cants ice cream, cream cheese, meat and vegetables.
Prices/Payment: Asparagus from 80p to £2.20. Raspberrries £1.50 per lb,

Strawberries £1.10 per lb. Cash and cheques only.
Hours: April-August, 9.30am-6.30pm seven days.
Notes: Disabled access. Also stockists of Botany Bay plants, glass, pots and furniture.

DORSET

DENHAY FARMS LTD
Broadoak
Bridport
DT6 5NP
Tel: 01308 458963
Fax: 01308 424846
Contact: Amanda Streatfield
Produce: Denhay Farmhouse Cheddar made in 27kg traditional rinded cylinders, 20kg Farmhouse blocks, mild and mature. 2kg Dorset Drums cloth wrapped in presentation box. Denhay Air Dried ham: ham on the bone from Denhay's whey-fed pigs, cured in apple-juice honey, curing salts and local herbs, lightly smoked and air dried for several months. Denhay Dry Cured Bacon, produced from the same pigs as the ham. De-rinded and packed in a range of sizes. A small quantity of cured meat, sausages and farmhouse butter is also produced. Also stock other locally produced items. Mail Order: cheese and bacon are sent by Interlink U.K, ham by first class post. Gift service available. 'Phone for details.
Prices/Payment: From 115g air dried ham £5.40 - Dorset Drum £20.75. Mastercard, Visa, cash, cheques.
Hours: Mon and Thurs, 9am-5pm
Notes: Denhay supply a range of outlets across Southern England.

R.J.BALSON & SON
9 West Allington
Bridport
DT6 5BJ
Tel: 01308 422638
Contact: Richard Balson

Produce: Fresh meat, poultry, local lamb, mutton, veal, venison, turkey, chicken, duck, pheasant, pigeon, partridge, mallard, guinea fowl, ostrich, kangaroo, rabbits, hare, wild boar. Home-made speciality sausages. Home-made faggots, burgers, home cooked hams, hogs pudding, cooked chickens, kebabs and black pudding. Also stock bacon, gammon, frozen foods. Mail Order on demand. Please 'phone for details.
Prices/Payment: Cash and cheques only
Hours: Mon, 6.45am-1pm. Tues-Sat, 6.45am-4.30pm.
Notes: Disabled access. Frequent tastings available. Members of the Q Guild of Butchers. R.J. Balson supply to the trade.

S. MOORES
The Biscuit Bakery, Morcombelake
Bridport
DT6 6ES
Tel: 01297 489253
Fax: 01297 489253
Email:
106444.3547@compuserve.com
Contact: Marie Dare
Produce: Biscuits and cakes. Mail Order available. No min. order charge, but minimum charge for postage.
Prices/Payment: Visa, Mastercard, Switch and Delta.
Hours: Mon-Fri, 9am-5pm.
Notes: No disabled access. Bakery open to the public. S. Moores are interested in supplying to the trade.

TAMARISK FARM
West Bexington
Dorchester
DT2 9DF
Tel: 01308 897784
Fax: 01308 897735
Contact: Josephine Pearse
Produce: All organic, most field and protected vegetables, fruit, stoneground organic wheat flour. Delivery box scheme.
Prices/Payment: Local seasonal

prices for vegetables. Flour 16kg £8.50 & 32kg £16. Delivery box scheme £6.00 worth vegetables/fruit in season; farm's selection, usually 9-12 items. Orders taken and boxes available on Thursdays.Min. orders £3 plain and £6 standard. Cash and cheques only
Notes: No disabled access. Tamarisk also supply Fruits of the Earth (Bridport)

W G S & P S BEST
Manor Farm, Godmanstone
Dorchester
DT2 7AH
Tel: 01300 341415
Fax: 01300 341170
Contact: Will or Pam Best
Produce: Organic wholemilk, semi-skimmed milk, farmhouse cream. Organic lamb, cut to order, whole or half lambs. Milk available from farm shop; lamb, please 'phone to place order.
Prices/Payment: Milk from 56p per litre. Cash, cheques only.
Hours: Mon-Sat, 8.30am-6pm. Closed Sun.
Notes: Possible for wheel chair access. Manor Farm supply to outlets throughout London & the South.

WHISTLEY CRAYFISH
Whistley Waters, Milton-on-Stour
Gillingham
SP8 5PT
Tel: 01747 840666
Fax: 01747 840666
Contact: Chris Campbell
Produce: Signal Crayfish. A sweet tasting fresh water crayfish (looks similar to a small lobster). Supplied alive in 5 lb or 10 lb boxes with 8-10 crayfish per lb weight. During season from Jun - Oct. Mail Order service available by overnight carrier, or collect. Min. order normally 5 lbs.
Prices/Payment: £6.50 per lb plus freight. Cash and cheques only.
Hours: Daylight hours from June-Oct.
Notes: Disabled access. Lakes and gardens to view. Whistley Crayfish's main outlets are hotels and restaurants.

THURSDAY COTTAGE LTD
Carswell Farm
Uplyme
LYME REGIS
DT7 3XQ
TEL: 01297 445555
FAX: 01297 445095
EMAIL: jams@thursday-cottage.com
INTERNET: www.thursday-cottage.com
CONTACT: Hugh Corbin
PRODUCE: Marmalades, jams and curds. Mail Order available. Min. order 12 jars.
PRICES/PAYMENT: Approx. £1.70 - £1.90 per jar, plus carriage. Cheques only.
HOURS: 'Phone for Mail Order.
NOTES: Thursday Cottage supply numerous outlets and are interested in supplying more to the trade.

THE REAL MEAT COMPANY
14 Bournemouth Road
Lower Parkstone
Poole
Tel: 01202 747972
(See Main Entry under Warminster, Wilts)

WOODLANDS PARK DAIRY
Woodlands
Wimborne
BH21 8LX
Tel: 01202 822687
Fax: 01202 826051
Email: sales@woodlands-park.co.uk
Internet: www. woodlands-park.co.uk
Contact: Richard or Rieta Murray
Produce: Sheep and goat's milk yoghurt - both natural (plain) and fruit flavoured, from animals fed only on feed of vegetable origin. Also stock frozen sheep & goats milk, sheep & goat's milk cheese and sheep's milk ice cream.

Prices/Payment: Cash and cheques only
Hours: Mon-Fri, 9am-5pm. Other times by appointment.
Notes: Disabled access to dairy. The Murrays supply many good health food shops and are interested in supplying to the trade.

HAMPSHIRE

BREBILAIT PRODUCTS
Wield Wood
Alresford
SO24 9RU
Tel: 01420 563151/564182
Fax: 01420 561018
E:mail: olivia-mills@msn.com
Internet: www.hampshirefare.co.uk/sheep.html
Contact: Christine Newens – dairy manager
Produce: 'Walda' semi-hard sheep cheese with vegetarian rennet. Pepper 'Walda' as above with green peppercorns; pure sheep milk Feta cheese; plain yogurt - no additives; flavoured yogurt - Swiss style, no added sugar. Sheep milk, lamb meat, lean lamb sausages, mutton.
Also stock 'Quantoch Blue' sheep cheese, apple juice, honey, chutney, sheep milk ice cream. By Mail order – chill van can deliver within a 50 mile radius. Min order £20.00.
Prices/Payment: 'Walda' cheese £12.00kg. Cash or cheques only.
Hours: 9am-1pm
except Wed. All other times by appointment.
Notes: No disabled access at the moment. Suppliers to several other outlets and interested in supplying to the trade.

DAVID BOWTELL
Home Farm Shop
East Tisted
Alton
GU34 3QP
Tel: 01420 588418

Fax: 01420 587360
Contact: David or Toby Bowtell
Produce: Home farm reared beef, pork, bacon, lamb, sold in the fresh meat shop. Barn reared additive free chicken. Venison. Sausages. Also stock vegetables, ice cream, jam, cakes, water and apple juice.
Prices/Payment: All major credit cards taken.
Hours: Thurs, 10am-5pm. Fri, 10am-7pm. Sat, 8am-5pm. Sun, 10am-1pm.
Notes: Disabled access. Farm open to inspection during shop hours.

K.A. GARDNER FAMILY BUTCHER
16 High Street
Ludgershall
Andover
SP11 9PZ
Tel: 01264 790318
Fax: 01264 790518
Contact: Mr Allan Gardner
Produce: 32 varieties of award winning sausages including Champion pork, Olde Wiltshire, pork and apple, onion and chive, Boozey Banger and hickory smoked pork. Traditional dry cured bacon and smoked bacon (smoked on the premises), boiled Wiltshire ham, home-made faggots, and chicken & ham pie. Also stock own label jams & pickles, cheeses, pies and pasties, fruit & veg.
Prices/Payment: Cash, cheques and Switch, Delta. No credit cards.
Hours: Closed Mon, Tues-Fri, 8.30am-5.30pm; Sat, 8.30am-4pm.
Notes: Disabled access. Gardners are interested in supplying to the trade.

THE MANYDOWN CO
Upper Farm
Wootton St Lawrence
Basingstoke
RG23 8PE
Tel: 01256 460068
Fax: 01256 329288
Contact: Richard Stirling
Produce: Farm shop/butchery. Own beef, lamb, potatoes and other farm produce.
Hours: 7.30am to 5pm, Tuesday and Wednesday. Thursday and Friday, 7.30am to 6pm. Saturday closes at 3pm.
Notes: Manydown's motto is "Farming and Conservation Working together".

NORTHDOWN ORCHARD
South Litchfield
Basingstoke
RG25 3BP
Tel: 01256 771477
Contact: Mike Fisher
Produce: Organic potatoes, vegetables and salads - grown all year round for box scheme in the Basingstoke area.
Prices/Payment: Vegetable bags £4.50, boxes £7 & £9. Minimum order £4.50. Cash and cheques only
Hours: Deliveries Tues - Fri.
Notes: Not open for direct sales.

BLACKBURNE & HAYNES
Meadow Cottage Farm, Churt Road
Headley
Bordon
GU35 8SS
Tel: 01428 712155
Fax: 01428 714001
Contact: Celia Haynes (Mrs)
Produce: Farmhouse Jersey ice cream: apricot & mango, butter toffee, creme caramel, coconut & pineapple, coffee, dairy milk chocolate, extra chocolate, hazelnut praline, Jamaican rum and raisin, peach liqueur, pistachio & toasted almond, strawberry, vanilla and stem ginger. Fruit sorbets, lemon, mango, raspberry. Sucrose free ice cream (suitable for diabetics), sheep's milk ice cream, unpasteurised Jersey milk/cream and cheesecakes.
Prices/Payment: Ice cream £3.40 per litre, milk 80p per 2 pints, cream £1.20 per half pint. Cash and cheques only.
Hours: 9am-6pm seven days a week, but any time by arrangement.
Notes: No specific disabled access, but no real problems. Blackburn & Hayes do supply to the trade.

BEAULIEU CHOCOLATES
High Street, Beaulieu
Brockenhurst
SO42 7YA
Tel: 01590 612279
Contact: Anne Smith
Produce: Hand-made natural ingredients, chocolates, New Forest Bark and fresh cream truffles. Loose chocolates and presentation boxes. Chocolate animals, bars and specialities. Also stock preserves, pickles, honey from Dart Valley and The New Forest Jam& Chutney Co. Delivery scheme and chocolates by post.
Prices/Payment: Boxes from £1.20 upwards. Chocolates/Truffles £11.84 lb. Mastercard, Amex accepted
Hours: Mon -Fri, 10am-5pm. Sat & Sun, 10am- 5.30pm.
Notes: Also suppliers to Sweet Seductions, Priorys of Christchurch.

HOCKEYS
South Gorley
FORDINGBRIDGE
SP6 2PW
TEL: 01425 652542
FAX: 01425 655499
CONTACT: Mr Michael Rust
PRODUCE: Natural farm produce including free range beef from (MAFF certified) own B.S.E. free herd. Free range lamb from sheep grazed on Salisbury watermeadows. Naturally reared pork, poultry, game. Bacon, home-made pies, pizzas, sauces etc. Also stock cakes, jams, chutneys made for Hockeys plus organic wines, cordials and juices. Available from countrywide outlets (a distribution network) in London counties. No min. order.
PRICES/PAYMENT: All major credit cards. Not American Express or Diners.
HOURS: Mon-Sat, 9am-5.30pm.
NOTES: Disabled access. Tasting promotions, deer park, farm walks and hospitality area.

DOWN TO EARTH
Pitmore Lane
Lymington
SO41 8LL
Tel: 01590 674020
Contact: Mr Chris Hewitson May
Produce: Legumes, brasicas, salads, root vegetables, peppers, chillis, aubergines, celery, tomatoes, asparagus, courgettes, spinach, onions (red & yellow), sweet corn, leeks, pumpkin, melon, strawberries, raspberries, rhubarb. Box scheme available. Local (5 mile radius) home delivery.
Prices/Payment: Prices are seasonal. Min order box scheme £5. Cash and cheques only.
Hours: Summer; Mon-Sun, 9am-5pm. Winter; weekdays 10am-2pm.
Notes: Disabled access. Down to Earth are interested in supplying to the trade.

"LINZI'S PATISSERIE"
9 High Street
Lymington
SO41 9AA
Tel: 01590 678980
Contact: Linzi Luker
Produce: 'Linzi's Amazing Cake'® - A healthy fruit cake made in 14 varieties. No added fat (98% fat free). No added sugar, no eggs or dairy products. Amazing Cakes also made luxury style for Christmas; also Christmas puddings. Also stock New Forest Jam and Chutney Company, Moore's Dorset biscuits, Terracotta Foods (Australian style chutneys). Cakes available by Mail Order. Min. order 2xbar cakes or 1x7" cake £9.99 with first class P&P.
Prices/Payment: 'Bar' Tin size £2.95, 7" round size £5.95. Cash and cheques only.
Hours: 9.30am-5.pm.
Notes: Disabled access. Tea rooms/ coffee shop offering light lunches, cream teas and patisserie. "Linzi's Patisserie" supply to The Old Station Tearooms (Holmsley). They are interested in supplying to the trade.

DURLEIGHMARSH FARM SHOP
Durleighmarsh, Rogate Road
Petersfield
GU31 5AX
Tel: 01730 821626
Contact: Roger and Alison Grange
Produce: Asparagus and new
potatoes are a speciality. PYO
strawberries, raspberries, blueberries,
tayberries, sunberries, currants,
gooseberries, broad beans, runner
beans, carrots, calabrese, sweetcorn,
pumpkin, etc. Farm shop stocks
honeys, chutneys, preserves, cheeses,
sheep's milk products, free range
meat, smoked fish, cakes, quiches,
wines and ciders.
Prices/Payment: PYO strawberries,
£1.08 per lb, raspberries £1.40 per lb.
Cash and cheques only.
Hours: Mon-Sat, 9am-5.30pm. Sun,
9am-1pm. (Sept-May)
9am-7pm every-day (June, July, Aug)
Notes: Disabled access to shop.
Tastings of various products; apple
tastings in Autumn. Durleighmarsh
supply local pubs and caterers.

A&M JOHNSON, HONEY AND HIVE PRODUCTS
Grasmead, Limekiln Lane
Dean, Bishops Waltham
Southampton
SO32 1FY
Tel: 01489 892390/890072
Fax: 01489 892390
Email: am.johnson@btinternet.com
Internet: www.hampshirefare.co.uk
Contact: Mrs Margaret Johnson
Produce: Natural honey gathered by
honeybees from the Hampshire
countryside. Five different honey
mustards and honey marmalade.
Heather honey fudge. Also stock a
range of beeswax candles, beeswax
skin creams and beeswax furniture
polish. Mail Order and delivery to the
Hampshire area. Min. order charge
£10.
Prices/Payment: 8oz of clear Hampshire honey, £1.30. Gift packs with
honey and beeswax items, from £4.75
to £15. Cash and cheques only.

Hours: 10am-5pm; always advisable
to 'phone first.
Notes: Limited disabled access. Bee
keeping and honey extraction
demonstrations by appointment. A &
M Johnson supply Ringwood Brewery
(Hampshire), Selfridges (London),
plus many local outlets throughout
Hampshire and are interested in
selling more to the trade.

CHALCROFT FARM SHOP
Chalcroft Farm
Burnetts Lane
West End
Southampton
SO30 2HU
Tel: 01703 600558/
01703 692206
Fax: 01703 602110
Email: rowtonbutchers@btinternet.com
Contact: Dave Morgan
Produce: Hampshire Sausage
(venison, watercress & red wine),
pork, ginger & spring onion sausages
plus many other varieties. Also stock
kangaroo, ostrich, emu, crocodile
tail. Smoked meats. Available by
home delivery within the Southamp-
ton area. Min order £25.
Prices/Payment: All major cards
except American Express.
Hours: Mon-Fri, 7am-5pm. Sat, 7am-
4pm.
Notes: Disabled access. Chalcroft
Farm supply to the trade.

PIROUET SEAFOODS
3 Redcar Street
Shirley
Southampton
SO15 5LL
Tel: 01703 788139
Fax: 01703 322263
Contact: Mr D Pirouet
Produce: Fresh fish and shellfish, live
lobster and crabs, frozen fish and
shellfish, Scottish salmon. Whole
salmon cooked to order.
Prices/Payment: Cash and cheques
only.
Hours: Tues-Sat, 9am-5pm.

TERRACOTTA FOODS

Terracotta Room, Wickham Vineyard
Botley Road, Shedfield
Southampton
SO32 2HL
Tel: 01329 835454
Email: terracotta@freenet.uk.com
Contact: Chris Muir
Produce: Australian chutneys made with unique Australian Bush foods and local (Hampshire) produce made at the Terracotta Room Restaurant at Wickham Vineyard.
Prices/Payment: Five chutneys range in price from £1.90 to £2.40 per jar. Visa, Mastercard accepted.
Hours: Seven days a week 10.30am-5pm
Notes: Chutneys available for sale in the restaurant – there is disabled access. Terracotta Foods supply R Owten (farm shop). They are interested in supplying more to the trade.

THE ANCHORAGE

Salisbury Road, Broughton
Stockbridge
SO20 8BX
Tel: 01794 301234
Contact: S.L.Tidy
Produce: Vegetables, eggs, chickens and fruit, in season.
Prices/Payment: Eggs from £1.60 per doz, chicken £2 per lb. Cash and cheques only.
Hours: Mon-Sat,10am-6.30pm.
Notes: Disabled access. The Anchorage supply Harroway Organic Gardens Farm Shop.

ISLE OF WIGHT

PHILLIPS FINE FOODS

Units 1&2, 290 Newport Road
Cowes
PO31 8PE
Tel: 01983 282200
Fax: 01983 281768
Contact: Jeff Dove
Produce: Smoked salmon, trout, halibut, eel, mussels, oysters, prawns, sprats, cheeses, chickens, duck,

gravadlax. Also stock all types of fresh and frozen fish and shellfish. Mail Order available for smoked salmon. No min. order charge.
Prices/Payment: Smoked salmon £9.50 per lb. Credit cards taken.
Hours: Mon-Fri, 9am-5pm. Sat, 9am-1pm
Notes: Disabled access. Tastings of all produce always available. Phillips Fine Foods also supply Alldays, Gowans, Wavells (all Isle of Wight).

GODSHILL ORGANICS

Newport Road
Godshill
PO38 3LY
Tel: 01983 840723 **Fax:** 01983 840723
Contact: Ruth Illman
Produce: 4 hectare organic symbol small holding growing wide range of crops for sale. Also stock organic groceries, fresh, chilled and ambient. Organic meat. Wine and beer. Box scheme and home service delivery. No min. order.
Prices/Payment: Visa and Mastercard taken.
Hours: Mon-Sat, 9am-5pm. Sun, 10am-5pm.
Notes: Disabled access. Natural wetland area.

BENEDICT'S FINE WINES & DELICATESSEN

28 Holyrood Street
Newport
PO30 5AU
Tel: 01983 529596
Fax: 01983 826868
Contact: Lynne Holland
Produce: A range of home-made food including quiches, cakes, salads etc. New range of home-made freezer meals now in stock. 'Home from Home' dinner party catering service. Picnic baskets and gift hampers made to order. Also stock a wide range of speciality cheese and meats. Wine department boasting more than 200 wines from around the world. South African Biltong. Handmade chocolates, a variety of speciality Isle of

Wight products: Minghellas ice cream, I.O.W honey. Available by Mail Order, for gift hampers, catering and picnic services and general purchases. Catalogue on request.
Prices/Payment: Freezer meals, luxury fish pie, £4.50, roasted fennel Niçoise £2.99. All major credit cards. American Express. Switch, Delta.
Hours: Mon-Sat, 9am-5.30pm.
Notes: Disabled access. Food and wine tastings – please 'phone for details. Benedict's are interested in supplying to the trade.

KINGCOB MERSLEY FARMS
Mersley Farms, Newchurch
Sandown
PO36 0NR
Tel: 01983 865229
Fax: 01983 862294
Email: kingcob@msn.com
Contact: Mr Gary Cadle
Produce: Processed garlic, ginger, smoked purée. Pre-packed sweetcorn. Prepared sweetcorn. Pre-packed garlic.
Prices/Payment: Cash and cheques only
Hours: Garlic farm shop is seasonal. 10am-6pm.
Notes: No disabled access.

ROSEMARY VINEYARD
Smallbrook Lane
Ryde
PO33 2UX
Tel: 01983 811084
Fax: 01983 812899
Contact: Mr C Gauntlett
Produce: Jams and mustards, produced at this vineyard, also producing juices, wines and ciders. Mail Order service available. No min. order.
Prices/Payment: Mustard, jams from £1.80. All major credit cards taken, cash and cheques.
Hours: Mon-Sat, 10am-5pm. Sun, 11am-4pm.
Notes: Disabled access. Vineyard trail, cafe and terrace, tastings. Rosemary Vineyard supply to the trade.

OXFORDSHIRE

PEACH CROFT FARM
Radley
Abingdon
OX14 2HP
Tel: 01235 520094 **Fax:** 01235 522688
Contact: W.J. Homewood
Produce: Traditionally reared free range Christmas poultry. Turkeys and geese. Reared exclusively for the Christmas market. Dry plucked, slow growing strains, grown to maturity. PYO strawberries, raspberries, currants, blackberries, tayberries and rhubarb in season. Pumpkins and squashes for Autumn and Halloween. Christmas trees from early Dec. Also stock speciality hams from Sandridge Farmhouse Bacon in Wiltshire. Overnight delivery service available across U.K. for poultry. Cost of delivery extra (about £15).
Prices/Payment: Bronze turkeys approx. £6.10 per kg. All major cards.
Hours: Seasonal opening of Farm Shop and PYO. Starting late April and ending July. Then Nov & Dec.
Notes: Disabled access. Tea shop and garden. Peach Croft Farm supply to local butchers only at Christmas. May wish to supply more to the trade.

THE NATIONAL HERB CENTRE
Banbury Road, Warmington
Banbury
OX17 1DF
Tel: 01295 690999
Fax: 01295 690034
Contact: Mr Peter Turner
Produce: Marmalade, conserves, fruit syrup, ginger syrup, lemon syrup, rosemary syrup, chutneys, jelly, flavoured vinegars, coriander pesto.
Prices/Payment: From £1.10-£3.35. All major credit cards and Switch for sales over £5.
Hours: Mon-Sun, 9.30am-5.30pm.
Notes: Disabled access. Herb shop, bistro, display gardens, plant centre and nature walks.

ELLIS ORGANICS
Little Bottom Farm, Colliers Lane
Rotherfield Peppard
Henley-on-Thames
RG9 5LT
Tel: 0118 972 2826 **Fax:** 0118 972 2826
Email: ellis-organics@clara.net
Contact: Aidan
Produce: Home grown fruit and
vegetables; salads a speciality. Also
stock a complete range of certified
organic foods (currently over 400
product lines). Home delivery only.
Prices/Payment: Cash and cheques only
Hours: Not open to the public.
Weekly home delivery orders taken
by fax, phone or e-mail.

CORNER FARM
Oakley Road, Horton-cum-Studley
Oxford
OX33 1BJ
Tel: 01865 358933
Fax: 01865 358806
Contact: Sheila Ayers
Produce: Organic fruit and vegeta-
bles; apples, blackcurrants, spinach,
cucumbers, lettuce, tomatoes etc.
Also stock organic meat, bread, ice
cream, grains, fruit, spreads, sweets,
cheese, yogurts, drinks, turkeys at
christmas, plus organic compost.
Delivery scheme around Oxford.
Min. order £20.
Prices/Payment: Cash, cheques only.
Hours: Tues, Wed, Thurs, 9am-5.pm.
Sat, 9am-1pm.
Notes: Disabled access to farm.
Corner Farm supply one hotel.

THE OLD DAIRY FARM SHOP
Path Hill Farm, Whitchurch on Thames
Reading
RG8 7RE
Tel: 0118 984 2392
Fax: 0118 984 1764
Contact: Elizabeth Rose
Produce: Free range, organic beef and
lamb from their own farm. Pork and
chicken from other organic farms.
Own range of oak-smoked bacon and
gammon. Free range turkey and wild

game from the estate. Fruit & vegetables from the market garden. Milk and
guernsey cream. Free range eggs.
British farmhouse cheese. Also stock
luxury ice cream, goat's milk cheese,
fresh bread baked daily; oatie cobs,
rich rye, cheese & onion and tea
breads. Stoneground organic flours,
biscuits, cakes, etc. Box scheme –
contact Tolhurst Organic Produce.
(0118 9843428)
Prices/Payment: Visa, Mastercard,
Delta, Switch.
Hours: Wed-Sat, 10am-5pm.
Notes: No disabled access. Food
events and guided tours of walled
gardens and farm by arrangement. Are
interested in supplying to trade.

SHAKEN OAK PRODUCTS
Shaken Oak Farm, Hailey
WITNEY
OX8 5UX
TEL: 01993 868043
FAX: 01993 868043
CONTACT: Bruce Young
**PRODUCE: Mustards: Original, Hot,
Mustard with Chillies, Mustard with
Herbs, Mustard with Garlic, Hot
and Smooth, Arthur's Peppercorn
Mustard, Mustard with Ginger.
Mustard and Garlic Dressing,
Picante Sauce. Also made are
chutneys, jams and jellies. These
are seasonal and stocks are limited.
Mail Order catalogue available
(Parcel Force). Minimum order 1
case (12 items).**
**PRICES/PAYMENT: Mustard from
£1.20, dressing £2.50, sauces from
£1.20. Cash and cheques only.**
**HOURS: 9.30am-5.30pm most days
please 'phone in advance.**
**NOTES: Disabled access. Tastings,
demonstrations upon request.
Shaken Oak also supply Wells
Stores (Abingdon), Gluttons (Ox-
ford), Mayby's Delicatessen (Stow-
on-the-Wold) and Mrs Bumbles
(Burford).**

The following are SHOPS within this region which do not produce but do sell quality or organic foods.

FRUGAL FOOD
17 West Saint Helen Street
Abingdon
Oxford
Oxfordshire
OX14 5BL
Tel: 01235 522239
Produce: Wholefoods, cheese, wine, chocolates, speciality foods (gluten free etc.), breads, savouries and sweets, frozen foods. A big selection of organic foods across the range. Home delivery for local elderly and disabled.
Hours: Mon-Fri, 9am-5.30pm. Bank Holiday weekends, 9am-1pm.
Notes: Disabled access. Tastings.

TIME FOR CHANGE LTD
167 Fawcett Road
Southsea
Hampshire
PO4 0DH
Tel: 01705 818786
Internet: listed under vegan village.
Produce: 100% animal and dairy-free (i.e. vegan) wholefoods, snacks, chilled and frozen goods, fresh organic produce, ready meals, spreads, pastas, wheat free and yeast free products, fresh bread.
Hours: Mon-Sat, 9.30am-6pm.
Notes: Disabled access.

M. NEWITT & SONS
10 High Street
Thame
Oxfordshire
OX9 2BZ
Tel: 01844 212103
Fax: 01844 217715
Produce: Quality butchers. Aberdeen Angus certified beef, from his own farm. Home-made sausages over 50 varieties including venison, pork, red wine. Boar, game, organic chicken.

Also home-made pies and ready meals. Free range eggs.
Hours: Mon, 8am-5.30pm. Tues, 7am-5.30pm. Wed, 8am-1pm. Thurs, 7.30am-5.30pm. Fri, 7am-6pm. Sat, 6.30am-5pm.

AVON

BATH BAKERY
3-4 Chelsea Road
Bath
BA1 3DU
Tel: 01225 421702
Contact: Sarah Jolly
Produce: Freshly baked bread, cakes and rolls. A full range of speciality breads including wholemeal, white organic, oat bread, black and green olive bread, tomato bread, ciabatta, onion, barley mill, three-seeded, traditional overnight loaf and 100% rye.
Prices/Payment: Rolls 13p to 28p. Bread 86p to £1.75. Wed special-split, farmhouse, bloomers, wholemeal loaves 70p. White/wholemeal rolls 9p. Cash and cheques only.
Hours: Mon-Fri, 7.30am-5.30pm. Sat, 7am-4pm.
Notes: Disabled access. Tastings, and one-off days of special bread not on usual list. Bath Bakery deliver daily to shops, cafes and hotels. Also suppliers to Guildhall Market, Weston Shop, Harvest and Fairfield (all Bath).

NORWOOD FARM
Bath Road
Norton St. Philip
Bath
BA3 6LP
Tel: 01373 834356
Fax: 01373 834765
Contact: C.M. Mack
Produce: Organic beef, lamb, pork and poultry, sausages and burgers. Organic potatoes. Organic wheat, oats and triticale (for poultry and pig feed). Also stock organic dairy produce and Dart Valley jams & pickles. Delivery at 10% charge. Min order £5 per mile distance.
Prices/Payment: Credit cards taken in 1999. Switch now.
Hours: March to Sept: every day 10.30am-6pm. Oct to early March:

Mon, Tues, 10am-4pm. Wed, 10am-5pm. Thurs and Fri, 10am-6pm. Sat, 8am-5pm.
Notes Disabled access. Norwood Farm supply to Hinton Stores, Hinton Charterhouse, Sagebury Cheese (Frome).

RADFORD MILL FARM
Timsbury
Bath
BA3 1QF
Tel: 01761 472549
Fax: 01761 472549
Contact: Susan Seymour
Produce: Organic fruit, vegetables, herbs, yogurt, soft cheese, lamb, beef, pork, eggs and turkeys (at Christmas only). Also stock imported organic fruit and vegetables, e.g. bananas, kiwi and ginger. Organic wholefoods. Delivery service in Bath and Bradford-on-Avon areas. No min. order.
Prices/Payment: Cash and cheques only.
Hours: Produce available at the farm by prior order only.
Notes: Annual open day. Market stalls in Glastonbury and Bath and Bristol Farmers Market. Also supply Radford Mill Farm Shop (Bristol). Possibly interested in supplying to the trade.

SALLY LUNN'S REFRESHMENT HOUSE & MUSEUM
Sally Lunn's House
4 North Parade Passage
Bath
BA1 1NX
Tel: 01225 461634
Fax: 01225 447090
Contact: Julian Abraham
Produce: Sally Lunn's bakes and serves the world famous and historic Sally Lunn's bun. The bun is a rich round and generous brioche style bread created by Sally Lunn's in the 1680's. Sally Lunn a French refugee, came to Bath in 1680 and found work with a local baker. Sally Lunn's

House, the old bakery, the oldest house in Bath. The refreshment rooms are open all day. The Sally Lunn bun can be served as sweet or savoury. The cellar musuem is open daily and shows the history of this house and shows the kitchen Sally Lunn would have used in 1680.

Prices/Payment: Buns to take away are £1.18, sweet treats in the refreshment rooms start from around £3 with meals/snacks from £4. Credit and some debit cards taken for evening meals but not Amex, Diners, JCB or Switch.

Hours: Mon-Sun, 10am-6pm. Evening meals from 6pm.

Notes: Disabled access is difficult due to the nature of this very old building. Lunn's do not sell their products through any other suppliers.

THE REAL MEAT COMPANY

7 Haynes Place, Bear Flat
Bath
Tel: 01225 335139
(See Main Entry – Warminster, Wilts)

THE SAUSAGE SHOP

7 Green Street
Bath
BA1 2JY
Tel: 01225 318300
Fax: 01225 318300
Email: joe-cole@hotmail.com
Contact: Joe Cole
Produce: Handmade gourmet and traditional sausages, made with the finest fresh ingredients. 32 recipes including; The Newmarket Chipolata, lamb & mint, the scrumpy sausage, pork & chestnut and The Mongolian Firepot. 4 vegetarian sausages; mushroom & tarragon, spinach leek & cheese, Indonesian, tomato & garlic. Mail Order service available. Min order 10 lbs.

Prices/Payment: Sausages from £2.15 -£3.95. Cash & cheques only.
Hours: Mon-Sat, 9am-5.30pm.
Notes: Disabled access. Hot food available in the shop. The Sausage Shop supply to the trade.

CORNWALL

TRELAY FARM MEATS

Trelay, St. Gennys
Bude
EX23 0NJ
Tel: 01840 230378
Contact: Andrea Tippett
Produce: "Devon Red Ruby Beef". The traditional breed reared on grass and silage and they are B.S.E. free. Meat hung 2 weeks for the traditional taste. Lamb grass reared, hung 1 week. Traditional sausages. Side of lamb or pork available. The beef is available by Box Scheme. No min order.

Prices/Payment: Sirloin steak £4.98 per lb, Topside £2.68 per lb. Cash & cheques only.
Hours: Please 'phone for best times.
Notes: Disabled access. Working farm. Trelay Farm Meats supply to Wainhouse Country Store (Bude). They are interested in supplying to the trade.

DUCHY CONFECTIONERY CO.

Stoke Climsland
Callington
PL17 8NZ
Tel: 01579 370331
Fax: 01579 370191
Contact: Paul Cheetham
Produce: Caramelised and spiced nuts. Clotted cream fudge and toffees. Also stock clotted cream shortbreads. Mail order service available; 'phone for details.

Prices/Payment: All major cards taken
Hours: 10am-5pm.
Notes: Duchy Confectionery Co. are interested in supplying the trade with personalised packs.

PENGOON FARM

Nancegollan
Helston
TR13 0BH
Tel: 01326 561219
Contact: Mr & Mrs East
Produce: Free range eggs, clotted

cream (traditional Cornish/Jersey), butter and unpasteurised milk. Home delivery service and Mail Order. No min. order.
Prices/Payment: From 65p per 1/4 lb cream. Prices on application. Cash and cheques only
Hours: 9am-9pm, all week.
Notes: Disabled access to farm. The Easts already supply to other shops in Cornwall and they are interested in any commercial venture.

ROSKILLY CREAM & ICE CREAM
Tregellast Barton
St Keverne
Helston
TR12 6NX
Tel: 01326 280479
Fax: 01326 280320
Contact: Rachel & Joe Roskilly
Produce: Dairy farm producing cream, ice cream, fudge etc, from the farm's own milk from Jersey herd. Cream, fudge and home-made truffles sent by post.
Prices/Payment: Clotted cream fudge £3.85, jams, chutneys, mustards 2 jars £7.50. Cash and cheques only. Truffles £9.99
Hours: 9am to dusk.
Notes: Disabled access. Public viewing area to watch milking. Farm Trail. Roskilly Cream & Ice Cream supply to Logans (Penzance), Ice Queen (St Ives), Jacobs (Falmouth) and Nauti but Ice (Porthleven). They are interested in supplying to the trade.

PHILIP WARREN & SON
1 Westgate Street
Launceston
PL15 7AB
Tel: 01566 772089 & 777211
Fax: 01566 774271
Contact: Philip Warren / Keith Yelland
Produce: British traditional breeds of beef suckled and grassfed, i.e. Red Ruby Devon, Angus, South devon, Galloway and Hereford. Gloucester

Old Spot, Tamworth and Saddleback pigs. Also stock dry cured Wiltshire bacon. All stock slaughtered by Philip Warren & Son.
Prices/Payment: Cash and cheques only.
Hours: Mon-Sat, 8am-5pm
Notes: Disabled access. Philip Warren & Son supply to the trade.

TALA CHEESE
North Beer Farm, Boyton
Launceston
PL15 8NR
Tel: 01566 785607
Contact: Hans White
Produce: Sheep's milk cheese, plain or lightly smoked in 1 lb or 5 lb sizes. Unpasteurised/vegetarian rennet. "Davatty" sheep's milk firm curd cheese balls in olive oil made to order - 280g or 400g. Mail Order available, but during summer at customer's risk. No min. order charge.
Prices/Payment: Plain Tala £3.80 per lb, smoked Tala £4.05 per lb. Davatty £3.15/£4.55. Cash or cheques only.
Hours: By appointment only.
Notes: No disabled access. Tala Cheese supply to Country Cheeses (Devon), Caseus (New Covent Garden, London), La Fromagerie, International Cheese Centre (London) and Arundell Arms Hotel (Devon). They are interested in supplying to the trade.

LYNHER DAIRIES
Netherton Farm, Upton Cross
Liskeard
PL14 5BD
Tel: 01579 362244
Fax: 01579 362666
Contact: Mrs Catherine Mead
Produce: Cornish Yarg cheese, Cornish pepper cheese, Cornish herb & garlic cheese. Also stock other foods, gifts and books.
Prices/Payment: All majors credit cards taken. Cheese by post £12 kg.

Min. order 1kg.
Hours: Easter to October daily,
10am-4pm. Sat, 10am-2pm. Sun,
closed.
Notes: Disabled access. Farm has a
tour of cheesemaking, teashop,
woodland walks and rare breeds.
Lynher Dairies supply some of the
major supermarkets and are interested in supplying hotels and
restaurants.

STEIN'S DELICATESSEN
8 Middle Street
Padstow
PL28 8AP
Tel: 01841 532221
Fax: 01841 533566
Contact: Julie Kirby
Produce: Fish cakes, fish terrines,
wild boar terrine, liver & bacon and
pork pâtés, pasties, bread, cakes and
tarts (incl. lemon tart, prune &
brandy, apricot & almond), salmon
koulibiac, tiramisu, fresh salads, Thai
fish cakes, bread & butter pudding,
tarte tatin and spanish omelette. Also
stock Carluccio's (pasta, olive oil,
etc.) Tracklements, pork pies, local
and continental cheeses. Wine,
cheese biscuits, tea, coffee beans &
ground coffee, "Seafood Restaurant" T
shirts, "Stein's Delicatessen" aprons.
Mail order available, by 'phone or
postal request. Carriage charge £6.50
- only ambient goods sent.
Prices/Payment: Please 'phone for
price list. All major credit cards
taken. Not American Express.
Hours: Mon-Sat, 9am-5pm.
Notes: No disabled access. Café next
door. Wine loft above deli, stocking
some of the Seafood Restaurant wines.

STONEYBRIDGE ORGANICS
Tywardreath
Par
PL24 2TY
Tel: 01726 813858
Contact: David Pascoe
Produce: A wide selection of
organic vegetables, fruit and herbs;

grown to Soil Association organic
standards. Also stock organically
reared meat (Soil Assoc. certified)
lamb, beef, chicken, pork, sausage,
bacon etc. Organic cheddar cheese,
fruit juices, beer, cider and wines.
Two box schemes to drop-off points
in Fowey and St. Austell. Local only
home delivery. Will also make up
veg. boxes for holiday makers staying
in Fowey. Min. order £5.
Prices/Payment: Prices change
weekly. Cash and cheques only.
Hours: Easter to 31st Oct: Tues-Fri,
9am-6pm. Sat, 9am -12.30pm.
Winter: Wed-Fri 9am-dusk (5pm).
Notes: Disabled access. Visitors are
welcome to walk around the nursery.
Stoneybridge Organics supply Good
Nature (Fowey), The Bran Tub
(Bodmin) and are interested in
supplying more to the trade.

MENALLACK FARMHOUSE CHEESES
Menallack Farm, Treverva
Penryn
TR10 9BP
Tel: 01326 340333
Fax: 01326 340333
Contact: Caryl Minson
Produce: Farm cheeses, handmade
from milk of cow, goat, buffalo and
sheep. Hard (matured) and fresh soft
cheeses. Organic cheese in the
pipeline. Farm baked bread. Also
stock all Cornish small business foods
i.e. chutneys, jams, smoked fish,
100% sausage and hogs pudding.
Mail Order available according to
customer's own price structure.
Prices/Payment: Farmhouse cheese,
£3.15 per lb (farm gate price). Cash
and cheques only.
Hours: Usual shop hours.
Notes: Disabled access difficult.
Tastings and viewings available.
Group visits. Menallack Farm supply
to Country Cheese (Tavistock), Di's
Dairy (Rock), Lavenders (Penzance)
and Market Garden (Truro). They
also supply to many hotels and
restaurants and can supply all of
Cornwall's 19 different cheeses.

THE CORNISH SMOKED FISH CO LTD
Charlestown
St Austell
PL25 3NY
Tel: 01726 72356
Fax: 01726 72360
Contact: Martin Pumphrey
Produce: Smoked foods; salmon, trout, herring, mackerel, eel, cod's roe, mussel, prawns, haddock, chicken breast, duck breast, cheese, gravadlax and gravadmackerel. Also stock Denhay bacon and dried ham. Mail Order or next day home delivery available. No min. order charge.
Prices/Payment: Please 'phone for price list. Cash and cheques only.
Hours: Mon-Fri, 8am-5pm. Sat (in summer), 10.30am-12.30pm. (Retail shop).
Notes: Disabled access. The Cornish Smoked Fish Co Ltd supply to Martins Deli (Castle Carey). Mr Christians Deli (Elgin Crescent) and Freshlands 196 Old Street (both London). Wholesale supply is the core of the business.

THE LIZARD PASTY SHOP
Sunny Corner
The Lizard
TR12 7PB
Tel: 01326 290889
Fax: 01326 290889
Internet: lizardpasty@connexions co.uk
Contact: Ann Muller
Produce: Traditional Cornish Pasties half way between puff and shortcrust with skirt of beef, turnips (called swedes outside Cornwall), potatoes, onions, salt, black pepper and nothing else! Vegetarian pasty available. All freshly baked. Cornish Pasties with a choice of customer's ingredients (within reason) made to order. Also James White single variety apple juices. Mail order by Interlink Express available (next day delivery). No min. order charge.
Prices/Payment: Medium pasty £1.50, small pasty £1.10. Large (made to order) £2.20. Cash and cheques only.
Hours: Daily, 9am-5pm. Closed Sundays.
Notes: Disabled access. Demonstrations during the morning. The Lizard Pasty shop supplies to Hattons at Mullion.

DI'S DAIRY AND PANTRY
Rock Road
Rock
Wadebridge
PL27 6NW
Tel: 01208 863531
Fax: 01208 863531
Contact: Mr or Mrs Dunkerley
Produce: Made on the premises; a wide range of savouries and sweets, e.g. steak & kidney or mushroom, chicken and veg, turkey and ham pies, quiches, pasties, lasagne, shepherds pie, moussaka, fresh fruit trifles, fruit pies and crumbles and a wide range of cakes, scones and marmalade. Also stock all general groceries, up to 100 cheeses, large deli counter, fresh fruit and veg, frozen foods, local ice cream and wines and spirits. Delivered locally if required, and Mail Order if required. No min. order. Please 'phone for price list.
Hours: Summer: Mon-Fri, 8am-8pm. Sat, 8am-7pm and Sun, 8.30am-6pm. Winter: Mon-Fri, 8am-6pm. Sat, 8am-5.30pm and Sun 8.30-2pm.
Notes: Disabled access.

DEVON

ACLAND ORGANIC MEATS
East Acland Farm, Landkey
Barnstaple
EX32 0LD
Tel: 01271 830216
Contact: Dr. Charles Morrish
Produce: Organic beef from this herd of pure beef Devon cattle – no dairy crossbreds. Organic lamb, traditionally reared and fattened at grass.

Home delivery possible for local people
Prices/Payment: Beef £5.50kg. Lamb
£5.00kg. Cash & cheques only.
Hours: By arrangement – please 'phone
Notes: Acland is interested in supply-
ing to the trade.

THE BIG SHEEP DAIRY CO.
Bideford
EX39 5AP
Tel: 01237 472366
Fax: 01237 477916
Contact: Ric Turner
Produce: Ewe's milk cheese, fudge
and ice cream made by traditional
methods with milk from their own
sheep. Mail order service available.
Prices/Payment: Approx £10-£12.20
kg. Mastercard & Visa accepted.
Hours: 10am-6pm seven days a
week, all year.
Notes: Disabled access. Licenced
restaurant and tea room. The Sheep
Shop (knitwear) and all-weather
attractions, including nature trail and
sheep shearing, racing, milking etc.

RIVERFORD ORGANIC VEGETABLES
Wash Barn
Buckfastleigh
TQ11 0LD
Tel: 01803 762720
Fax: 01803 762718
Contact: Jo Field
Produce: Over 85 different varieties of
organically grown vegetables, salads &
fruit. Plus free-range organic eggs.
Occasionally stock exotic organic
fruits. Home delivery and box scheme.
Prices/Payment: Boxes, hampers £5,
£7 & £9. Cash, cheques only.
Hours: Daily, 8am-4.30pm
Notes: Disabled access. Farm walks.
Riverford's already supply to shops and
are interested in supplying to the trade.

TORDEAN FARM
Dean Prior
Buckfastleigh
TQ11 0LY
Tel: 01364 643305

Contact: Adrian & Sue Dawe
Produce: Local naturally produced
additive free meats and meat products.
Also stock hog's pudding made to 150-
year old recipe. Organic vegetables.
Mail Order & Home Delivery.
Prices/payment: Cash and cheques only
Hours: Mon-Thurs, 7am -5pm. Fri,
7am-6.30pm; Sat, am by appointment
only; closed Sun.
Notes: Disabled access. Farm shop is
in rural setting with a view of
Dartmoor.

OTTERTON MILL & BAKERY & RESTAURANT
Otterton
Budleigh Salterton
EX9 7HG
Tel: 01395 568521
Fax: 01395 568521
Contact: Desna Greenhow
Produce: 100% wholemeal organic
flour, organic breads and cakes from
their own and other flours, including
unbleached white, spelt and 100%
rye flours.
Prices/Payment: Large loaf £1.10,
Small 60p. Flour in bulk 30p per lb
for 28lbs or above. Visa, Mastercard,
Delta taken.
Hours: 10.30a -5pm daily.
Notes: Disabled access. The mill is
open to the public and craft workshops
are housed in the complex. Pretty
gardens and countryside with well
known riverside walks. Otterton Mill
supplies Seasons (Exeter) and Guy's
(Exeter). Otterton Mill are interested in
supplying flour to the trade.

PURE JERSEY ICE CREAM
Rookbeare Farm, Cheriton Fitzpaine
Crediton
EX17 4BE
Tel: 01363 866057
Fax: 01363 866424
Email: rookbeare@mcmail.com
Contact: Jamie Marsh
Produce: Wide range of ice cream
made from: fresh Jersey milk, double
Jersey cream, unrefined cane sugar,

milk powder, free range eggs plus authentic fruits, nuts, liqueurs and nothing else. Fruit sorbets. Ice cream flavours include: mango and passion fruit, pineapple, coconut and stem ginger, espresso mocha, after dinner mint and zabaglione.
Prices/Payment: Cash and cheques only.
Hours: Please 'phone ahead and Rookbeare farm will sell direct.
Notes: Rookbeare Farm is interested in supplying to the trade.

PIPERS FARM
Cullompton
EX15 1SD
Tel: 01392 881380 (24 hour messages)
Fax: 01392 881600
Contact: Peter Greig
Produce: Full range of naturally reared meats using a style of continental butchery for the minimum of preparation and cooking, including home-made fresh herb stuffings and marinades. They farm slow growing, old fashioned breeds reared in small groups on diets of grass or cereal. Red Devon Beef is hung for 4 weeks; also lamb, pork, chicken, venison, mutton and Bronze turkeys. Traditionally cured hams and bacon plus a range of sausages. Nationwide Mail Order service available. Min order £40.
Prices/Payment: Please 'phone for a price list. All major credit cards taken including Amex, Switch.
Hours: Mon-Fri, 9am-5pm
Notes: Also shop in Exeter – see over

P.T.S. WHITEMAN
Lower Turley Farm
Cullompton
EX15 1NA
Tel: 01884 32234
Contact: P. Whiteman
Produce: Organic vegetables from early July to end of February. Mostly sold through a box scheme and at farm gate. No min. order charge.
Prices/Payment: Cash and cheques only.

Hours: By appointment.
Notes: No disabled access. P.T.S. Whiteman supply to Joshua's Harvest Store (Ottery St. Mary). They are interested in supplying to the trade by arrangement.

THE CARVED ANGEL LTD
2 South Embankment
Dartmouth
TQ6 9BH
Tel: 01803 832465
Fax: 01803 835141
Contact: Miss Zoe Wynne
Produce: Jams, pickles, preserves and Christmas puddings made by this well known restaurant.
Prices/Payment: £10 for 2lb Christmas puddings. Visa, Mastercard, Switch, Delta accepted
Hours: Restaurant: Tues-Sat, 9am-10.30pm. Sun, 9am-4pm..
Notes: Cafe in Foss Street, Dartmouth. Disabled access to both. Supply The Garden Store, Salcombe.

HIGHFIELD HARVEST
Highfield Farm
Clyst Road
Topsham
Exeter
EX3 0BY
Tel: 01392 876388
Fax: 01392 876388
Contact: Ian or Lyndsay Shears
Produce: One of the largest ranges of organic food in the West Country. Fruit, over 50 types of vegetables, groceries, wholefoods, free range eggs, over 40 organic wines. Organic pork from Highfield Farm's Gloucester Old Spot Pigs. Organic dairy and soya products, milk, cream, butter yogurts, Rocombe Farm' ice creams and sorbets. Organic veg box and home delivery in Exeter/Topsham area only. Min. order varies.
Prices/Payment: Cheques and cash only
Hours: Tues-Sat, 9am -6pm; Sun, 10am-1pm
Notes: Disabled access. Farm trail, play tractor.

GIBSON'S PLAICE FISHMONGERS
38 Magdalen Road, St Leonards
Exeter
EX2 4TD
Tel: 01392 495344
Contact: Jon Bond
Produce: Fresh fish selected daily
from Brixham market. Also shellfish,
smoked fish and exotics. Free of
charge service for skinning, filleting,
de-boning any fish for customer
requirements. Free delivery service
throughout Exeter and surrounding
area every Tues, Thurs and Fri
afternoon. No min. order.
Prices/Payment: From £1.35/ lb for
dabs to 5.95/ lb Scottish halibut. Cash
and cheques only.
Hours: Mon - closed. Tues-Wed,
9.30am-5pm. Thurs-Fri, 9.30am-
5.45pm. Sat, 9am-3pm.
Notes: Disabled access. Gibson's
Plaice offer a full wholesale price list,
fresh and frozen, specifically for
hotels and restaurants.

PIPERS FARM
27 Magdalen Road
Exeter
EX2 4TA
Tel: 01392 881380 24 hour
answerphone.
Fax: 01392 881600
Contact: Peter Greig
Produce: Full range of naturally reared
meats using a style of continental
butchery for the minimum of preparation and cooking, including home-
made fresh herb stuffings and
marinades. They farm slow growing,
old fashioned breeds reared in small
groups on diets of grass or cereal. Red
Devon Beef is hung for 4 weeks; also
lamb, pork, chicken, venison, mutton
and Bronze Turkeys. Traditionally
cured hams and bacon plus a range of
sausages. Nationwide Mail Order
service available. Min order £40.
Prices/Payment: Please 'phone for a
price list. All major credit cards
taken including Amex, Switch.
Hours: Mon-Fri, 9am-5.30pm. Sat,
9am-2pm.

Notes: Limited disabled access.
Available also at the farm (see
Cullompton).

RIVER EXE SHELLFISH FARMS LTD
Lyson
Kenton
Exeter
EX6 8EZ
Tel: 01626 890133
Fax: 01626 891789
Contact: David L Jarrad
Produce: Pacific oysters, mussels.
Grown in West Country waters. Mail
Order service available, 'phone for
details. Min. order twelve oysters.
Prices/Payment: All major credit
cards taken.
Hours: Mon-Fri, 9am-5pm.
Notes: River Exe Shellfish are
interested in supplying to the trade.

WESTCOUNTRY ORGANIC FOODS
Natson Farm
Tedburn St Mary
Exeter
EX6 6ET
Tel: 0164 724724
Fax: 0164 724031
Email: westorg.btinternet.com
Contact: Bruce Burton
Produce: A range of organic meat
and meat products, cut and packed to
your requirements. Beef, lamb, pork
and poultry. Dry cured and smoked
bacon. Also stock organic speciality
sausages, burgers and cooked meats.
Organic cheese, wine and vegetarian
pies and burgers. Pies (vegetarian),
organic tofu products,wine. All
available by Mail Order nationwide.
No min. order.
Prices/Payment: Lean minced beef,
£6 per kg, pork sausages £5.10 per kg
and whole chicken £5.85 per kg. All
primary cards accepted, not Switch.
Hours: Retail shop hours, early
closing Wed.
Notes: Easy access from main street.
Also supply wholesale; bulk or
prepacked.

THORNE FARM NATURAL DAIRY ICE CREAM LTD
Holsworthy
EX22 7JD
Tel: 01409 253342
Fax: 01409 253751
Contact: Mr & Mrs Clarke
Produce: Luxury Ice Cream.
Prices/Payment: £2.25 per litre. Cash and cheques only.
Hours: 9am-5pm
Notes: Nature trail. Thorne Farm are interested in supplying to the trade.

AVON OYSTERS
Stakes Hill, Bigbury
Kingsbridge
TQ7 4AN
Tel: 01548 810876
Fax: 01548 810876
Contact: Peter/Fay Lewis
Produce: Pacific Gigas oysters grown on the oyster farm. Mussels harvested on the River Teign. Clams, crabs and lobsters and crayfish. Also stock a range of smoked fish products from Dartmouth Smokehouse, frozen shellfish etc. Mail order service available for oysters. Generally min. order 4 stone or over.
Prices/Payment: Oysters retail at £5 per doz. Cash and cheques only.
Hours: Winter 5 days per week, Closed 12.30pm-2.30pm.
Summer 7 days per week.
Notes: Part disabled access. Also the Oyster Shack seafood bistro open in summer. Purification centre, exhibition room and shop. Avon Oysters supply four local shops, hotels and restaurants.

SALCOMBE SMOKERS LTD
54 Fore Street
Kingsbridge
TQ7 1NY
Tel: 01548 852006
Fax: 01548 852006
Email: salcombe@globalnet-co.uk
Contact: Mr B Benson
Produce: Smokers of all kinds of fish and shellfish. Please 'phone for details. Full Mail Order service is

available. No min order.
Prices/Payment: All major credit cards, Delta, Switch, Amex and JCB.
Hours: Mon-Sat, 8.30am-5pm.
Notes: No disabled access. They are interested in selling to the trade.

LITTLE ASH ECO-FARM
Throwleigh
Okehampton
EX20 2GQ
Tel/Fax: 01647 231394
Contact: Alex Armstrong
Produce: Organic vegetables, fruit, jams, flour, oats. Sheep and llama wool and woolen garments. Also stock wooden items, willow baskets, macramé work. Box scheme for all products, local delivery only. Min. order, regular £4 box.
Prices/Payment: Veg in box scheme from £4, fruit from £1, flour and oats from 80p/lb. Cheques, cash only.
Hours: Normal working hours.
Notes: Limited disabled access. Some open days, ballets and rides during the year. Little Ash is interested in supplying to the trade.

MID DEVON FALLOW
Keyethern Farm, Hatherleigh
Okehampton
EX20 3LG
Tel: 01837 810028
Fax: 01837 810028
Contact: Peter and Susan Kent
Produce: "Westcountry Venison" from their own fallow deer herd and selected Westcountry producers. Butchered and processed at premises on the farm. Venison butchered to requirements, sausages & burgers made. Mail order or local delivery, also Christmas hampers.
Prices/Payment: From £2.75 per lb for sausages and burgers to £7 per lb for loin & fillet. Cash & cheques only.
Hours: Daytime - by appointment.
Notes: No disabled access. Mid Devon Fallow; member of 'Taste of the West', supply some pubs, hotels & restaurants and some wholesale.

LANGAGE FARM
Plympton
Plymouth
PL7 5AW
Tel: 01752 337723
Fax: 01752 339712
Contact: Mr P Tremain – sales manager
Produce: Dairy products from their own Channel Island milk. Clotted cream, liquid creams, live yoghurt, soft cheeses inc. cottage cheese and premium dairy ice cream (26 flavours). Also stock niche products, shortbread, jams, etc. Mail Order available for clotted cream by post. Min. order 4oz.
Prices/Payment: Cash and cheques only.
Hours: Seven days a week, both shops. 9am-5.30pm and 9am- 6pm.
Notes: Disabled access. Langage Farm already supply to Tesco and Somerfield.

MELCHIOR CHOCOLATES
Tinto House
Station Road
South Molton
EX36 3LL
Tel: 01769 574442
Fax: 01769 574442
Contact: C Melchior
Produce: High quality chocolate truffles and pralines, novelties and liqueurs. Over 100 different items, all totally handmade using the finest couverture and natural ingredients. Available by Mail Order. No min order charge.
Prices/Payment: Please 'phone for full price list. Mastercard or Visa are accepted
Hours: 9am-5pm
Notes: No disabled access. Demonstrations available by pre-booking only. Melchior Chocolates supply to Fortnum & Mason, (London), Chatsworth Farm Shop (Bakewell), Hudson Coffee House (Birmingham) and The Ramsbottom Victuallers Co Ltd (Bury). They are interested in supplying to the trade.

MOORLAND LARDER
113 East Street
South Molton
EX36 3DB
Tel: 01769 573554
Fax: 01769 573554
Contact: Pat or Graham Wright
Produce: Fresh venison, hand-made venison pies, pasties and pâté, sausages and burgers. Now producing a range of fresh free range chicken meat. Also stock; Head Mill trout, Otter Vale Kitchen Garden Preserves, Brendan Hill Crafts, jams, chutneys and mustards. Delivered locally (25 miles) or will arrange carriage at cost. No min. order.
Prices/Payment: Venison in red wine with redcurrant, 6 portions £8.50. Venison sausages £6.57 per kg. Cash and cheques only.
Hours: Mon-Fri, 9.30am-5.30pm. Sat, 9.30am-1pm.
Notes: No disabled access. Regular tastings of new and unusual products. Moorland Larder are interested in supplying to the trade.

QUINCE HONEY FARM
North Road
South Molton
EX36 3AZ
Tel: 01769 572401
Fax: 01769 574704
Contact: Jean Wallace
Produce: Devon honey, Exmoor heather honey, comb honey, honey marmalade, chutney, mustard; packed in a variety of glass and ceramic containers. Also stock skincare and textiles. Mail Order catalogue available. No min. order.
Prices/Payment: 340g Devon honey £1.95. All major credit cards, no Switch Mail Order, cash, cheques.
Hours: 9am-5pm daily.
Notes: Disabled access to shop and cafeteria. Exhibition of living honey-bees. Quince Honey Farm supply Selfridges (London) with jars; The Conran Shop and Fortnum & Mason (London) with comb honey, and would like to supply more to the trade.

TOTNES HEALTH SHOP & SEEDS BAKERY
35 High Street
Totnes
TQ9 5NP
Tel: 01803 862526
Contact: Barry Pope
Produce: Bakery making savoury flans, filled rolls, pizza, cakes from organic flour. Also retail shop, organic veg, milk, cheese, bread, grains, pulses, range of wholefoods, organic herbs (dried) and essential oils. Mail Order for vitamins and minerals, herbs. No min order charge.
Prices/Payment: Large organic wholemeal with sunflower £1.33. Organic wholemeal £1.18. 2 pints of organic milk 88p. Cash and cheques only.
Hours: 9am-5pm six days a week.
Notes: Limited disabled access. Totnes Health supplies to Pudding & Pie (Bovey Tracey) and Willow Restaurant (Totnes).

MRS GILL'S COUNTRY CAKES
Link House, Leat Street
Tiverton
EX16 5LG
Tel: 01884 242744
Fax: 01884 242744
Email: mrs_gills_country_cakes@compuserve.com
Contact: Jacqueline Gill
Produce: Award winning traditional fruit cakes, gourmet Devon fruit cake, christmas, wedding, birthday and simnel cakes. Made with butter, black cherries, muscovada sugar. Also stock Christmas puddings, almond and Dundee cake. Mail order service available by Business Post, nationwide & worldwide, no min. order.
Prices/Payment: From £1.75 - £400. Cash, cheques only.
Hours: 9am-5pm.
Notes: Disabled access, open working kitchen all day. Mrs Gill also supplies famous London West End stores and is interested in supplying to hotels & restaurants.

RIVERFORD FARM FOODS
Staverton
Totnes
TQ9 6AF
Tel: 01803 762523
Fax: 01803 762571
Contact: Ben Watson
Produce: Cured bacon and sausages from own farm pork, organic beef, Riverford vegetables, bakery, wine, frozen meals, all made on the premises. Also stock a wide range of additive free, organic and quality grocery and deli items.
Prices/Payment: All major cards – not American Express.
Hours: Easter to Christmas - Mon-Sat, 9am-6pm. Wed (staff training), 10am-6pm. Sun, 10am-4pm. Closed Sun Christmas-Easter.
Notes: Also a second farm shop at Kitley, Yealmpton, nr Plymouth. Tel: 01752 880925. Interested in supplying to the trade.

SHARPHAM PARTNERSHIP LTD
Sharpham Estate
Ashprington
Totnes
TQ9 7UT
Tel: 01803 732203
Fax: 01803 732122
Contact: Duncan Schwab
Produce: Unpasteurised soft cheeses from their own Jersey milk. They also stock a range of estate bottled wines. Also available by Mail Order to any U.K. address with no min. order charge.
Prices/Payment: Cheese £10 per kg. Wines from £5.99 - £19.99. Visa, Mastercard, Switch, Delta.
Hours: Mon-Fri, 2pm-5pm April to Sept.
Notes: No disabled access. Vineyard trail. The Sharpham Partnership supply cheese to Riverford Farm Foods (Totnes), Ticklemore Cheese Shop (Totnes), Jeraboams (London) and Country Cheeses (Tavistock and Exeter). They supply wine to Tesco, Threshers, Dartmouth Vintners, Cider Press & many more local outlets.

TICKLEMORE CHEESE
1 Ticklemore Street
Totnes
TQ9 5EJ
Tel: 01803 865926 **Fax:** 01803 865926
Contact: Sarie Cooper
Produce: Hand-made speciality
cheeses; Beenleigh Blue, Devon
Blue, Harbourne Blue, Ticklemore
Goat and Ticorino. Also stock a full
range of cheese, ice cream, biscuits
and preserves.
Prices/Payment: From Ticklemore
goat's cheese at £11.20 per kg to
Ticorino at £12.10 per kg Cash and
cheques only.
Hours: Mon-Fri, 9am-5.30pm. Sat,
9am-4.45pm.
Notes: Small step into shop. Supply
to shops/wholesalers throughout UK

TIDEFORD FOODS
Higher Tideford
Cornworthy
TOTNES
TQ9 7HZ
TEL: 01803 712276
FAX: 01803 712388
CONTACT: Diana Cooper
**PRODUCE: Fresh, chilled organic
soups, pestos and sauces sold in
returnable kilner jars available by
Mail Order. Also prepared meals.
No min order charge, but P&P £6.**
**PRICES/PAYMENT: Cash and cheques
only.**
HOURS: By arrangement.
**NOTES: No disabled access. Tideford
Foods supply to Waitrose and
Ticklemore Cheese. They are
interested in supplying more to the
trade.**

CUSGARNE ORGANIC VEGETABLES
Cusgarne Wollas, Cusgarne
Truro
TR4 8RL
Tel: 01872 865922
Contact: Greg & Teresa Pascoe
Produce: Organic vegetables - 60

varieties a year. Organic wild boar
cross, pork and sausages. Organic
suckler herd reared beef.
Box scheme in Truro, Point, Mylor,
Falmouth, Gweek, Stithians, Redruth,
Blackwater. Min order £6.
Prices: From the farm, pork £1.80
per lb, sausages £2 per lb, beef from
per £1.55 lb. Veg box £6 delivered
locally. Cash and cheques only.
Hours: Visits by appointment only.
Notes: Limited disabled access.
Annual farm walks. Also suppliers to
Country Store (Falmouth & Helston),
Carley & Co (Truro), Highfield Harvest
(Exeter), Organic Marketing (Ledbury).

HIGHER HACKNELL FARM
PARTNERSHIP
Higher Hacknell Farm, Burrington
Umberleigh
EX37 9LX
Tel: 01769 560292
Fax: 01769 560909
Internet: www.gratton.co/hacknell
Contact: Jo Budden
Produce: Home produced organic
meat - all reared to organic Soil Assoc
standards. Mail Order box system
selling direct to customer. Min. order
£50.
Prices/Payment: Organic beef £6.50
per kg, organic lamb £5.95kg,
organic pork £5.80 per kg. Cash and
cheques only.
Hours: Orderline open 24 hours.
Notes: No disabled access. Farm
walks are open to customers. Higher
Hacknell Farm also supply Marshford
Farm Shop, Highfield Harvest and are
interested in supplying to the trade.

SOMERSET

NATURAL BEEF
Moorland Farm, Moorland Street
Axbridge
BS26 2BA
Tel: 01934 733341
Fax: 01934 733341
Contact: Elizabeth Scott

Produce: Natural reared home produced beef . Available by box scheme or local delivery.
Prices/Payment: Boxes from £50 - £120 including delivery. Containing fillet, sirloin and rump steaks, mince and braising steak, beefburgers and two joints of beef. Please 'phone for details. Cash and cheques only.
Hours: Please 'phone ahead as times vary throughout the year. Usually Thurs, Fri and Sat, 10.30am-5.30pm.
Notes: No built disabled access as such but easy to access. Natural Beef supply to The Butchers Shop (Axbridge). They are interested in supplying to the trade.

STAWELL FRUIT FARM
Stawell
Bridgwater
TA7 9AE
Tel: 01278 722732
Contact: Charles or Rowena Graham
Produce: Apples, approx 30 varieties, strawberries and 4 types of fresh pressed apple juice from Stawell Farm apples. Strawberries sold ready picked, apples available as PYO; delivery by arrangement.
Prices/Payment: Cash and cheques only
Hours: Apples: Mid Aug-March, Wed-Sun, 11am-4pm. Jan-March, open weekends only. Strawberries, open every day through the season,11am-4pm. Other times by arrangement.
Notes: Disabled access. The Grahams are interested in supplying to trade.

ALVIS BROS LTD
Lye Cross Farm, Redhill
Bristol
BS40 5RH
Tel: 01934 863663
Fax: 01934 862213
Contact: Jane Lindley
Produce: Full range of farmhouse cheddars, all suitable for vegetarians; mild, mature, extra mature, vintage, oak smoked, black wax. Non GMO rennet. Also organic Cheddar and Double Gloucester. Organic Certification U.K.5 P1542) Home produced beef, pork, bacon and sausages. Also stock dairy produce, fresh fruit and vegetables, preserves, bread and cakes, biscuits.
Prices/Payment: Cash and cheques only.
Hours: Mon-Fri, 8am-5.30pm, Sat, 8am-12.30pm.
Notes: No disabled access. Alvis Brothers supply to The Cheese & Wine Shop (Wellington, Somerset). They are interested in supplying to the trade within a 50 miles of Bristol.

ARCADIA ORGANICS
Waterworks House, Chapel Lane
Claverham
Bristol
BS49 4LT
Tel: 01934 876886 & 0976 835341
Contact: Rosey Knifton
Produce: A 10 acre holding growing a variety of in season organic vegetables, supplying own box scheme.
Prices/Payment: 3 sizes of boxes, £4, £6, £10 including delivery in North Somerset. Cash and cheques only.
Notes: Arcadia Organics have a possible interest in supplying to the trade. Not open to public at present.

ARNE HERBS
Limeburn Nurseries, Chew Magna
Bristol
BS40 8QW
Tel/Fax: 01275 333399
Contact: Jenny Thomas
Produce: Suppliers of culinary, aromatic and medicinal herbs in pots, to create your own herb garden. Mail Order available, 24hr courier, and own van delivery. No min. order.
Prices/Payment: Herbs from £1.30-£250. Courier delivery £14.00. Cash and cheques only.
Hours: 10am-4pm most days - 'phone first.
Notes: No disabled access. Suppliers of cut herbs to the catering trade. Also supply London wholesale.

K.G. CONSULTANTS
The Bailiff's Cottage, The Green
Compton Dando
Pensford
Bristol
BS39 4LE
Tel: 01761 490624
Fax: 01761 490624
Contact: Keith Goverd
Produce: Cider vinegar, produced
from single variety English apple
juice. Also single variety English
apple and pear juice. Available by
Mail Order. Home delivery service
locally, i.e. Bristol and Bath area.
Min. order 1 doz bottles of mixed
varieties.
Prices/Payment: Most products are
£2 per 75cl bottle. Cash and cheques
only.
Hours: Most daylight hours by
arrangement, please phone to arrange.
Notes: Disabled access. Tastings and
demonstrations can be arranged. Also
supply to Real Cheese & Wine (Bristol),
Nancassick Farm Shop (Truro), Paxton
& Whitfield (Bath) and Clives Fruit
Farm (Upton-on-Severn) and are
possibly interested in supplying to the
trade.

MAGDALEN FARM
Winsham
Chard
TA20 4PA
Tel: 01460 30277
Fax: 01460 30144
Contact: Christina Ballinger
Produce: Organic vegetables.
Organic pork, beef and pink veal
from the farm. Box scheme available:
pick up point in Chard and
Crewkerne or collect from the farm.
Prices/Payment: Cash and cheques
only.
Hours: Normal working hours – but
please phone first.
Notes: Disabled access. Circular
footpath around the farm. On site 35
bed educational centre. Magdalen
Farm supply to Manor Court Delicates-
sen (Chard), Naturalife (Crewkerne)
and Provender (S. Petherton).

SWADDLES GREEN FARM
Hare Lane, Buckland St Mary
Chard
TA20 3JR
Tel: 01460 234387
Fax: 01460 234591
Contact: Charlotte Reynolds
Produce: Complete range of award
winning organically produced meats,
poultry, bacon, sausages, hams,
charcuterie, pies, pâtés and ready
prepared meals. Also stock a range of
organic dairy products and groceries.
Available by Mail Order to whole of
U.K. Weekly delivery service to
London. No min. order charge.
Prices/Payment: Please 'phone for
price list. All major credit cards
taken. Switch. Not Amex or Diners.
Hours: Please 'phone first

THE CHEDDAR SWEET KITCHEN
Daghole Cottages
Cheddar Gorge
BS27 3QJ
Tel: 01934 743810 **Fax:** 01179 406656
Contact: Mrs A. Mizen-Jenkins
Produce: Old fashioned boiled
sweets, toffees, fudges, peanut brittle
and lollipops. Also stock chocolates
and jellies. Mail Order and Home
Delivery available. Min. order £10.
Orders over £25 carriage free.
Prices/Payment: From 10p to £12. All
major credit cards taken. No Switch.
Hours: 11am-5.30pm daily, Easter to
October. Weekends in Winter.
Notes: Disabled access. Demonstra-
tions 12pm-5pm when shop is open.
The Cheddar Sweet Kitchen supplies
to The Bath Sweet Shop. They are
interested in supplying to specialist
confectioners, farm shops etc.

WHATLEY VINEYARD & HERB GARDEN
Whatley
Frome
BA11 3LA
Tel: 01373 836355
Fax: 01373 836579
Contact: Robin Witt

Produce: Culinary herbs sold in pots. A range of still wines and one bottle fermented sparkling wine. Also stock local jams & cider. Mail Order available for wines. Min order £50.
Prices/Payment: Wines from £4.20 to £10. Cash and cheques only.
Hours: April 1st-Sept 30th, 10am-6pm. Closed Mon and Tues.
Notes: Disabled access is limited. Group tours which include wine tasting, slide show and a meal. Whatley Vineyard & Herb Garden are interested in supplying to the trade.

BROWN & FORREST

The Smokery, Bowdens Farm
Hambridge
Langport
TA10 0BP
Tel: 01458 250875
Fax: 01458 253475
Email: brownforrest@btinternet.com
Contact: Michael Brown
Produce: Smoked eel, smoked salmon, smoked trout, smoked duck breast, smoked chicken breast, smoked ostrich, lamb, sausages, a range of smoked fish pâtés. Speciality is smoked eel, hot smoked over beech & apple wood, using wood-fired smokers. Also stock; chutneys, chocolates, olive oil, honey, books and guides. Mail Order available. No min order charge. Please 'phone for details.
Prices/Payment: Smoked eel fillets, £9.50 per 8oz including 1st class p&p. £4.25 for smoked fillets of trout. All major credit cards taken. Not American Express or Diners.
Hours: Mon-Fri, 10am-4pm. Sat, to 1pm
Notes: Disabled access. Visit/tour of smokery to explain smoking methods.

ALHAM WOOD CHEESES

Higher Alham Farm, West Cranmore
Shepton Mallet
BA4 6DD
Tel: 01749 880221
Fax: 01749 880771
Contact: Frances Wood
Produce: Cheeses made from the farm's own herd of water buffalo, Iambors cheese, Iambors little cheese and Junas cheese. Sheep's milk cheese; Arthur's cheese. Ricotta and yoghurt also sometimes available. From 1999 meat will sometimes be available. Mail Order available. Min order £20.
Prices/Payment: From £1 per 100g or small young cheese from £2.25 each. Cash and cheques only.
Hours: Tue-Fri, 10am-5.30pm. Sat, 9.30am-1.30pm. Prior arrangement advisable for large numbers or trade enquiries.
Notes: No disabled access. The animals can be seen by arrangement. Alham Wood Cheeses supply to Sagebury Cheese (Frome), Bruton Delicatessen (Somerset), Country Foods (Exeter), Ticklemore Cheese and Oxford Cheese and they are interested in supplying more to trade.

CHARLTON ORCHARDS
Creech St. Michael

TAUNTON

TA3 5PF
TEL: 01823 412959/ 412979
FAX: 01823 412959
CONTACT: **Matthew Freudenberg**
Produce: Traditional apples (25 varieties), pears, plums, damsons, gooseberries, soft fruit. Ready picked strawberries available mid Jun to late Sept. Apple juice (individual varieties), jams & chutneys. Squash. Also stock vegetables and ice cream. Mail Order on apples and juice. Min. order 12 bottles or 6lb apples. Gift packs available.
PRICES/PAYMENT: **Apple juice £1.65, jam £1.25/£1.50. Cash & cheques only.**
HOURS: **Mon-Fri, 10am-6pm. Sat, 10am-5pm. Sun, 2pm-5pm.**
NOTES: **Disabled access. Farm walks, open days and tastings. Suppliers to Granny Smiths (Taunton), Fermoys Garden Centre (Devon) and Dawes Farm Shop (N. Petherton).**

HAMBLEDEN HERBS
Court Farm, Milverton
Taunton
TA4 1NF
Tel: 01823 401205
Fax: 01823 401001
Contact: Gaye Donaldson
Produce: Organic top quality dried herbs and spices. Organic herbal teas, infusions, cocoa, flower waters, tinctures. See mail order section for full details.
Prices/Payment: All major credit cards. Switch and Delta.
Hours: Mail Order only.
Notes: Hambleden Herbs supply to Planet Organic, Bluebird and Selfridges (all London).

OAKE BRIDGE FARM/OAKE ORGANICS
Oake
Taunton
TA4 1JA
Tel: 01823 461317
Contact: Keith Martin
Produce: Soil Assoc approved organic vegetables (over 40 lines). Mostly home grown, some are bought in from local sources for resale. Available by Box Scheme. No min order as such; however boxes are in three sizes small, medium and large.
Prices/Payment: £4 for small, £6 for medium, £8 for large. Cash and cheques only.
Hours: Most produce is delivered. That which is collected is between 2pm-6pm on Tuesday or by prior arrangement.
Notes: Disabled access possible once over the cattle grid. Oake Bridge Farm supply to Natural Path (Taunton), Country Harvest (Taunton) and Peacocks (Bristol). All other collection points are private houses.

C L G & J WADMAN & SONS
Elliscombe Farm
Holton
Wincanton
BA9 8ED
Tel: 01963 32393

Fax: 01963 32393
Contact: C L G Wadman
Produce: Jersey cream and milk and eggs. Potatoes.
Prices/Payment: Cream £2 per litre. Milk 60p per litre. Cash and cheques only.
Hours: 7am-9pm
Notes: No disabled access. CLG Wadman supply to Camelot Fruit Farm, Martins Stores, Dovecote Delicatessen and W.I. Market. They are interested in supplying more to the trade.

BARROW BOAR
Fosters Farm
South Barrow

YEOVIL

BA22 7LN
TEL: 01963 440315
FAX: 01963 440901
CONTACT: Christina Baskerville
PRODUCE: A wide range of exotic & traditional game meats, fresh and frozen speciality meats, traditionally cured and smoked meats; wild boar, bison, kid, ostrich, venison, kangaroo, crocodile, alligator, peacock, emu, locusts. Other game includes: pheasant, pigeon, wild rabbit, partridge, wild duck, full range of gourmet sausages. Fosters Farm butcher their own meats and take great care to hang the meat further enhancing flavour & tenderness. Mail Order next day courier service. No min. order.
PRICES/PAYMENT: From £3.50 per lb for wild boar and apple sausages - £15.76 per lb for bison/buffalo fillet steak. Mastercard, Visa and Delta.
NOTES: No disabled access. No shop but customers can collect their order by prior arrangement. Barrow Boar supply famous London, West End stores and are interested in supplying to more hotels & restaurants.

WILTSHIRE

MARSHFIELD BAKERY
Westend Farm
Marshfield
CHIPPENHAM
SN14 8JH
TEL: 01225 891709
FAX: 01225 892284
EMAIL:
info@marshfield.demon.co.uk
INTERNET: www.wiltshire-web.
co.uk/marshfield
CONTACT: Mr Paul White
Produce: 16 varieties of snack bars
(shortbread, tiffin, flapjacks). Fruit
cakes. "Maggie Ramage"- a 1940's
recipe fruit cake to eat with
cheese. (Launched July 1998)
Available by Mail Order. No min.
order charge.
PRICES/PAYMENT: Mail Order; Fruit
Cakes £10-£20. Maggie Ramage
£6.50 each. Prices include postage
& packing. Cheques only.
HOURS: 8.30am-6pm for Mail
Order. People can visit to see
bakery in operation.
NOTES: Disabled access.
Marshfield Bakery supply many
local shops, restaurants, schools,
hospitals and universities nation
wide. Major customers include
British Airways, John Lewis,
National Trust, P&O Ferries,
Fortnum & Mason. They are
interested in appointing new
distributors, especially in London
& South East. They also supply
own label.

R & J M ARTINGSTALL
22 High Street,
Marshfield
Chippenham
SN14 8LP
Tel: 01225 891304
Contact: R. Artingstall
Produce: Rare breeds meat. Tradi-
tional beef, lamb, pork, chicken etc.
Game. Home cooked pies and hams.
Local fruit and vegetables. Also stock
honey, jam and Marshfield Bakery
cakes and biscuits.
Prices/Payment: Visa taken, not
Switch.
Hours: Mon, Wed, 8am-1pm. Tues,
Thurs, Fri, 8am-5.30pm. Sats, 8am-
1pm.
Notes: R & J M Artingstall supply to
Artingstall Butchers (Corsham) and
are interested in supplying to the
trade.

SANDRIDGE FARMHOUSE BACON
Bromham
Chippenham
SN15 2JL
Tel: 01380 850304
Contact: Mrs Rosemary Keen
Produce: Wiltshire cured bacon.
Speciality 'village' hams; The
Brumham dry cured ham with
molasses, The Devyses, with the
flavour of hops, The Trubridge,
similar to York Ham, The
Chippenham traditional ham with a
deep pink colour and The Golden
Rind, smoked over oak and beech
sawdust. Oak smoked bacon.
Farmhouse sausages. Also stock
cheese and mustard/jellies. Available
by Mail Order (First Class post or
overnight carrier).
Prices/Payment: Cash and cheques
only. Please ring for price list and list
of stockists.
Hours: Mon-Sat, 9am-5pm.
Notes: No disabled access. Visitors
are able to see the pigs on the farm.

KIT FARM
Southview, Little Cheverell
Devizes
SN10 4JJ
Tel: 01380 818591
Contact: Lynn Rooke
Produce: Beef from Sussex breed and
Sussex cross cattle. All animals
single suckled and grass reared. Kit
Farm produce Soil Symbol registered

carcasses. Delivered locally to order. Other deliveries considered. Min. order £50.
Prices/Payment: Cash and cheques only.
Hours: Please 'phone to place order.
Notes: Kit Farm supply Rushall Mill Farm Shop.

MARTIN PITT
Levetts Farm
Clench Common
Marlborough
SN8 4DS
Tel: 01672 512035
Fax: 01672 514976
Contact: Martin Pitt
Produce: Free range eggs.
Prices/Payment: Cash and cheques only.
Hours: 7.30am-4pm every day.
Notes: Disabled access. 400 acre farm growing & making chicken food. Martin Pitt supplies to 150 shops in and around London and the Thames Valley. Also some in Bristol & Bath area. Send S A E for stockists. He is interested in supplying to the trade.

WILD FOOD TAMED
31-32 Lower Horsehall, Hill Cottages
Chisbury
Marlborough
SN8 3HX
Tel: 01672 870639/ 0171 735 4475
Contact: Louisa Maskell
Produce: Old English fruit cheeses with original modern additions; damson, elderberry, sloe, etc. Sauces made from wild herbs, nuts, funghi. Pickled wild mushrooms/walnuts. Nettle, sorrel and wild garlic paste etc.
Prices/Payment: Cash and cheques only.
Hours: Please 'phone to arrange.
Notes: Wild Food Tamed supply to Neal Street Shop, Drone's, Mortimer & Bennett (all London) and Mackintosh's (Marlborough) and have a possible interest in supplying to the trade.

RUSHALL FARM SHOP
Devizes Road, Rushall
Pewsey
SN9 6DR
Tel: 01980 630335
Fax: 01980 630095
Contact: Mrs Elizabeth Ball
Produce: Rushall organic flour, a wide variety of wholemeal bread products, wholemeal fruit cakes, pizza, biscuits, buns, dog biscuits. Also stock organic fruit and vegetables, organic dairy produce, organic rice, pasta, pulses, organic cordials, organic babyfood, organic breakfast cereals, organic oils and vinegars.
Prices/Payment: 3kg organic wholemeal flour, £1.65, large wholemeal loaves £1, slice of pizza 95p chelsea buns 30p. Cash and cheques only.
Hours: Tues-Fri, 8am-5pm. Sat 8am - 1pm.
Notes: Possible disabled access. Mill and bakery tours including bakery demonstrations and refreshments by appointment only. Rushall Farm Shop supply bread and flour to Londis (Pewsey), McIntosh (Marlborough) and Wild Thymes (Marlborough) and would consider supplying to the trade.

A. PRITCHETT & SON
5 Fish Row
Salisbury
SP1 1EX
Tel: 01722 324346
Contact: Mr V. Aldridge
Produce: Home made sausages, faggotts, burgers etc. Home cured bacon. Also stock local beef, pork and lamb. Home delivery service. Min. order £5.
Prices/Payment: Sausages £1.88 per lb, greenback bacon £3.20 per lb, faggots 40p each. Cash and cheques only.
Hours: 7am-5pm six days per week.
Notes: Disabled access. Occasional tastings. A. Pritchett & Son supply to the trade and are interested in supplying more.

PURE ORGANICS LTD
Stockport Farm
Stockport Road
Amesbury
SALISBURY

SP4 7LN
TEL: 01980 626263
FAX: 01980 626264
EMAIL: mail@pure.organics.org
INTERNET: www.organics.org
CONTACT: Pauline Stiles
PRODUCE: Organic gluten free meat
and vegetarian products. "Kids
Organic Club" range - unadulter-
ated organic children's food in a
convenient format. Pure Organics
range - organic meats, burgers and
sausages. Home delivery scheme in
operation. Min weight 5kg.
PRICES/PAYMENT: Please 'phone for
price list. Mastercard, Visa and
Switch.
HOURS: 8am-8pm.
NOTES: Not open to the public.
Pure Organics supply to organic
health food shops such as Planet
Organic Ltd (London), Out of this
World (Gosforth, Bristol, Cheltenham, Nottingham) Marshford
Organic Nursery (Bideford) and
Iceland stores. Pure Organics are
interested in supplying to the trade.

PERTWOOD ORGANIC CO-OP LTD
Lower Pertwood Farm
Hindon
Salisbury
SP3 6TA
Tel: 01747 820763
Contact: Miranda Tunnicliffe
Produce: Farm based box scheme.
Some vegetables from the farm in the
boxes; each box contains fruit and
vegetables, also available is a fruit
box. Organic lamb and beef freezer
packs, Wiltshire Horns and Welsh
Blacks reared on the farm to your
door. Also stock hemp goods. Boxes
are available by 24hr answerphone.

Delivery to drop-off points.
Prices/Payment: Boxes £6, £8 and
£10. Fruit box £8. £2.70 per lb.
Cash and cheques or standing order.
Hours: Public open days only ' phone
for details.
Notes: Pertwood Organic Co-op also
supply Rushell Mill Bakery and
Edwards of Mere and are interested in
supplying to the trade.

TRUFFLES
72 Belle Vue Road
Salisbury
SP1 3YD
Tel: 01722 331978
Contact: Barbara Bayfield
Produce: Plum puddings made by
hand to a recipe more than a hundred
years old. Made with high quality
ingredients including dark musca-
vado sugar, fresh eggs and wholemeal breadcrumbs. Available with
brandy, Cointreau, rum or whisky.
Also with vegetarian suet. Two new
puddings available this year, fig and
ginger with cider brandy and apricot
and pineapple with rum. Mail order
service available. No min. order.
Prices/Payment: From £3 for 227g to
£7 for 908g. Plus postage charge for
Mail Order.
Hours: By appointment only.
Notes: No disabled access. Truffles
supplies Hockleys Farm Shop (Hants),
Windmill Hill City Farm (Bristol),
Goose Green Deli (Cheshire) and
Confisserie Verdanh (Salisbury) and
are interested in supplying more to
the trade.

BERKELEY FARM DAIRY
Berkeley Farm
Swindon Road
Wroughton
Swindon
SN4 9AQ
Tel: 01793 812228
Fax: 01793 845949
Contact: N.J. Gosling
Produce: Guernsey (C.I.) cow's milk
from which Guernsey cream,

Guernsey handmade butter both salted and unsalted. Also stock Wiltshire honey, local free range eggs, ice cream made locally using Berkeley Farm cream. Also sold on local milk rounds.

Prices/Payment: Butter from 90p per half pound. Cash and cheques only.

Hours: 8.30am-2.30pm.

Notes: No disabled access, but will deliver out to the car. Butter making demo, milking if prior arrangement. Berkeley Farm supply four local outlets and are interested in supplying to the trade.

THE WILTSHIRE TRACKLEMENT CO
The Dairy Farm
Pinkney Park
Sherston
Malmesbury
SN16 0NX
Tel: 01666 840851
Fax: 01666 840022
Contact: Guy Tullberg/Shirley Bailey
Produce: A wide range of mustards, jellies and sauces, available mainly by mail order. See Mail order section for full details.
Notes: Local stockist: Skidmores (Sherston).

COOKIE CRAFT
'Michaelmas'
Common Platt
Purton
Swindon
SN5 9LB
Tel: 01793 770250
Fax: 01793 770250
Contact: Michael Keaveny
Produce: Traditional tea cakes. Victoria sponge cakes, cookies, flapjacks, shortbreads, slices and scones.
Prices/Payment: £2.90 for a large Victoria sponge. Whiskey cake £5.75. Mail Order on long shelf life products. No min. order; p&p charged.
Hours: 8.30am-6pm
Notes: No disabled access. Cookie

Craft also supply St. Peters Church (Marlborough), Grovelands Farm Shop (Reading), Country Bumpkins (Leamington Spa) and Chesterton Farm Shop (Cirencester). They are interested in supplying to the trade and can arrange wholesale terms.

EASTBROOK FARMS ORGANIC MEAT LTD
50 High Street, Shrivenham
Swindon
SN6 8AA
Tel: 01793 790460 - Office
01793 782211 - Shop
Fax: 01793 791239
Contact: Graham Burroughs
Produce: Fresh organic beef, lamb, pork, chicken, sausage & home cured bacon. Turkey & geese at Christmas time. Also stock a wide range of organic dry goods, vegetables & dairy products. Mail Order available by nationwide home delivery for all fresh meats. No min. order, delivery charge varies according to the amount spent.
Prices/Payment: Access, Visa, Switch, only on Mail Order.
Hours: Mon-Fri, 8am-5.30pm. Sat, 8am-1pm.
Notes: Disabled access. Eastbrook Farms supply to; Sunnyfields, Garlands Farm, Smithy Farm Shop and Godshill Organics. They are interested in supplying more to the trade.

WILLOW FARM SHOP
Willow Farm
Inglesham
Highworth
Swindon
SN6 7QZ
Tel: 01367 252163
Contact: Miles & Megan Saunders
Produce: Organic lamb & beef, free range Gloucester Old Spot pork, all frozen.
Prices/Payment: Cash & cheques only.
Hours: Saturdays. In week, evenings etc, please 'phone for appointment.
Notes: Disabled access.

DEVERILLS FISH FARM
The Marsh, Longbridge Deverill
Warminster
BA12 7DZ
Tel: 01985 841093
Fax: 01985 841093
Contact: Steve Holloway
Produce: Wet fish: including fresh rainbow trout, whole plaice, fresh haddock, fresh Scottish salmon, red mullet, John Dory, oysters, skate wings, fresh squid, live crab, dressed crab, cooked and live lobster, tiger prawns, live crayfish, whelks, cockles etc. Smoked produce includes; local oak smoked trout, salmon, smoked haddock, smoked kipper cutlets, smoked duck breast, whole smoked eel, smoked pâté. Organic watercress and organic eggs.
Prices/Payment: Please 'phone for price list. All major credit cards taken and Switch.
Hours: 10am-6pm seven days a week.
Notes: Disabled access possible if required. Occasional tastings. Local delivery van service for larger orders. Deverills Fish Farm supply local pubs and restaurants.

JOHN HURD'S ORGANIC WATERCRESS
"Stonewold" Watercress Farm
Hill Deverill
Warminster
BA12 7EF
Tel: 01985 840260
Fax: 01985841246
Produce: Organic watercress. Dial-in delivery service. Min. order £10.
Notes: Watercress available from the shop below. Aside from this, Hurds are also interested in direct supply to the catering trade.

THE REAL MEAT COMPANY
51 Market Place
Warminster
BA12 9AZ
Tel: 0345 626017
Fax: 01985 218950

Email: richard@realmeat.co.uk
Internet: www.realmeat.co.uk
Contact: Arabella Collins
Produce: High welfare additive free meats. Beef, lamb, pork, chickens, bacon, ham and seasonal poultry i.e turkeys at Christmas. Specialities include cushion of lamb (apricot or plum and ginger stuffing encased in boneless lamb), bacon chops, mini roasts, koftas, kebabs, chicken breasts with herby garlic butter. Sausages and burgers.
Prices/Payment: From £2.59 per lb for pork chipolata sausages to £14.99 per lb for beef fillet steak. All sent by next day delivery. Min. order £35. All major credit cards. Amex. Switch and Delta.
Hours: Mon-Fri, 8.30am-5pm. Sat, 9am-12pm. Also 24 hour answer phone.
Notes: Not open to the public. There are Real Meat Co shops in Sheffield, Bath, Poole, Leicester and Carshalton Beeches.

LATE ENTRIES

HOLSWORTHY ORGANICS
Little East Lake Farm, East Chilla
Beaworthy
Devon
EX 21 5XF
Contact: Moyra on 01409 221417 or Jemima on 01288 381216
Produce: All summer and winter vegetables, soft fruit, apples, Box scheme. Telephone order by Sun, for delivery Wed.
Prices/Payment: Boxes at £5, £7.50, £10. Cash and cheques only.
Notes: Holsworthy Organics may be interested in supplying to the trade.

R. A. DUCKETT & CO LTD
Walnut Tree Farm
Heath House
Wedmore
Somerset
BS28 4UJ

Tel: 01934 712218
Contact: Chris Duckett
Produce: Caerphilly cheese - made with raw cow's milk and vegetarian rennet, Wedmore cheese made as above. Wedmore cheese includes a layer of chopped chives.
Prices/Payment: Caerphilly, £2 per lb mini. Wedmore £2.15 per lb mini. Cash and cheques only.
Hours: Mon-Sat, 9am-5pm.

The following are SHOPS within this region which do not produce but do sell quality or organic foods.

CAUSEWAY HEALTHFOODS & HOME BREW
4 Causeway
Chippenham
Wiltshire
SN15 3DT
Tel: 01249 659431
Produce: Wide selection of organic groceries, Doves Farm, Whole Earth, Evernat, Meridian, Swedish Organic. Vegetable and fruit box scheme for Pertwood Organics.
Hours: Mon, Tues, Thurs, Fri, 9am-5.30pm. Wed, Sat, 9am-5pm.
Notes: No disabled access.

GOOD NATURE
2 Esplanade
Fowey
Cornwall
PL23 1HY
Tel: 01726 832110
Produce: Wide range of authentic and processed organic foods and wholefoods; also chilled and frozen. Herbal supplements and remedies. Aromatherapy oils, toiletries. Organic vegetable boxes on a weekly basis.
Hours: Open daily. Hours vary, summer more, winter less.
Notes: No disabled access.

MALMESBURY WHOLEFOODS
29 Abbey Row
Malmesbury
Wiltshire
SN16 0AG
Tel: 01666 823030
Produce: Wholefoods, vegetarian, organic foods. Nuts, pulses, rice, cereals, flour, herbs, spices, tea, coffee, honey, jams, dairy products. Home delivery scheme within 15 miles of Malmesbury. £5 discount for bulk buys.
Hours: Mon-Sat, 9am-5.30pm.
Notes: Disabled access.

TORBAY HEALTH STORE
28 Hyde Road
Paignton
Devon
TQ4 5BY
Tel: 01803 527251
Fax: 01647 441069
Produce: Organic wholefoods, loose herbs & spices. Specialists in ethnic food. Mail Order available.
Hours: Mon-Sat, 9am-5pm.
Notes: No disabled access.

CARLEYS
34,35,36, St Austell Street
Truro
Kernow
Cornwall
TR1 1SE
Tel: 01872 277686
Fax: 01872 277686
Produce: Soil Assoc. No. P1584. Extensive range of organic foods. Breads, cakes, nut butters, frozen meals, herb purées, pesto, pasta sauces, breakfast cereals. Thousands of products available including organic cat and dog food. Produce supplied to three local box schemes; please 'phone for details.
Hours: Mon-Sat, 9am-5.30pm.
Notes: Disabled access. Free customer car park. Tastings. Carleys are interested in supplying to the trade.

EAST YORKSHIRE

THOMAS THE BAKER
(See Main Entry under York)
16-17 Market Place
Driffield
YO25 7AP
Tel: 01377 255554

NORTH YORKSHIRE

CRAKEHALL WATER MILL
Little Crakehall
Bedale
DL8 1HU
Tel: 01677 423240
Contact: Peter H Townsend
Produce: Stone ground wholemeal flour produced from a mixture of Canadian spring wheat and English hard wheat.
Prices/Payment: 1.5 kg, £1.05 - 12.5kg, £7.20. Cash, cheques only.
Hours: Mill: Easter-end Sept; Tues, Wed, Thurs, Sat, Sun, 10am-5pm. When closed buy at the Mill House.
Notes: No disabled access for wheel chairs. Tour of Water Mill built in 1086. Crakehall Water Mill supply four other outlets.

THE BIG SHEEP AND LITTLE COW FARM
Aiskew Watermill
Aiskew
Bedale
DL8 1AW
Tel: 01677 422125
Fax: 01677 425205
Contact: Jared Clark
Produce: Award winning ewe's milk ice cream, made on the farm. Ewe's milk and naturally reared Dexter beef. Also stock Shepherds Purse speciality ewe's milk cheese, Yorkshire country wines and Black Sheep Ales.
Prices/Payment: Ewe's milk ice cream £2.99 per 500ml, ewe's milk 80p per pint, minced steak £4.40 per kg, best steak £7.70 per kg. Cash, cheques only.
Hours: Apr-Sept: 10am-5pm every day. Oct-Dec: 11am-4pm weekends only.
Notes: Disabled access. Farm visitor centre, tea shop, under cover children's play area. The farm is interested in supplying to the trade.

BETTYS & TAYLORS OF HARROGATE
Pagoda House, Prospect Road
Harrogate
HG2 7NX
Tel: 01423 886055 (Mail Order), 0800 418898 (customer queries.
Fax: 01423 881083 (Mail Order)
Produce: Over 600 specialities are made daily at Bettys Craft Bakery including cakes, chocolates, biscuits and bread. Preserves are handmade in small batches. They also roast, blend and sell speciality coffees and teas. Mail Order available. No min. order charge.
Prices/Payment: Please 'phone for catalogue. All major credit cards taken. Switch.
Hours: Mail Order: Mon-Fri 8.30am-5.30pm. Bettys York every day 9am-9pm; Bettys Harrogate, every day 9am-9pm; Bettys Ilkley, every day 9am-6pm; Bettys Northallerton, Mon-Sat, 9am-5.30pm, Sun 10am-5.30pm.
Notes: Disabled access. At café tearooms; occasional musical evenings, talks on the history of Bettys.

BETTYS CAFÉ TEAROOMS
1 Parliament Street
Harrogate
Tel: 01423 502746

THOMAS THE BAKER
Unit 11
Victoria Garden Shopping Centre
Harrogate
HG1 1AF
Tel: 01423 526868

J.W. COCKETT & SON
Main Street
Hawes
DL8 3QL
Tel: 01969 667251
Contact: John Cockett
Produce: Cakes, biscuits and pastries. Speciality is a rich Wensleydale fruit cake which is suitable for Christmas, weddings, christenings and anniversaries. Available as square, round and hexagonal from 5 and a half inch to fourteen inches. Mail Order system being set up. No min order charge.
Prices/Payment: Rich Wensleydale fruit cake retails at £2.55 per lb.
Hours: Mon-Sat, 8am-5pm.
Notes: Disabled access. J.W. Cockett & Son supply to 'Westwoods' (Leyburn), T. Robinson (Kirkby Stephen), Post Office, Romansy (Northallerton), Reahs (Masham) and Pawson (Gargrave).

THOMAS THE BAKER
The Baker's Yard
Helmsley
YO62 5DQ

THOMAS THE BAKER
2 Church Street
Kirkbymoorside
YO62 6AZ
Tel: 01751 432420
and at:
15 Market Place
Kirkbymoorside
YO62 4AA

THOMAS THE BAKER
12 Market Place
Knaresborough
HG5 8AG
Tel: 01423 861170

DEREK FOX
25 Market Place
Malton
YO17 7LP
Tel: 01653 600338
Contact: Shaun or Melanie Fox
Produce: Speciality Yorkshire Pot,

four birds boned out, stuffed and re-assembled. Duck, chicken, pheasant, partridge, venison with three different stuffings. Feeds 10-12 people. 18 varieties of sausages, all home-made. Mail Order available. No min. order charge.
Prices/Payment: Credit cards taken .
Hours: 8am-5pm, six days per week.
Notes: Disabled access. Cheese and sausage tastings. Derek Fox is interested in supplying to the trade.

THOMAS THE BAKER
Wheelgate House,
26 Wheelgate
Malton
YO17 7IP
Tel: 01653 600167

BETTYS CAFÉ TEAROOMS
188 High Street
Northallerton
Tel: 01609 775154

THOMAS THE BAKER
175 High Street
Northallerton
DL7 8JZ
Tel: 01609 771774

THE ORGANIC FARMSHOP
Standfield Hall Farm
Westgate Carr Road
Pickering
YO18 8LX
Tel: 01751 472249
Fax: 01751 472249
Contact: Mike or Pam Sellers
Produce: All types of organic vegetables and organic beef. Soil Assn no PS21N. Home-made organic vegetarian frozen meals, flans, pizzas, bread, sausages and burgers, all organic. Also stock a vast range of organic vegetables, imported fruit, wholefood, dried fruit, beef, pork, lamb and chickens. Organic flours, dairy products, ice cream, cheeses. Home delivery 10 mile radius. Box

scheme in Malton and Scarborough.
Min. order £6.
Prices/Payment: Frozen meals £2.25
to £4. Cash and cheques only.
Hours: Wed, Thur, Fri, 9am-6pm.
Saturday 9am-2pm and at other times
by appointment.
Notes: Disabled access to shop. Farm
walks by appointment with free teas.
Possible interest in supplying to hotels.

THOMAS THE BAKER
33/34 Market Place
Pickering
YO18 7AE

CURRANT AFFAIRS
Riverview Cottage
Grange Road
Brompton-on-Swale

RICHMOND

DL10 7HJ
TEL: 01748 811770
CONTACT: Gillian or Alex Ives
Produce: Producers of luxury
fruitcakes which are mixed and
decorated by hand. Their luxury
cakes are baked to recipes which
have been adapted by Currant
Affairs from a time proven family
recipe. The vine fruits are soaked
in brandy for 48 hours and the
cakes themselves are matured for
6 months at least until they are
considered to be at their best.
Traditional Yorkshire fruitcakes,
Poachers cake, Apricot and Ginger
cake, Drunken Apricot cake.
Currently compiling a Mail Order
brochure. No min order charge.
PRICES/PAYMENT: Please 'phone for a
price list. Cash and cheques only.
Hours: Please 'phone for details.
Also mail order – see mail order
section.
NOTES: Currant Affairs sell to Lewis
& Coopers (Northallerton) and
Philberts of Darlington. They are
interested in supplying more to the
trade.

THOMAS THE BAKER
27 Market Place
Richmond
DL10 4QG
Tel: 01748 821157

THOMAS THE BAKER
20 Market Place
Ripon
HG4 1BW
Tel: 01765 605232

THOMAS THE BAKER
7 Aberdeen Walk
Scarborough
YO11 1BA
Tel: 01723 501181
and at;
76-78 Newborough
Scarborough
YO11 1EP
Tel: 01723 355009

SIMPLY ORGANIC
Sandylands
Market Weighton Road
Barlby
Selby
YO8 7LB
Tel: 01757 708540
Fax: 01757 708540
Contact: Kathryn Patrick
Produce: The farm produces organic
fruit and vegetables, eggs, lamb in
season. A Box scheme operates
through the farm shop which
customers call to collect. No min.
order.
Prices/Payment: Cash, cheques only.
Hours: Wed-Thurs, 1pm-7pm. Fri-Sat,
9am-5pm.
Notes: Disabled access. Small
coffee shop and outside garden area
for picnics etc.

THOMAS THE BAKER
20-22 Gowthorpe
Selby
YO8 4ET
Tel: 01757 213816

ROSEBUD PRESERVES
Rosebud Farm
Healey
RIPON
HG4 4LH
TEL: 01765 689174
FAX: 01765 689174
CONTACT: Elspeth Biltoft
PRODUCE: Range of preserves
including chutneys, pickles,
relishes, herbs and wild fruit jellies,
jams, marmalade, lemon curd,
mustard and mincemeat. Mail
Order Brochure. No min order
charge.
PRICES/PAYMENT: Please 'phone for
price list. Cash and cheques only.
Hours: Mon-Fri, 9am-5pm.
Notes: No disabled access. Rose
bud Preserves supply to;
Ramsbottom Victuallers (Bury),
Archimbolds (Harrogate),
Villandry (London), Wensleydale
Dairy Products (Hawes) Limoncello
(London). They are interested in
supplying to the trade.

KILNSEY PARK & TROUT FARM
Kilnsey
Skipton
BD23 5PS
Tel: 01756 752150
Fax: 01756 752224
Contact: Vanessa Roberts
Produce: Fresh rainbow trout,
smoked trout, cold smoked trout
fillets, pâté etc. Home-made cakes &
biscuits. Spring bottled water. Also
stock a large range of jams, jellies,
chutneys and cheese. Limited Mail
Order available on smoked products.
No min. order.
Prices/Payment: Major credit cards
taken. Switch.
Hours: 9am-5.30pm every day of the
year except Christmas Day.
Notes: Disabled access. Restaurant,
tea shop, park and aquarium. Herb
talks. Kilnsey Park & Trout Farm
supply to hotels and restaurants.

THE CELEBRATED PORK PIE ESTABLISHMENT
9 Mill Bridge
Skipton
BD23 1NJ
Tel: 01756 793477
Contact: David Holmes
Produce: Pork pies, sausage rolls,
black puddings, sausage. Quality
meats.
Prices/Payment: Cash and cheques
only.
Hours: Mon, Wed, Thurs, Fri, Sat,
6am-5pm. Tues, 6am-1.30pm.

SMITHY FARMSHOP
Baldersby
Thirsk
YO7 4PN
Tel: 01765 640 676
Contact: Susan Brown
Produce: Home baking; rich fruit
cakes, Yorkshire fruit loaves, sticky
toffee puddings, steak pies. Also stock
organic meats, dairy products,
vegetables, drinks, handmade pâtés,
puddings and supper dishes. Local
Deliveries. Min. order £50.
Prices/Payment: Credit and debit
cards taken.
Hours: Mon-Sat, 9.30am-5.30pm
Notes: Disabled access.

THOMAS THE BAKERS
45 Market Place
Thirsk
YO7 1HA
Tel: 01845 525949
30A Market Place
Thirsk
YO7 1LB

C F & E T PADMORE
Bank House Farm
Glaisdale
Whitby
YO21 2QA
Tel: 01947 897297
Fax: 01947 897297
Email: chrisemmap@aol.com
Contact: Chris & Emma Padmore

Produce: Organic beef and lamb. Woodland reared pork. All frozen.
Prices/Payment: Cash and cheques only.
Hours: Office hours but 'phone first before arriving.
Notes: No disabled access. The Padmores are interested in supplying to the trade.

E. BOTHAM & SONS LTD
35/39 Skinner Street
Whitby
YO21 3AH
Tel: 01947 602823
Fax: 01947 820269
Email: mj@botham.co.uk
Internet: www.botham.co.uk
Contact: Michael Jarman
Produce: Craft bakery products. Following their original recipes, the finest ingredients, skillfully combined to produce biscuits, plum bread, Yorkshire Brack and cakes to a high standard. Available by world wide mail order for baked goods, hampers, preserves etc. No min. order charge.
Prices/Payment: Visa and Mastercard taken. No Switch.
Hours: 8.30am-5.30pm.
Notes: Disabled access except to 1st floor cafe. Tearooms at; 35 Skinner Street, Whitby and 30 Baxtergate, Whitby. E. Botham & Sons Ltd are interested in supplying to the trade.

FORTUNES WHITBY KIPPERS
22 Henrietta Street
Whitby
YO22 4DW
Tel: 01947 601659
Contact: Derek & Barry Brown
Produce: Curers of herrings to produce traditional kippers.
Price/Payment: £1.34 per lb. No credit cards.
Hours: Mon-Sat, 9am-4pm. Sun all year round, 10am-12pm & 1.30pm-2.30pm
Notes: Disabled access. Smoke house & shop can be visited. No credit cards.

BETTYS CAFÉ TEAROOMS
6-8 St Helen's Square
York
Tel: 01904 659142

BRUNSWICK ORGANIC NURSERY
Appleton Road, Bishopthorpe
York
YO23 2RF
Tel: 01904 701869
Fax: 01904 701869
Contact: Adam Myers
Produce: Home grown organic vegetables, fruit and herbs. Plants in pots, bedding plants, cottage garden perennials, herbs. Also stock organic produce from other growers.
Prices/Payment: Cash and cheques only
Hours: Mon-Fri, 10am-4pm plus Sat and Sun from May to Sept.
Notes: Disabled access. Brunswick Organic supply to Alligator Wholefoods (York). Limited restaurant supply.

HOLME FARMED VENISON
Thorpe Underwood
York
YO26 9SR
Tel: 01423 331212
Fax: 01423 330855
Email: nigel@hfvenison.demon.co.uk
Produce: Full range of venison products. Sausages, burgers, grills, diced steak, joints and pâtés, pies and special order items (for dinner parties). Also mince, liver, stirfry, mini joints, T.bones and cutlets. Also a full range of English wild boar and ostrich. Also stock game pies and pâtés. Available by Mail Order, overnight delivery. Special boxes. Min. order charge £50.
Prices/Payment: Venison sausages, £6.61 per kg. Steak £17 per kg. Whole boneless haunch £14.33 per kg. Diced steak £10.47 per kg. All major credit cards taken.
Notes: No disabled access. Holme Farmed Venison supply to Selfridges, Harrods (London) and Booths (Lancashire & Cumbria).

TAYLORS
46 Stonegate
York
Tel: 01904 622865

THOMAS THE BAKER
The Baker's Yard, Sawmill Lane
Helmsley
York
YO62 5DQ
Tel: 01439 770870 **Fax:** 01439 771131
Contact: Simon Thomas
Produce: Freshly baked bread, rolls,
pies, pastries and savouries. Freshly
made sandwiches. Speciality
decorated cakes to order. Best
known for sausage rolls and Yorkshire
curd tarts and award winning mince
pies. Also stock soup and drinks.
Prices/Payment: Picnic sausage roll
16p, Small Yorkshire curd tart 32p.
Cash and cheques only.
Hours: 8am-5.30pm.
Notes: Disabled access at most of the
shops. They are interested in
supplying to other outlets. Also at:

3 Market Place, Helmsley
York
YO62 5BJ
Tel: 01439 771352

13 Lendal
York
YO1 2AQ
Tel: 01904 642449

22 Spurriergate
York
YO1 1QR
Tel: 01904 655189

Unit 7, Coppergate
York
YO1 9NT

99 Low Petergate
York
YO1 2HY

59 York Road, Acomb
York
YO24 4LN
Tel: 01904 782311

Haydale
Spring Street, Easingwold
York
YO61 3BJ
Tel: 01347 822613

Tang Hall Shop
153A Tang Hall Lane
York
YO1 3SD
Tel: 01904 430591

25 Bishopthorpe Road
York
YO23 1NA
Tel: 01904 621863

12 Church Street
7 Kings Square
York
YO1 2QE
Tel: 01904 658872

SOUTH YORKSHIRE

ROUND GREEN VENISON CO.
Round Green Farm
Worsbrough
Barnsley
S75 3DR
Tel: 01226 205577
Fax: 01226 281294
Contact: Richard Elmhurst
Produce: Venison - Full range of
joints, steak, pies, sausages. Rare
breed pork. Also stock game in
season including wild boar. Local
honey, local preserves & chutneys.
Mail Order available. Overnight
chilled delivery to home. No min.
order charge, but carriage charged.
Prices/Payment: Credit cards taken
shortly. Until then cash & cheques
only.
Hours: 9am-5pm six days a week.
'Phone for Sun opening times.
Notes: Disabled access. Round Green
Venison Co supply to Park Farm
(Snettisham, Norfolk), Jedforest Deer
& Farm Park (Jedburgh), Windmill
Farm Equestrian Centre (Harrogate).
They are suppliers to the trade.

WOMERSLEY CRAFTS AND HERBS
Womersley

DONCASTER

DN6 9BH
TEL: 01977 620294
FAX: 01977 620200
CONTACT: **Martin Parsons**
PRODUCE: **Ten fruit condiments, six herb condiments and 15 herb jellies. Suitable for uses ranging from cordials in the summer, hot toddys in winter to transforming salad dressings and use in soups, casseroles and jellies and particularly used for flavouring sauces. Also stock a wide range of herbs (plants or seeds), herbal teas, essential oils, products by Floris of London, Crabtree & Evelyn, Weleda and Applewoods. Also pottery, woodturning and other crafts. Carrier service available for condiments. Min. order 1 box (12 mixed jars).**
PRICES/PAYMENT: **From £1.80 for 285g jar chutney to £3.50 for 300ml mulberry fruit condiment. All major credit cards taken, not Switch.**
HOURS: **Jan-Feb, Sun only, 2pm-5pm. Mar-Dec, Sats and Bank Holidays 10.30am-6pm. Sun, 12pm-6pm. 10th Dec - Christmas, weekdays 2pm-5pm. Weekdays during year - press bell for attention**
NOTES: **Disabled access not very good. Tastings available. Womersley also supply Clarkes of Kensington (London), Corbridge Larder (Northumberland), Mooreland Foods (Wilmslow), Burford Garden Co (Oxfordshire) and are happy to supply more to the trade.**

RONEYS "GOING THE WHOLE HOG"
276 Sharrowvale Road
Sheffield
S11 8SH
Tel: 01142 660593
Fax: 01142 660593
Contact: Mr Adrian Rubenstein
Produce: Traditional and rare breeds of meat, pork, beef, lamb and chicken including Tamworth, Gloucster Old Spot, Middle White pork and bacon; White Park beef and North Ronaldsay lamb, also Ixworth chickens and Norfolk broad breasted Bronze turkeys. Mail Order available. Min. Order charge, £45.
Prices/Payment: Dry cured Tamworth bacon £4.50 per lb. Pork, Stilton and Celery Sausage, £3.50 per lb. All major credit cards taken. Switch and Delta.
Hours: 7am-5.30pm six days a week.
Notes: Disabled access.

WEST YORKSHIRE

KOLOS BAKERY & CO
128/132 Parkside Road
West Bowling
Bradford
BD5 8EH
Tel: 01274 729958
Fax: 01274 729958
Contact: Mr Prytulak
Produce: Continental and traditional bread. Organic, wheat free bread. None of products contains any additives or preservatives or animal fats. Also stock pizza bases, fresh yeast and all types of flour. Mail Order service, next day delivery. Min order 10 loaves.
Prices/Payment: Cash and cheques only.
Hours: Mon-Fri, 7am-6pm. Sat, 7am-1pm. Closed Sun.
Notes: No disabled access. Kolos Bakery & Co supply to Rackhams, Selfridges, Fenwicks and Yorkshire Co-op. They are interested in supplying to the trade.

CHARLOTTES REAL DAIRY ICE CREAM
The Meadows Lane Top Farm
Whitley Road, Whitley
Dewsbury
WF12 0NQ
Tel: 01924 494491
Fax: 01924 494491
Contact: Audrey Wraithmell
Produce: Ice cream in 18 flavours made from their own Jersey milk on the farm. Served in their own ice cream parlour.
Prices/Payment: From 60p for cones, to take home packs at £2.50-£9.50. Cash and cheques only.
Hours: 10.30am-6pm seven days a week, 8pm Sat and Sun, July to end of Sept.
Notes: Disabled access and toilets. Tastings, tea/coffee shop, ice cream parlour, seating inside 50, outside 30. Playground. Charlottes Real Jersey Ice Cream are interested in supplying to the trade.

NATURAL CHOICE
72 Westbourne Road
Marsh
Huddersfield
HD1 4LE
Tel: 01484 513162
Contact: Graham Rushworth
Produce: Organic fruit and vegetables. Organic bread, muesli etc. All types of wholefoods, specialist diet foods plus standard fruit and vegetables. Also stock Suma wholefoods. Free home delivery and box scheme.
Prices/Payment: Please 'phone for price list.
Hours: 9am-5.30pm, six days a week.
Notes: No disabled access. Natural Choice are interested in supplying to the trade.

R&J LODGE FOODS
4 Greens End Road, Meltham
Huddersfield
HD7 3NW
Tel/Fax: 01484 850571
Contact: Raymond or Janice Lodge

Produce: Handmade stand pies; pork, game, fidget, harvest (veggie), turkey/ham/cranberry, pork/apple/stilton. Sausages - Approx 12 varieties in total, a range of small pies etc. Home-made sticky parkin. Coleslaw. Also stock dry cured bacon and farmhouse cheeses. Mail Order by Interlink.
Prices/Payment: Prices on request; cash & cheques only.
Hours: Mon closed. Tues, Thurs, Fri, 8.30am-2pm; Wed, 8.30am-1.30pm; Sat, 8.30am-12.30pm.
Notes: No disabled access.

BETTYS CAFÉ TEAROOMS
(See main entry for Harrogate)
32 The Grove
Ilkley
Tel: 01943 608029

LISHMANS OF ILKLEY
25 Leeds Road
Ilkley
LS29 8DP
Tel: 01943 609436
Fax: 01943 816007
Contact: David Lishman
Produce: Naturally home reared rare breed pork; Saddleback, Gloucester Old Spot. Rare breed and conventional beef and lamb. Championship sausage. Dry cured bacon. Cooked meats and pies. Mail Order available. Min order £45 plus delivery.
Prices/Payment: Yorkshire champion pork sausage £1.70 per lb. Dry cured rare breed bacon £2.72 per lb. Visa, Mastercard, Delta and Switch taken.
Hours: Mon-Sat, 8am-5.30pm.
Notes: Disabled access.

WEEGMANN'S
4-6 Market Place
Otley
LS21 3AQ
Tel: 01943 462327
Fax: 01943 462327
Contact: Richard Smithson
Produce: Pork products. Pork pies,

special sausages, home cured bacon, pies to cook. Hot pork and beef sandwiches. All made on the premises. Home cooked meats; boiled ham, roast ham, roast pork, black pudding and polony. Fresh Yorkshire beef, lamb and pork all locally fed.
Prices/Payment: Cash & cheques only
Hours: Mon-Fri, 8am-5.30pm. Sat, 8am-5pm.
Notes: Disabled access is possible.

BRICKYARD ORGANIC FARM
Badsworth
Pontefract
WF9 1AX
Tel: 01977 617327
Fax: 01977 617327
Contact: John Brook
Produce: A range of organic seasonal field vegetables, salad and fruit. Box Scheme available in Wakefield and Leeds area. Min. order £9.50.
Prices/Payment: Cash and cheques only.
Hours: Sat, 9am-4pm.
Notes: Disabled access to shop. Brickyard Organic Farm supply to Natural Food Store (Leeds).

THOMAS THE BAKER
3 Horsefair Centre
Wetherby
LS22 4FL
Tel: 01937 581550

LATE ENTRY

SLATER ORGANICS
The Oasis Garage
Long Riston
Hull
East Yorks
HU11 5JF
Tel: 01964 562250
Contact: Bob Slater
Produce: Growers of fresh organic summer and winter vegetables. Soil Assoc. No G1917. Box scheme

available. Min order £5.
Prices/Payment: Cash and cheques only
Hours: 8am-6pm, six days a week.
Notes: Slater Organics also supply to Hull Food (Hull) and Country Store (Beverley).

The following are SHOPS within this region which do not produce but do sell quality or organic foods.

THE GREEN HOUSE
5 Station Parade
Harrogate
North Yorkshire
HG1 1UF
Tel: 01423 502580
Produce: Fresh organic fruit and vegetables. Packaged goods, organic wines.
Hours: Mon, 10am-5.45pm. Tues-Sat, 9am-5.45pm.
Notes: Disabled access. Café.

HALEY & CLIFFORD DELICATESSEN
43 Street Lane
Leeds
West Yorks
LS8 1AP
Tel: 0113 237 0334
Produce: Variety of cooked dishes. Cooked to order if given a few days notice. Salads, desserts. Also a selection of breads and home-made pickles. Large range of cheeses.
Hours: Mon-Fri, 9am-5.30pm. Sat, 9am-5pm. Sun, 9am-12pm.

APPLETONS OF RIPON
6 Market Place
Ripon
North Yorks
HG4 1BP
Tel: 01765 603198
Produce: Cold meats and pork pies. Breaded savoury duck and roast belly of pork.
Hours: Mon, Tues, Thurs, Fri, 8am-5.30pm. Wed, Sat, 8am-5pm.

STANFORTHS OLD PORK PIE SHOP
11 Mill Bridge
Skipton
North Yorks
BD23 1NJ
Tel: 01756 793477
Produce: Home-made fine pork pies;
also their speciality is hot stand pies.
Hours: Mon, Wed, Thurs, Fri, 6am-
5pm. Tues, 6am-1pm. Sat, 6am-
4.30pm.

THE GOOD FOOD SHOP
9 Scarcroft Road
York
North Yorks
YO23 1ND
Tel: 01904 637445
Produce: Pâtés, cheeses, bacon,
home cooked ham on the bone. Also
a range of home made cakes and
puddings.
Hours: Mon-Sat, 9.15am-5.30pm.

EAST

CLEAN BEAN
37e Princelet Street
E1 5LP
Tel: 0171 247 8349
Contact: Neil McLennan
Produce: Makers of fresh Tofu from organic soybeans, sold every Sunday at Spitalfields Market.
Prices/Payment: Regular Tofu £1.50 per 250g. Cash and cheques only.
Hours: Spitalfields Market every Sunday 9am-5pm.
Notes: Disabled access. Clean Bean supply to Planet Organic, BumbleBee Whole Foods, Freshlands, Spitalfields Organics (all London). They are interested in supplying to the trade.

GRAMMA'S
P.O. Box 218
E6 4BG
TEL: 0181 470 8751
FAX: 0181 548 8755
CONTACT: Ms Dounne Alexander
PRODUCE: Traditional Caribbean Herbal Foods. A range of four concentrated herbal pepper sauces (mild, hot, extra-hot & super hot) and four concentrated herbal seasonings (original, hot & spicy, curry, creole) available individually or in gift boxes. Mail Order service; no minimum order.
PRICES: Herbal pepper sauces £3.50, herbal seasonings £3.95, gift sets £12.50.
HOURS: Orders sent by post Mon-Sat; allow 14 days delivery. Cash, cheques only.
NOTES: Tasting demonstration can be arranged for groups/clubs; ring in advance. Suppliers to Fortnum & Mason. Ms Alexander is interested in supplying to restaurants, hotels and airlines.
Otherwise, not open to the public.

WEST

NEALS YARD BAKERY LTD
6 Neals Yard
Covent Garden
WC2H 9DP
Tel: 0171 836 5199
Fax: 0171 379 1544
Contact: John Loffler
Produce: Wide range of breads, cakes & pastries made from organic whole-wheat flour. Daily changing lunchtime hot meals, soup and at least four different salads. Pizzas and savoury croissants. Everything made on the premises. Also stock 100% sourdough rye bread.
Prices/Payment: 800g organic wholewheat loaf £1.30. Range of baps £1.85 £2.20. Cash, cheques only.
Hours: Mon - Sat10.30am - 5.pm
Notes: Upstairs tea-room. Disabled access to shop but not to tea-room. Neals Yard Bakery also supply Bumblebee Wholefoods, Sesame, Planet Organic and Harvey Nichols; all in central London.

BLAGDEN FISHMONGERS
65 Paddington Street
W1M 3RR
Tel: 0171 935 8321
Fax: 0171 935 8321
Email: blagfish@vossnet.co.uk
Contact: D.J. Blagden
Produce: A wide range of fresh fish including; fresh tuna steaks and fillet, rainbow trout, John Dory, silver pomfret & dorade, Loch Fyne kippers, New Zealand mussels etc. Also stock; game, quail's eggs, free range eggs and samphire. Home delivery in West and North West London. No min. order.
Prices/Payment: Wild smoked salmon £22 per lb. Cash and cheques only.
Hours: Mon-Fri, 7.30am-5pm. Sat, 7.30am-1pm.
Notes: Easy access for disabled. Recipes provided by computer database. Blagden Fishmongers are interested in supplying more to the trade.

SOUTH LONDON

PATISSERIE FRANCAISE
127 Queensway
W2 4SJ
Tel: 0171 221 7923
Fax: 0171 221 0504
Contact: Phillip Klein
Produce: High class patisserie and bread products. Made in the bakery. Also stock chocolate, snacks etc.
Prices/Payment: Cash and cheques only
Hours: 8am-6pm approx.
Notes: No disabled access. Branches at 80 Queensway, 27 Kensington Church Street and 4 Chepstow Road (all London).

& CLARKE'S
122 Kensington Church Street
Kensington
W8 4BH
Tel: 0171 229 2190
Fax: 0171 229 4564
Contact: Sarah Bilney
Produce: Selection of fresh breads, cakes and tarts. Handmade chocolate truffles. Also stock; dry store goods, California wines, British cheese, Irish cheese, olive oils etc. Limited Mail Order available. No min. order charge.
Prices/Payment: Handmade chocolate truffles £15 per lb. All major credit cards. Switch, Amex.
Hours: Mon-Fri, 8am-8pm. Sat, 9am-4pm
Notes: Limited disabled access. & Clarke's supply bread, biscuits and truffles to: Jeroboams, Harvey Nichols, Selfridges and Mortimer & Bennett (all London).

C LIDGATE
110 Holland Park Avenue
Holland Park
W11 4UA
Tel: 0171 727 8243
Fax: 0171 229 7160
Contact: David Lidgate

Produce: Organic lamb, beef, pork and poultry (beef and lamb from The Prince of Wales home farm Highgrove when available). Free range also available (grass fed no antibiotics). Home-made pies from above meats and home-made sausages (24 varieties) and hams. Also stock various conserves, sauces and organic cheeses. Available by Mail Order nationally and own van deliveries London; North, NorthWest, Central and West. No min. order.
Prices/Payment: Pies £3 per portion 2-16 portions. All major credit cards except American Express and Diners.
Hours: Mon-Fri, 7am-6pm. Sat, 7am-5pm.
Notes: Disabled access. Tastings constantly available. C. Lidgate do not supply to the trade.

GREENWICH MARKET
SE10
ASH GREEN ORGANIC FOODS
Tel: 01892 838070
Fax: 01892 838070
Contact: Mark Temple/Lesley Howard
Produce: Bramleys, eating apples, pears and plums. Also stock other fresh and dry goods, locally whenever possible and always from certified suppliers. Home delivery service on any of their produce. Min. order £15 though this is flexible.
Prices/Payment: Cash and cheques only.
Hours: Every Sat 10am-5pm. Also at Little Darmon Farm, Paddock Wood (see South East Section).
Notes: Disabled access. Ash Green Organic are interested in supplying fruit and veg on a wholesale basis.

CONDON FISHMONGERS
363 Wandsworth Road
Lambeth
SW8 2JJ
Tel: 0171 622 2934
Contact: Ken Condon
Produce: Condon's own smoked fish.

Also service for smoking fish caught by customers (salmon & trout etc). Hiring of fish kettles. Also stock fresh fish and shellfish.
Prices/Payment: Cash and cheques only.
Hours: Tues, Wed, Fri and Sat, 8.45am-5.30pm. Mon, Thurs, 8.45am-1pm.
Notes: Disabled access, open fronted shop.

O'HAGAN'S SAUSAGE & SOUTH AFRICAN PRODUCTS
192 Trafalgar Road
Greenwich
SE10 9TZ
TEL: 0181 858 2833
FAX: 0181 293 0072
CONTACT: Bill O'Hagan
PRODUCE: Over 40 varieties of fresh sausage including hi fibre pork sausages in 16 varieties, beef and game sausages, Moroccan lamb, lamb & mint, lamb & rosemary, lamb & coriander sausage, 11 flavours of gluten free sausage, 4 flavours of poultry sausage, 4 smoked British sausages, salmon, trout, eel, their own dry cure bacon and hams, poultry and game plus biltong when available. Available by Mail Order. Min order £30 includes p&p.
PRICES/PAYMENT: Please 'phone for price list. All major credit cards taken.
HOURS: Mon-Sat, normal shop hours. Sun 11am-3pm.
NOTES: Disabled access. O'Hagan's have other shops at The Butter Market, North Street, Chichester. Tel: 01243 532833 and Delling Lane, Bosham, Tel: 01243 574833. (See South East Section)

NORTH LONDON

DUGANS CHOCOLATES
149a Upper Street
Islington
N1 1RA
Tel: 0171 354 4666
Contact: Annie Dugan-Webster
Produce: A range of handmade fudges, Belgian chocolate, orangette, vanilla butter, rum & raisin, peanut butter and stem ginger. Also stock organic chocolates, coffee, luxury Belgian chocolates (over 70 varieties), Yesteryear sweets, novelties. International Mail Order on all items.
Prices/Payment: All major credit cards taken. Switch and American Express.
Hours: Mon-Sat, 10.30am-6.30pm. Sun,11am-5pm.
Notes: Can be accessed by the disabled.

ACKERMANS CHOCOLATE LTD
Unit 11
St Pancras Commercial Centre
63 Pratt Street
St Pancras
NW1 0BY
Tel: 0171 267 5375
Fax: 0171 267 5357
Email: 100533 2406@Compuserve.com
Contact: Carolym de la Force
Produce: Handmade chocolate delux. Mail Order available.
Prices/Payment: Amex, Switch, Visa, Mastercard taken.
Hours: 8am-5pm

THE CAKE COMPANY
Basement, 2-4 Sentinel Square
Hendon
NW4 2EL
Tel: 0181 202 2327
Fax: 0181 202 2327
Contact: Karen Barsam
Produce: Kosher cakes, biscuits, patisserie. Novelty cakes, wedding cakes and desserts. Can be delivered

for a charge. No min. order charge.
Prices/Payment: 200g biscuits £1.99.
Cash and cheques only.
Hours: 8am-5pm
Notes: Disabled access. The Cake Co
supply to Tesco, Waitrose, Kosher
King and Moshe. They are interested
in supplying more to the trade.

THE PURE MEAT COMPANY &
B & M SEAFOOD
258 Kentish Town Road
Kentish Town
NW5 2AA
Tel: 0171 485 0346
Fax: 01462 851561
(See Main Entry under Henlow, Beds.)

**The following are SHOPS within this
region which do not produce but do
sell quality or organic foods.**

ALL THINGS NICE
86 Royal Hill
Greenwich
SE10 8RT
Tel: 0181 488 6764
Produce: Fresh organic fruit and
vegetables, daily. A large variety of
pulses, beans, seeds, pastas, teas, fruit
spreads, honey, juices, breads, biscuits,
chilled and frozen products – all
organic. Supplements and beauty
products. Fruit and vegetable box
scheme.
Hours: Tues-Fri, 9.30am-5pm. Sat,
9.30am-5.30pm. Sun, 10am-1pm.
Notes: Disabled access.

BARSTOW & BARR
24 Liverpool Road
Islington
N1 0PU
Tel: 0171 359 4222
Fax: 0171 359 4222
Produce: Fine range of cheeses,
including Isle of Mull. Whey butter
and bread.
Hours: Mon-Fri, 10am-8pm. Sat, 9am-
6pm. Sun, 10am-4pm.

BARSTOW & BARR
32 Earls Court Road
Kensington
W8 6EJ
Tel: 0171 937 8004

THE CHEESE BOARD
26 Royal Hill
Greenwich
SE10 8RT
Tel: 0181 305 0401
Fax: 0181 305 0401
Produce: Over 100 different cheeses.
Also stock breads, butter, home-made
pickles and wine.
Hours: Mon-Sat, 9am-5pm. Thurs,
9am-1pm.

FRANK GODFREY
7 Highbury Park
London N5 1QJ
Tel: 0171 226 2425
Produce: Aberdeen Angus beef.
All meat is Aberdeen Angus. Also
cheaper cuts of the same for stewing
etc. Cawl fat available
Hours: Mon-Fri, 8am-6pm. Sat, 8am-5pm

FRESHLANDS
196 Old Street
London
EC1V 9FR
Tel: 0171 250 1708
Produce: Over 1,000 certified organic
foods in an extensive food hall.
Vegetarian take-away meals are freshly
prepared by their chefs on the premises
Hours: Mon-Fri, 10.30am-6.30pm. Sat,
10.30am-4.30pm.
Notes: No disabled access.
Natural remedy centre, with trained
staff to advise.

THE HIVE HONEY SHOP
93 Northcote Road
Battersea
SW11 6PL
Tel: 0171 924 3638
Produce: Honey from their own hives
from around the area and Surrey. Also

flavoured honeys with nuts or fruits. Honey, sauces, confectionery, mustards and other honey related products.
Hours: Mon-Sat, 10am-6pm.

HAMISH JOHNSTON
48 Northcote Road
Battersea
SW11 1PA
Tel: 0171 738 0741
Produce: Speciality cheeses. Single and Double Gloucester, Llanboidy, Devon Blue etc. Pies from The Harrow. The Toffee Shop fudge. Also stock cordials.
Hours: Mon-Fri, 9.30am-7pm. Sat, 9am-6pm.

KOSHER KING
235 Golders Green Road
Golders Green
NW11
Tel: 0181 455 1429
Fax: 0181 201 8924
Email:kosherking@compuserve.co
Produce: Extensive range of Kosher foods. Grocery, chilled and frozen. Under the supervision of the London Beth Din.
Hours: Sun-Fri, 8am-late.
Notes: Party arrangements catered for.

MORTIMER & BENNETT
33 Turnham Green Terrace
Chiswick
W4 1RG
Tel: 0181 995 4145
Fax: 0181 742 3068
Produce: Fresh salad leaves, wild mushrooms, fresh pasta, olive oils, free range eggs, breads, biscuits and cheeses.
Hours: Mon-Fri, 8.30am-6.30pm. Sat, 8.30am-5.30pm.

PLANET ORGANIC LTD
42 Westbourne Grove
W2 5SH
Tel: 0171 221 7171
Fax: 0171 221 1923
Produce: 5,000 square foot natural food supermarket. All foods you would find in a conventional supermarket except organic wherever possible; no preservatives or additives, no refined sugar or hydrogenated fat. Home delivery.
Hours: Mon-Sat, 9am-8pm. Sun, 11am-5pm.
Notes: Disabled access. Demonstrations, tastings, free nutritional advice, juice bar, community noticeboard.

REALFOOD
14 Clifton Road
Little Venice
W9 1SS
Tel: 0171 266 1162
Contact: Doug Taylor

also at:

Joy
507-511 Finchley Road
Hampstead
NW3 7BB
Tel: 0171 435 7711
Contact: Alistair Cameron

Love,
62-64 Weymouth Street, W1
Tel: 0171 487 LOVE
Contact: Nexhat Dedushi

Love
515 Finchley Road
Hampstead
NW3 7BB
Tel: 0171 794 2121
Contact: Ramon Segad.
Fax: Group 0171 435 7007
Produce: A wide range of food and upscale groceries made with integrity. Over 6,000 lines. Addresses with Love in are Café-Bars. Full grocery and ready meals delivery, extensive Mail Order. Events catering. No min order.
Payment: Please 'phone for price list. All major credit cards. No Diners.
Contact Hours: Mon-Fri, 8am-9pm. Sat, 8am-7pm.
Love at 515 Finchley Road, Tues-Sat, 6pm-11.30pm.
Notes: Disabled access at all locations. Always regular tastings.

MARQUESS MEATS (FARM SHOP)
38 Oldstone Hill
Muckamore
Antrim
BT41 4SB
Tel: 01849 465180
Fax: 01849 465180
Contact: Harry or Jean Marquess
Produce: Meat; (beef cattle raised as
near organically as possible), pork,
lamb, chicken. Some Aberdeen
Angus meat. Potatoes, fresh vegeta-
bles and jam. Also stock goat's milk
and ice cream.
Prices/Payment: Fresh mince £1 per
lb, home-made sausages 80p per lb.
Switch cards accepted.
Hours: Tues-Sat, 9am-6pm. Friday,
9am-8pm.
Notes: Disabled access. Marquess
Meats will be opening a small open
farm in the near future. They are
interested in supplying to the trade if
the price is acceptable for top quality
products.

WOODVIEW FARM SHOP
Woodview House
137 Portadown Road
Armagh
BT61 9HL
Tel: 01762 871329
Contact: George Hutchinson
Produce: Most types of soft fruit,
grown on the farm. Also stock jam.
Prices/Payment: Strawberries from £1
per lb. Cash and cheques only.
Hours: 9am-7pm daily.
Notes: Disabled access. Occasional
tastings. Woodview Farm are
interested in supplying to the trade.

BALLYLAGAN ORGANIC FARM
12 Ballylagan Road
Straid
Ballyclare
BT39 9NF
Tel: 01960 322867
Fax: 01960 322129
Contact: Tom Gilbert

Produce: Organic beef and lamb.
Rare breed pork and bacon. The beef
is Aberdeen Angus. Some seasonal
organic vegetables.
Prices/Payment: Cash and cheques
only.
Hours: Sat, 9.30am-5pm or by
arrangement.
Notes: Disabled access. Rare breed
animals and Shetland pony stud.

THE MOTTE FARM SHOPPE
56 Ballygarvey Road
Ballymena
BT43 7HB
Tel: 01266 650550
Contact: Ruth or Robert Wilson
Produce: PYO soft fruits - strawberries, raspberries, blackcurrants, red
currants, gooseberries and tayberries.
Locally produced potatoes and other
fruit and vegetables. In tea rooms,
home-made soups e.g. carrot and
orange, turnip and bacon, broccoli
and bacon. Quiches and salads,
home baked cakes, buns, tray cakes,
scones and bread. Also stock
preserves and craft items incl metal
craft & concrete garden pots.
Prices/Payment: Cash and cheques
only.
Hours: Mon-Fri, 9am-7pm
Notes: Disabled access. Tea rooms.
Some small farm animals e.g. Soay
sheep and pot bellied pig. Hopefully
expanding to open farm by 2000.

MARTIN JAMISON
30 Graceystown Road
Banbridge
BT32 4DZ
Tel: 018206 62315
Fax: 018206 24962
Contact: Kate Russell or Martin
Jamison
Produce: Organic & traditional food
home-grown and imported. Vegeta-
bles: potatoes, carrots, parsnips,
turnips, cabbage, lettuce, tomatoes
etc. organic dairy products. Organic

fruit: apples, oranges, bananas, kiwis etc. Organic dried foods: porridge oats, muesli, pulses, rice, pasta, figs, dates, raisins. Some veg boxes available. Min order charge £5.
Prices/Payment: Cash and cheques only.
Hours: Thurs, Fri, Sat, 9am-6pm.
Notes: Disabled access. Hands-on experience with animals, play area.

EATWELL FOODS
413 Lisburn Road
Belfast
BT9 7EW
Tel: 01232 664362
Fax: 01232 664362
Contact: James Hunter
Produce: Organic breads - selection of dietary breads made without sugar, eggs, yeast, dairy products. Also wheat-free breads, made from flours such as rice, buckwheat, maize, soya. Vegetarian & vegan savouries, apple pies. Also stock organic cheese, yoghurt, dried fruit, cereals, beans, pulses, juice, teas, health & beauty products. Mail order service and home delivery.
Prices/Payment: From 18p for a fruit scone, 400g gluten & yeast free bread £1.40, 800gram organic wholemeal loaf 99p. All major cards taken and Switch, Amex
Hours: Mon-Sat, 8.30am - 6.00p.m.
Notes: No disabled access. Eatwell Foods are interested in supplying to the trade.

CULDRUM ORGANIC FARM
31A Ballylintagh Road
Aghadowey
Coleraine
BT51 3SP
Tel: 01265 868991
Contact: Brian Wallace
Produce: A wide range of organically grown vegetables. Organic chicken and Aberdeen Angus beef. Also stock a small range of dried organic foods, eg. nuts, pulses, jams, juices etc. Bread. Box scheme available.

No min. order charge.
Prices/Payment: Please 'phone for price list. Cash and cheques only.
Notes: Culrum Organic Farm are interested in supplying to the trade.

MOYALLON FOODS
76 Crowhill Road
CRAIGAVON
BT66 7AT
TEL: 01762 349100
FAX: 01762 349188
CONTACT: Jilly Acheson
PRODUCE: Their own wild boar, fallow, silka & red venison (both farmed and wild), rare breeds beef, lamb & pork, a range of game sausages (e.g. wild boar and bramley apple, venison & redcurrant), dry cured bacon and ham, smoked duck, chicken and pheasant fillet etc. Also pheasant, pigeon, duck and quail. Also stock Irish cheeses, fruit juices, speciality jams, chutneys, oils and mustards, organic muesli, porridge oats, dried fruit, pasta, free range eggs, local bakery goods, herbs & spices etc.
PRICES/PAYMENT: Please 'phone for a price list. Cash and cheques only.
HOURS: Mon-Sat, 9am-5.30pm.
NOTES: Disabled access. Some home delivery. Moyallon Foods supply to the trade.

CHAPMANS FARM FRESH FRUIT AND VEGETABLES
47 Dobbin Road
Portadown
Craigavon
BT62 4EY
Tel: 01762 330222
Fax: 01762 350333
Contact: Mr T. Brian Chapman
Produce: Fresh fruit & vegetables. Also stock; cakes, traybakes, tarts,

jams, chutneys and country butter.
Prices/Payment: Cash and cheques only.
Hours: Mon-Sat, 8am-7.30pm.
Notes: Disabled access. Tastings available. Chapmans Farm is interested in supplying to the trade.

OATLANDS FRUIT FARM
42 Kilwarlin Road
Hillsborough
BT26 6DZ
Tel: 01846 682223
Fax: 01846 682223
Contact: Hilda Law
Produce: June - Aug, all soft fruits. Strawberries, raspberries, red, white & blackcurrants, loganberries, fresh vegetables, peas and beans, tayberries, blackberries, red, yellow, green gooseberries. All year round; jams, frozen fruit, home catering for all occasions. Sept-Nov autumn raspberries. Also stock fresh free range eggs.
Prices/Payment: Cash and cheques only.
Hours: Fruit Season, Mon-Sat, 9am-9pm. All other times orders taken by telephone.
Notes: Disabled access. Tea rooms and farm animals. Home catering for parties etc. All home-made food. No min order. Oatlands Fruit Farm supplies to Palmers M1 Hillsborough, Arcadia, Greenmount Meats, Finaghy Quality Fruit Centre. Oatlands are interested in supplying to the trade.

CAMPHILL HOLYWOOD
8 Shore Road
Holywood
BT18 8HX
Tel: 01232 423203
Contact: Miriam Müller or Brigitta O'Connor
Produce: Soil Assoc. and Demeter standards. Fresh daily baked breads from the bakery. Full range of organic foods, including fresh vegetables, dairy produce and dry goods. Also

sold at market stalls on Sats.
Prices/Payment: Cash and cheques only.
Hours: Shop Tues-Sat, 9am-5.30pm. Coffee Shop Tues-Fri, 9am-4.30pm. Sat, 9am-5pm.
Notes: Disabled access. Coffee shop with an extensive lunch menu, soup, pizzas, quiches etc. Tea and coffee.

THE FARM SHOP
100 Comber Road
Newtownards
BT23 4QS
Tel: 01247 812635
Contact: Maurice Patton
Produce: A full range of fruit and vegetables; also home-made cakes and jam. The farm shop specialises in top quality floury potatoes like British Queen. Also stocks a range of exotic fruit & vegetables.
Prices/Payment: Cash & cheques only.
Hours: Mon-Sat, 9.30am-5.30pm.
Notes: Disabled access. The Farm Shop is interested in supplying to the trade.

GORTNAGARN FRUIT FARM
Gortnagarn House
79 Gortnagarn Road
Omagh
BT79 7SW
Tel: 01662 242851
Fax: 01662 250890
Contact: Carol Johnston
Produce: PYO fruit farm; strawberries, raspberries, blackcurrants, gooseberries, rhubarb. Selection of organic vegetables; broccoli, cauliflower, cabbage, swedes, potatoes. Home-made preserves/home baking.
Prices/Payment: Strawberries £1.20 per lb, PYO Veg mostly 50p. Preserves £1.20 per pot. Cash and cheques only.
Hours: 8am-9pm
Notes: Disabled access. Pony rides and horses. Gortnagarn Fruit Farm supply local hotels with fresh fruit and vegetables

The following are SHOPS within this region which do not produce but do sell quality or organic foods.

ORGANIC AND FINE FOODS N.I.
57 Central Avenue
Bangor
Co Down
BT20 3AU
Tel: 01247 456873/01247 271525
Ext. 242.
Fax: 01247 456873
Produce: Fresh fruit and vegetables, fresh herbs, breads, dairy produce, pasta, rice, dried fruit, nut and seeds, delicatessen goods, flour, preserves, cereals, beverages, tinned goods and eggs. Home delivery in the Greater Belfast Area, Co Down and Co Antrim. Special arrangements for further afield. Min. order charge £5.
Hours: Delivered weekly on Thurs and Fri.

EDINBURGH REGION

KNOWES FARM SHOP
Knowes Farm, by E. Linton
Dunbar
EH42 1XJ
Tel: 01620 860010 shop
01620 860221 office
Fax: 01620 861098
Contact: Hilary Cochran
Produce: Farm grown rarer varieties of potato. "Sun and dung" vegetables - grown without artificial fertilisers and minimum number of sprays. Herbs, herb vinegars, pâtés, soups. Pavlovas, "Hedgerow Harvest" marmalade, jams, jellies, chutneys. Also stock game, Scottish foods: honey, oatcakes, biscuits. Bread baking etc. Mail order considered on an individual basis.
Prices/Payment: Variable, especially seasonal goods. Cash/cheques only, accounts with references.
Hours: 10am-4.30pm – seven days a week.
Notes: Disabled access - ramp. Herb garden, visitors can walk through the farm to the river. The Cochrans supply local farm shops and local hotels and restaurants.

CROMBIES OF EDINBURGH
97/101 Broughton Street
New Town
Edinburgh
EH1 3R2
Tel: 0131 556 7643 admin
0131 557 0111 customer
Fax: 0131 556 3920
Internet: www.crombies.co.uk
Contact: Jonathan Crombie
Produce: Grass fed beef - pure Angus, free range pork, hill lambs, barn chickens, haggis, game, up to 50 varieties of sausage, home cured bacon. All their steaks are hung for a full 3 weeks. Also stock a large selection of deli items and cheese; also pickles and marmalades. Mail

Order boxes catalogue available, please 'phone for details. Free home delivery in Edinburgh for orders over £40, but no min order charge.
Prices/Payment: Mail order haggis as a gift from £10. Visa, Access, Mastercard, Switch and Solo.
Hours: Mon-Thur, 8am-6pm. Fri, 8am-7pm. Sat, 8am-5pm.
Notes: Disabled access. Various tastings throughout the day.
Crombies are interested in supplying sausages to the trade.

MACSWEEN OF EDINBURGH
Dryden Road
Bilston Glen
Loanhead

EDINBURGH

EH20 9LZ
TEL: **0131 440 2555**
FAX: **0131 440 2674**
CONTACT: **Miss Jo Macsween**
PRODUCE: **Handmade traditional haggis. Handmade vegetarian/vegan haggis (approved by the Vegetarian Society). Black pudding, white/mealy pudding, Lorne sausage, fruit pudding. Burns napkins, books, cassette. Available by International Mail Order. Min. order one and a half pounds.**
PRICES/PAYMENT: **£11.30 per 24oz haggis, gift boxed inc. carriage. £1.50 per 12oz black pudding + carriage. Major credit cards taken.**
HOURS: **Mon-Fri, 8.30am-5pm.**
NOTES: **Disabled access. Suppliers to a large number of shops in the U.K; please 'phone for details. Trade enquiries welcome.**

DAMHEAD ORGANICALLY GROWN FOODS

32A Damhead
Old Pentland Road
Lothianburn
Edinburgh
EH10 7EA
Tel: 0131 445 1490
Fax: 0131 445 5848
Email: sgerard@compuserve.com
Contact: Sue Gerard
Produce: Organic vegetables and wholesale and retail organic foods. Nationwide Mail Order Service. Free home delivery service in Edinburgh. Min order £30.
Prices/Payment: All major credit cards taken. Amex. Switch.
Hours: Mon-Sat, 9am-5pm. Sun, 10.30am-4.30pm.
Notes: No disabled access. Damhead Organically Grown Foods supply to Grass Roots (Glasgow), New Leaf,Hendersons Farm Shop and Fresh Fruits (all Edinburgh). They are interested in supplying more to the trade.

GEORGE BOWERS (BUTCHER)

75 Raeburn Place
Stockbridge
Edinburgh
EH1 1JG
Tel: 0131 332 3469
Fax: 0131 624 3469
Contact: Alex Smith
Produce: Wild boar, venison, roe, seika red deer, pheasants, pidgeon, guinea fowl, rabbits, grouse, partridge, mallard duck, barbary duck, 10 varieties of sausages. Smoke house on premises. Home delivery (10 mile radius) over £50 free.
Prices/Payment: Price list available, please 'phone. Cash and cheques only.
Hours: Mon-Fri, 8am-5.30pm. Sat, 8am-5pm.
Notes: No disabled access. George Bowers supply to Skippers Restaurant, Vinters, and Brash Butchers.

GRAMPIAN HIGHLANDS, ABERDEEN AND NORTH EAST COAST

CANDYCRAIG PRODUCTS

Cairnaquheen Cottage, Crathie
Ballater
AB35 5TP
Tel: 01339 742342
Contact: Charles Chamberlain
Produce: Fresh wild mushrooms/fungi (dried). Soft fruit, mange tout. Mail Order available. No min order.
Prices/Payment: Dried Cep, £5 per 28g. Fresh chanterall £5 per lb. Cash and cheques only.
Hours: Always open.
Notes: Supply to A&B Flowers (Ballater), T.D. McDonald (Blairgowrie)

H.M. SHERIDAN

11 Bridge Street

BALLATER

AB35 5QP

TEL. 013397 55718

FAX: 013397 56042

CONTACT: Michael Sheridan/Katrina Farquhar

PRODUCE: Scotch beef, Scotch lamb, pork, poultry, bacon and game. Own make sausages, burgers, pies, pâté, black pudding, haggis, white pudding, coleslaw, Granny Munros dumpling and bread. Also stock pickles, preserves and cheese. Available by Mail Order, next day delivery. No min. order charge. Home delivery throughout area.

PRICES/PAYMENT: Pork sausage, £1.70 per lb, pork and wine sausage £1.75 per lb. Large steak pie, £4.10 each. All major credit cards taken. Switch and Delta.

HOURS: Mon-Sat, 7am- 5.15pm.

NOTES: Disabled access. H.M. Sheridan also supply to Balmoral Estate Shop, Brough Butcher, Buckwells of Southsea. They also supply to the trade.

BALHAGAN CHEESE
Wester Lochagan
Banff
AB45 3BS
Tel: 01261 843244
Fax: 01261 843244
Contact: Pauline M. Mackinnon
Produce: Full fat-semi hard cheese made with pasteurised milk from their own pedigree Jersey herd.
Prices/Payment: Cash and cheques only.
Hours: Please 'phone.
Notes: Balhagan Cheese is available at I McIntosh, Grouse Inn (Cabrach) and Retail Outlet K.D.I. Possible interest in supplying more to the trade, especially over winter.

ISABELLA'S RELISHES
Lower Braiklay
Methlick
Ellon
AB41 7EY
Tel: 01651 806257
Fax: 01651 806232
Email: Isabellasrelishes@btinternet.com
Contact: Alastair Massie
Produce: A range of mustard and tomato relishes and apple jellies, made on an Aberdeenshire farm. All free from artificial colours and additives.
Prices/Payment: £1.40-£1.50 per jar. Cash and cheques only.
Hours: By appointment only.
Notes: Demonstrations and tastings available. Isabella's relishes supply to Chatsworth Farm Shop, Brodie Country Fayre, Loch Fyne Oysters and Hopeton House (Edinburgh). They are interested in supplying more to the trade.

MACBETH'S BUTCHERS
11 Tolbooth Street
Forres
IV36 0PH
Tel: 01309 672254
Fax: 01309 672254
Contact: Susan Gibson

Produce: Traditional breeds of Scottish beef (export status) from their own farms. All beef hung for 2-3 weeks. Full range of pork, lamb and game. Black pudding, haggis and sausages all made in house. Also stock complementary jellies and sauces from Moniack Castle. Mail Order service available; packed in insulated boxes. No min. order. Specially wrapped gift packs to your own specification, discount packs etc.
Prices/Payment: Gift packs from £25-£37.50, Discount packs £65-£240. Beef from £3.00 per lb. All major credit cards taken.
Hours: Mon and Sat, 8am-4pm. Tues, Thurs, Fri, 8am-5pm. Wed, 8am-1pm.
Notes: Disabled access to shop. Macbeth's are interested in supplying to the trade.

DRUMMUIR CASTLE WALLED GARDEN
Estate Office
Drummuir
Keith
AB55 5JF
Tel: 01542 810225/300
Fax: 01542 810383
Email: cilla@lineone.net
Contact: Priscilla Gordon-Duff
Produce: Vegetables, herbs, soft fruits, grown using organic and bio dynamic methods. Box scheme collected from garden.
Prices/Payment: £5 per box of produce. Cash and cheques only.
Hours: Mon-Fri, 10am-4pm.
Notes: Disabled access. Garden.

JOHN & MAGGIE FRASER
Burnorrachie
Bridge of Muchalls
Stonehaven
AB39 3RU
Tel: 01569 730195
Contact: John or Maggie
Produce: Biodynamically grown vegetables and fruit. Pork sometimes

available. Once a week delivery to Stonehaven area. No min order charge.

Prices/Payment: Wholesale carrots, £6 per 15kg, 60p per kg. Potatoes, £6-7 per 25kg, 40p per kg. Cash and cheques only.

Hours: By arrangement, please 'phone for details.

Notes: No disabled access. Farm walk by arrangement. John and Maggie are interested in supplying to the trade.

LEMBAS
Lorieneen, Bridge of Muchalls
Stonehaven
AB39 3RU
Tel: 01569 731746
Fax: 01569 731746
Contact: Paul or Freya van Midden
Produce: Fresh organic and biodynamic fruit and vegetables. Also stock bought-in organic vegetables to offer all year round variety. Available by pick up box scheme to individual choice. No min order. Delivery to regular bulk buyers only.
Prices/Payment: Cash and cheques only.
Hours: Order Wed/Thurs, pick up following Wed. Please 'phone for details.
Notes: Disabled access. Lembas supply to Newton Dee Village Store and Total Organic. Can supply to catering trade, dependent on quantities.

GREATER GLASGOW & CLYDE VALLEY

CARMICHAEL ESTATE FARM MEATS
Discover Carmichael Visitor Centre
Warrenhill Farm
(A73 between Lanark & Biggar)
Carmichael Estate
Biggar
ML12 6PG
Tel: 01899 308169
Fax: 01899 308481

Email: chiefcarm@aol.com
Internet: www.carmichael.co.uk/meats
Contact: Sandra Stewart
Produce: Home farm venison, beef and lamb. Grazed on home farm grass and crops, farm slaughtered. Also supply a range of country produce foods, gifts, kitchen wear. Mail Order available. Min. carriage cost £11.50.
Prices/Payment: All major credit cards accepted.
Hours: 9.30am-5.30pm seven days per week. Closed Christmas and New Years day and Jan 6- March 20.
Notes: Disabled access. Clan Farmhouse licensed restaurant, venison cookery demonstrations, deer park and other attractions. Carmichaels supply Alexander Taylor (Strathaven) and Tinto Hill (Thankerton). Also supply to the trade.

RAMSAY OF CARLUKE LTD
Wellriggs
22 Mount Stewart Street
Carluke
ML8 5ED
Tel: 01555 772277
Fax: 01555 750686
Email:
ramsay@wellriggs.demon.co.uk
Contact: Andrew Ramsay
Produce: International award winning traditional Ayrshire bacon and hams. Award winning cooked meats, sausages and black pudding. In summer months a large range of barbecue products. Mail Order available for a selection of products inc. gift ideas. No min. order.
Prices/Payment: Credit cards taken for Mail Order only.
Hours: Mon-Fri, 8am-4.30pm. Sat, 8am-12.30pm.
Notes: Disabled access. Ramsay supply to Harrods (London), Selfridges (London), Jenners (Edinburgh) and Fergusons (Airdrie). They are interested in supplying more to the trade.

BRADFORDS, BAKERS & CONFECTIONERS
Head Office, 70 Speirsbridge Road
Thornliebank
Glasgow
G46 7SN
Tel: 0141 638 1118
Fax: 0141 620 0035
Contact: Claire Bradford
Produce: Manufacturers and retailing bakers, confectioners and chocolatiers. Scotch pies and all types of pastry products. Wholesalers of bread, small cakes, wedding cakes and specialist patisserie lines. Also stock a range of fine quality coffees and tea. Mail Order for preserves, biscuits and a range of home filler products. No min. order charge.
Prices/Payment: Cash and cheques only
Hours: 8.30am-5.30pm.
Notes: Interested in supplying more to the trade. Bradfords branches at:

245 Sauchiehall Street, Glasgow G2 3EZ
Tel: 0141 332 1008

186 Fenwick Road, Giffnock Glasgow
Tel: 0141 638 9797

10 Torrisdale Street, Glasgow G42 8PZ
Tel: 0141 423 5246

4 Glasgow Road, Eaglesham G76 0JQ
Tel: 01355 302944

17 Fenwick Road, Giffnock, Glasgow G46 6AU
Tel: 0141 633 1815

196 Harvie Avenue, Newton Mearns G77 6LL
Tel: 0141 639 5348

48 Busby Road, Clarkston, Glasgow G46 7XJ
Tel: 0141 638 1411

50 Main Street, Neilston, Glasgow G78 3NJ
Tel: 0141 881 9876

23 Clarence Drive, Hyndland, Glasgow G12 9QN
Tel: 0141 334 7622

40 Calderwood Square, East Kilbride G74 3BQ
Tel: 013552 20164

11 Station Road, Milngavie, Glasgow G62 8PG
Tel: 0141 956 6655

306 Crow Road, Broomhill, Glasgow G11 7HS
Tel: 0141 334 8052

H.J. ERRINGTON & CO
Walston Braehead Farm, Carnwath
Lanark
ML11 8NF
Tel: 01899 810257
Fax: 01899 810257
Contact: H.J. Errington
Produce: Lanark Blue: semi-hard blue cheese made from raw milk supplied by their own flock of 400 dairy ewes. Traditional regional cheese recipe. Suitable for vegetarians. Dunsyre Blue: semi-hard blue, raw cows' milk supplied daily by Strathbogie Farm (a neighbouring farm), traditional recipe, vegetarian. Available by Mail Order outside of hot summer months. No min. order charge.
Prices/Payment: Approx £10 per kg for Lanark Blue; £8 per kg for Dunsyre. Cash and cheques only.
Hours: 7am-4pm weekdays, 7am-12pm weekends.
Notes: No disabled access. H.J. Errington & Co supply to Mellis (Edinburgh & Glasgow), Paxton & Whitfield (London, Birmingham, Bath and Stratford), House of Bruar (Blair Atholl) and Williams of Wem (Salop). They are willing to mail cheeses to restaurants and hotels.

OTTER FERRY SALMON LTD
Otter Ferry
Tighnabruaich
PA21 2DH
Tel: 01700 821226
Fax: 01700 821244
Email:
106271.2520@compuserve.com

Internet: www.otterferry.co.uk
Contact: Alice Russell
Produce: Hickory smoked salmon, smoke roasted salmon, smoked shellfish, pâtés. Also stock Moniack sauces and preserves, Walker's shortbread and oatcakes. Mail Order service, deliveries throughout U.K. and Europe. No min. order charge.
Prices/Payment: £11.97 for 250g pack of smoked salmon inc. gift box and delivery. Gift vouchers available from £12.50-£25.00. All major credit cards, Switch and Delta.
Hours: Summer months, 10am-4.30pm. Winter – by arrangement.
Notes: Suppliers to the trade.

THE HIGHLANDS AND SKYE

MOIDART SMOKE HOUSE
Dalnabreac Moidart
Acharacle
PH36 4JX
Tel. 01967 431211
Fax: 01967 431214
Contact: James Gillies
Produce: Traditionally oak or peat (your choice) smoked salmon, salmon pâté, trout, chicken; also haddock and kippers when herring is available. Smoked mussels and oysters. Smoked cheese; cream cheese with toasted oatmeal, smoked Dunlop cheese with chives, with paprika, with mixed herbs, with garlic & ginger or with cumin. Mail Order available. No min. order.
Prices/Payment: Unsliced side smoked salmon, £15.60 per kg sliced £16.50 per kg, smoked chicken £4.50 per kg, cheeses £1.15per pkt. Cash and cheques only.
Hours: 9am-6pm every day all year round. Mail order accepted anytime.
Notes: Disabled access. The Smoke House is situated on a croft overlooking Loch Shiel. The Moidart Smoke House already supply to some hotels and are interested in supplying more to the trade.

LETTERFINLAY SPECIALIST FOODS
Units 1+2, Annat Industrial Estate
Corpach
Fort William
PH33 7JW
Tel: 01397 772957
Fax: 01397 772181
Contact: Hazel or Roy
Produce: Fresh and traditionally smoked venison, salmon, trout, trout caviar, ham, beef and lamb. Hot smoked duck and turkey breast. Buckie kippers. Handmade Scottish cheeses, Caithness, smoked Caithness, Dunsyre Blue, Lochaber smoked, Highland Crowdie, Mull of Kintyre, Gruth Dhu, Isle of Mull, Isle of Gigha, Isle of Arran flavoured cheddar, handmade oatcakes, herb biscuits, jellies and preserves and chocolates. Letterfinlay selection boxes avail able, or combine your own selec tion. Mail Order available, 'phone for price list and order form.
Prices/Payment: Pack of two filleted trout £7.00. Selection boxes from £12-£50. Major credit cards taken, cash and cheques.
Hours: Mon-Fri 10am-4pm.
Notes: No disabled access. Letterfinlay supply to the trade.

GOLSPIE MILL
Golspie
KW10 6RA
Tel: 01408 633278
Contact: Fergus Morrison
Produce: Organic 100% wholemeal bread flour, Soil Assoc. symbol no P1651). Conventional oatmeal, unique beremeal and peasemeal all stoneground using water power. Sales direct by arrangement.
Prices/Payment: Cash and cheques only
Hours: Please 'phone first
Notes: Golspie Mill supply to Highland Wholefoods, Green City Wholefoods, Ryans Wholefoods and Sutherland Brothers (Scotland).

KYLE OF TONGUE OYSTERS
236 Achnahuaigh, Talmine
Lairg
IV27 4YT
Tel: 01847 601271
Fax: 01847 601371
Contact: Angela & Tom Mackay
Produce: Grade A oysters. Home delivery available.
Prices/Payment: Cash and cheques only
Hours: All hours.
Notes: No disabled access. Demonstrations and tastings, site visit. Kyle of Tongue Oysters supply direct to top hotels and restaurants all over UK

MACDONALD'S SMOKED PRODUCE
Glenuig
Lochailort
PH38 4NG
Tel: 01687 470266 **Fax:** 01687 470311
Contact: Simon Macdonald
Produce: Smoked foods including international award winning "Lochaber Smoked Cheese", award winning smoked salmon, smoked trout, smoked shellfish, smoked alligator, smoked ostrich and smoked duck. Mail Order service world-wide. No min. order
Prices/Payment: Smoked salmon, trimmed whole sides or packs unsliced, £9.85 per lb. Smoked duck breast, £10.50 per lb. Lochaber smoked cheese £1.75 per 4oz pack. Visa, Mastercard and Eurocard taken.
Hours: Mon-Sat, 9am-5pm. Mail Order service operates out of hours.
Notes: Disabled access. Macdonald's supply to Jenners (Edinburgh), Peter McLennan (Fort William) and The Cheese Shop (Glasgow). Also suppliers to top hotels, restaurants and airlines.

CAITHNESS CHEESE
Moorings, Occumster
Lybster
KW3 6AX
Tel: 01593 721309
Fax: 01593 721309
Contact: Sandy or Sandra Sutherland
Produce: A creamy semi-hard waxed cheese from their own herd of Friesian cows produced entirely on the farm. Flavours include plain, smoked, garlic, mustard, chives, caraway and black pepper. Also produced in their own smokehouse a unique quality of smoked salmon in a variety of pack sizes. Mail Order available. No min order charge. Local deliveries.
Prices/Payment: Cheese approx £2.20 to £2.50 for 225g truckle. Cash and cheques only.
Hours: 9.30am-8.30pm everyday.
Notes: Disabled access. Tastings available. Caithness Cheese supply; Gourmets Lair (Inverness), House of Bruar (Bruar), Baxters of Fochabers and Falls of Shin Visitor Centre. They also supply the catering trade

LETTERFINLAY SPECIALIST FOODS
The Boat House, Letterfinlay
SPEAN BRIDGE
TEL: 01397 772957
FAX: 01397 772181
CONTACT: Hazel or Roy
PRODUCE: Fresh and traditionally smoked venison, salmon, trout, trout caviar, ham, beef and lamb. Hot smoked duck and turkey breast. Buckie kippers. Handmade Scottish cheeses, Caithness, smoked Caithness, Dunsyre Blue, Lochaber smoked, Highland Crowdie, Mull of Kintyre, Gruth Dhu, Isle of Mull, Isle of Gigha, Isle of Arran flavoured cheddar, hand made oatcakes, herb biscuits, jellies and preserves and chocolates. Letterfinlay selection boxes available, or combine your own selection. Mail Order available, 'phone for price list and order form.
PRICES/PAYMENT: Pack of two filleted trout £7.00. Selection boxes from £12-£50. Major credit cards taken, cash and cheques.
HOURS: Mon-Fri 10am-4pm.
NOTES: No disabled access. Letterfinlay supply to the trade.

WEST HIGHLAND DAIRY

Achmore
Strome Ferry
By Kyle of Lochalsh
IV53 8UW
Tel: 01599 577203
Fax: 01599 577203
Contact: David Biss
Produce: Hard cheese, soft cheese, blue cheese, yogurt, ice cream. Made from their own sheep's milk, also from cow's and goat's milk bought in. Also stocks honey, oatcakes, shortbread and local pickles. Mail Order service according to requirements, no minimum order.
Prices/Payment: Visa
Hours: Dawn till dusk, all year.
Notes: The dairy runs cheese courses, has a picnic area and allows you to view a succesful small holding; help available for the disabled. Suppliers to The Healthy Deli (Dingwall) and to local shops & hotels.

HIGHLAND FINE CHEESES LTD & HIGHLAND FINE CELTIC FOODS

Knockbreck
Tain
IV19 1LZ
Tel: 01862 892034 & 892035
Fax: 01862 892489
Contact: Miss Susannah Stone
Produce: The original fresh soft cheeses of the Highlands & Islands of Scotland. Original methods and recipes used, with modern hygiene. Also stock handmade herb biscuits for eating with Scottish cheese. Six different sorts of herbs in packs of eighteen biscuits, and eighteen packs to the box. Available by Mail Order, retail and wholesale. No min. order charge.
Prices/Payment: Credit cards accepted.
Hours: 9.30am-4.30pm.
Notes: Disabled access. Free demonstrations and tastings. Suppliers to delicatessens and supermarkets in many Scottish towns, and are interested in supplying to the trade.

SUMMER ISLES FOODS LTD

The Smokehouse
Achiltibuie
Ullapool
IV26 2YR
Tel: 01854 622353
Fax: 01854 622335
Email: sifsalmo@globalnet.uk
Contact: Keith Dunbar
Produce: Smoked salmon, kippers, smoked fish, smoked game, poultry and meat. Also stock shortbreads, preserves and herring products. Mail Order service available. No min. order charge.
Prices/Payment: Smoked salmon, traditional sweet cure, £23 per 2lb pack. Smoked chicken, whole bird (approx 1.25kg) £17.50. All major credit cards taken. Switch.
Hours: Mon-Sat, 9.30am-5pm from Easter to October.
Notes: No disabled access. Viewing windows for visitors to watch processing.
Summer Isles Foods supply to Harrods, Selfridges (London), Peckham & Ryo (Glasgow and Edinburgh) and Margiotta Stores (Edinburgh). They are interested in supplying more to the trade.

OUTER ISLANDS

CHARLES MACLEOD

Ropework Park, Matheson Road
Stornoway
Isle of Lewis
HS1 2LB
Tel: 01851 702445
Fax: 01851 704445
Contact: Iain Macleod
Produce: Traditional Stornoway black pudding. Also stock a full range of meats. Available by Mail Order, telephone for details. No min. order.
Prices/Payment: Prices available on request. All major credit cards. Switch and Amex.
Hours: Mon-Sat, 8am-6pm
Notes: Disabled access. Macleods are interested in selling to the trade.

MERMAID FISH SUPPLIES
Clachan, Lochmaddy
North Uist
HS6 5HD
Tel: 01876 580209
Fax: 01876 580323
Email: mermaid.fish@zetnet.co.uk
Contact: George or Rosemary
Jackson
Produce: Peat smoked salmon is their speciality. It is a real taste of the Hebrides and is supplied by mail order throughout the UK and to many countries world-wide. Also other smoked fish, whitefish and shellfish are produced and sold locally, along with home grown fruit and vegetables in season.
Prices/Payment: All major cards taken. Switch. Delta.
Hours: Mon-Sat, 9am-6pm. Saturday, 9am-6pm (later by appointment)
Notes: They are always happy to explain and demonstrate the smoking process. Visitor are welcome.

ARGO'S BAKERY
50 Victoria Street, Stromness
Orkney
KW16 3BS
Tel: 01856 850245
Fax: 01856 851264
Email: george.argo@virgin.net
Contact: Grace Argo
Produce: Organic wholemeal bread, large range of handmade biscuits and Orkney farmhouse cheese. Also stock general groceries.
Prices/Payment: All major credit cards. Switch.
Hours: Mon-Sat, 7.30am-8pm.
Notes: Disabled access. Also supply to most shops in Orkney.

WHEEMS
Eastside, South Ronaldsay
Orkney
KW17 2TJ
Tel: 01856 831537
Contact: Michael Roberts (veg)
Christina Sargent (cheese)
Produce: Traditional and oriental vegetables; winter potatoes, roots, brassicas, summer salad, leaf veg, herbs, etc. all certified with Scottish Organic Producers Assoc. Organic, unpasteurised, semi-mature, cheese produced from Jersey cow's milk. Also supply organic wholefood products and organic fruit. Box scheme available, weekly Aug-Dec, fortnightly Jan-July. No min order charge. Delivered.
Prices/Payment: Vegetable prices compare well with local supermarkets. Cheese £6.60 per kg. Monthly payment for veg boxes. Cash and cheques only.
Hours: 9am-10am, 6pm-7pm.
Notes: No disabled access. Wheems also run a hostel for visitors to the island. Wheems wish to concentrate on local production and consumption but may consider supplying to trade.

WILLIAM JOLLY
Scott's Road, Hatston
Kirkwall
Orkney
KW15 1GR
Tel: 01856 873317/872417
Fax: 01856 874960
Contact: Karin Brown
Produce: Traditional oak smoked kippers, smoked salmon, "Hot Cure" smoked haddock and smoked mackerel. Fresh and frozen shellfish, e.g. crabs, scallops, prawns, mussels etc. Christmas hampers a speciality. Also stock Orkney cheddar cheese and farmhouse cheese. A selection of handmade biscuits, groceries etc. and Orkney ice cream. Mail Order available, catalogue out in Dec. and runs all year. No min. order.
Prices/Payment: Pre-sliced side smoked salmon, 700g – £21.85. Luxury selection box £33.10. All major credit cards taken. Switch.
Hours: Mon-Fri, 7am-5pm. Sat, 7am-1pm.
Notes: Disabled access. William Jolly supply to W. Lobban & Son and Cumming & Spence. They are interested in supplying more to trade.

SALAR LTD
The Pier
Lochcarnan
SOUTH UIST
HS8 5PD
TEL: 01870 610324
FAX: 01870 610369
CONTACT: Jane Twelves/Fiona
MacDonald
PRODUCE: Salar inform us that their
flaky smoked salmon is so ex-
tremely tasty and utterly delicious
it is simply irresistible! Winner of
the Great Taste Award Gold Medal
for smoked salmon 1998. Mail
Order available. No min. order
charge.
PRICES/PAYMENT: From £9.99 to
£22.95. Cheque with order. No
credit cards.
HOURS: Mon-Fri, 9am-5pm.
NOTES: Disabled access. Seasonal
tastings. Salar supply Jenners
(Edinburgh), Taste of Moray (Inver
ness), Ramus Seafoods (Harrogate)
and Ramsbottom Victuallers (Bury)
Salar are interested in supplying to
the trade.

PERTHSHIRE, ANGUS & DUNDEE AND FIFE

TOMBUIE SMOKEHOUSE
Aberfeldy
PH15 2JS
Tel: 01887 820127
Fax: 01887 829625
Contact: Mrs Sally Crystal
Produce: Smoked gourmet products;
bacon, lamb, venison, chicken, pork,
quail and salmon. Also smoked
cheeses; white cheddar, red cheddar
and three soft cheeses. Also stock ice
cream by Cream of Galloway (not
suitable for Mail Order). Mail Order
available. Please send for price list.

No min. order charge.
Prices/Payment: All major credit cards
Hours: Shop (in summer): Mon, Tues,
Thurs, Fri, 10am-5pm. Wed, 10am-
1pm. Sat 9am-5pm. Sun, 10am-
4pm. Shop closed Jan, Feb.
Notes: No disabled access. Tombuie
Smokehouse also supply to The
Scottish Deer Centre, Cupar (Fife) and
The Scottish Wool Centre, Aberfoyle
(Stirling). Trade enquiries welcome.

**R.R. SPINK & SONS
(ARBROATH) LTD**
33-35 Seagate
Arbroath
DD11 1BJ
Tel: 01241 872023
Fax: 01241 875663
Contact: Bob Spink
Produce: Arbroath smokies & trout
(local speciality hot-smoked haddock
and trout, smoked traditionally over
an open hardwood fire). No addi-
tives other than salt. The method used
is wholly 'accountable' under the
new food hygiene legislation.
Smoked salmon (special cure using
Drambuie Liqueur). Mail Order
available. No min. order charge.
Prices/Payment: Scottish smoked
salmon, £19 per whole side
(unsliced). Cash and cheques only.
Hours: Mail Order only.
Notes: R.R. Spink & Sons supply to
Tesco, Waitrose, Loch Fyne Oysters
and many others. Interested in
supplying to hotels and restaurants.

SCOTT'S FISH
5 Seagate
Arbroath
DD11 1BJ
Tel: 01241 872331
Contact: Ramsay Scott
Produce: Hand filletted haddock,
lemon sole, salmon, trout, genuine
Arbroath smokies, smoked haddock.
Seasonal herring, crabs, lobsters. Also
stock kippers, boneless kippers,
smoked mackerel and peppered
mackerel.

Prices/Payment: Cash and cheques only.
Hours: Mon-Fri, 8am-5pm. Sat, 9am-4pm. Sun, 12pm-4pm.
Notes: No disabled access. Viewings of filleting and smoking available.

DAVID RENDALL & SON
Stiellsmuir Fruit Farm
Woodlands Road, Rosemount
Blairgowrie
PH10 6LE
Tel: 01250 872237
Fax: 01250 872237
Email: stiellsmuir@compuserve.com
Contact: Mr David Rendall
Produce: Raspberries, strawberries, blackcurrants, brambles (black berries). Also processed gooseberries, redcurrants, blueberries, cranberries, apples, summer harvest fruit salad.
Prices/Payment: Please 'phone for price list.
Hours: All
Notes: Available through wholesale outlets to the hotel/catering industry.

MESSRS GEORGE McLAREN
Bankhead of Kinloch, Meigle
Blairgowrie
PH12 8QY
Tel: 01828 640265
Fax: 01828 640687
Contact: George McLaren
Produce: PYO strawberries, raspberries, blackcurrants, redcurrants and gooseberries.
Prices/Payment: Cash and cheques only.
Hours: For July and early August every day 9am-5pm.
Notes: No disabled access. Picnic area available.

FISHER AND DONALDSON
21-23 Crossgate
Cupar
KY15 5HA
Tel: 01334 652551
Fax: 01334 653729
Contact: Mr Milne

Produce: Premier handmade traditional and continental bakery and confectionery. Bread rolls, cakes, pastries, biscuits, confectionery and chocolates, all made on the premises.
Prices/Payment: 16p per roll to £1.50 speciality breads. Cakes 50p - £20. Cash and cheques + Visa.
Hours: 6.30am-5.15pm.
Notes: Disabled access inclusive of disabled toilets. Waitress service cafe at rear of shop. Fisher and Donaldson also supply to their two other shops in St. Andrews and Dundee. Also to G.H. MacArthur & Son (St Andrews) and to restaurants and hotels locally.

FLETCHERS OF AUCHTERMUCHTY
Reediehill Farm, Auchtermuchty
Cupar
KY14 7HS
Tel: 01337 828369
Email: fletchers.scotland@virgin.net
Contact: Nichola Fletcher
Produce: Free range venison produced and field-shot on the farm. Hung for 2-3 weeks for greater flavour. Huge range of venison cuts from osso buco to fillet steak. Joints on the bone, braising cuts etc. Home made additive free products, eg. sausages, smoked venison, wee pies, olives, carpaccio, etc. Available by Mail Order. Vacuum packed and despatched by overnight courier for delivery before noon next day. No min. order, carriage free for orders over £95. Please 'phone for brochure.
Prices/Payment: All major credit cards. Switch. Not Diners or American Express.
Hours: 9am-7pm seven days a week. Other times by arrangement. Closed Dec 25th and Jan 1st.
Notes: Disabled access limited. Manager will bring selection out for disabled customers. Fletchers supply to The House of Bruar (Blair Atholl), The Butterchurn (Kelty), Scotland's Larder (Upper Largo) and Lowes Country Store (Edinburgh).

SCOTHERBS

Kingswell
Castle Huntley Road
Longforgan
Dundee
DD2 5HJ
Tel: 01382 360642
Fax: 01382 360637
Contact: Mr Robert Wilson
Produce: Fresh culinary herbs. A wide selection available all year, including purple basil, rockette, lemon grass, savoury tarragon, coriander etc. Seasonal herbs include angelica, lemon balm, sweet cicely and lovage. Also available, seasonal flowers; borage, cowslips, heartsease, marigold, nasturtiums, sweet violet and chives. Available by Mail Order. Min. Order 3 x 50 gram bags.
Prices/Payment: £1.50 each for up to ten 50g bags. £1.40 for ten or more 50g bags. Cash and cheques only.
Hours: By Mail Order only.
Notes: Scotherbs supply major supermarkets in Scotland and Valona & Crolla (Edinburgh), Henderson Farm Shop (Edinburgh), Herbie's Deli (Edinburgh) and many hotels and restaurants.

DUNKELD SMOKED SALMON LTD

Springwells Smokehouse
Brae Street
Dunkeld
PH8 0BA
Tel: 01350 727639
Fax: 01350 728760
Email: dunkeldwildsam@zetnet.co.uk
Contact: Sandra Stewart
Produce: Smoked Scottish salmon, particularly wild. Hand sliced sides, wholesides, finely sliced packs. Smoked salmon pâté, smoked wild venison, smoked chicken breast. Christmas gifts, Scottish butcher pack, larder service. All available by Mail Order. U.K. deliveries up to 700g by First Class Mail, or for £3 Guaranteed next day delivery. Orders over 700 g guaranteed next day delivery. No min. order charge.

Prices/Payment: All major credit cards. Switch.
Hours: 8am-6pm
Notes: No constructed disabled access. Dunkeld Smoked Salmon supply Robert Menzies (Dunkeld), Hello Deli (Giffnock), The Delicatessen (Comrie). They are interested in supplying more to the trade

CAIRN O' MOHR WINERY

East Inchmichael
Errol
Perth
Tel: 01358 742507
Fax: 01358 742507
Email emmowatt@dircon.co.uk
Contact: Raymond Mowatt
Produce: Scottish country wines made from fruits, flowers and leaves grown both wild and on the farm, used in original recipes using mainly Scottish produce. Also stock Grozit Beer - made from gooseberries, Heather Ale - made from heather and Alba Pine - ale made from pine needles. Available by Mail Order. Min. order; case of 12 bottles.
Prices/Payment: Still wines £4.99 per bottle. Oak & Elder sparkling wines £6.50 per bottle. Braes of Gaurnie non-alcoholic wine £2.50. Cash and cheques only.
Hours: 10am-5pm.
Notes: No disabled access yet. Tastings of all wines available. Cairn O' Mohr supply to; Gourmets Lair (Inverness), Kelly of Cults (Aberdeen), Real Foods (Edinburgh), Ellerys (Perth) and Garrison Crafts.

ORGANIC MEAT PRODUCTS LTD

Jamesfield Farm
Abernethy
Perth
KY14 6EW
Tel: 01738 850498
Fax: 01738 850741
Contact: Mr Miller
Produce: Organic beef, lamb, mutton, sausages, turkeys, free range pork, chicken, haggis, wild venison,

salmon, sea trout. Organic vegetables and wholefoods. Mail Order available on organic meat, free range and wild meat. No min. order.
Prices/Payment: Mastercard and Visa taken.
Hours: 10am-5pm
Notes: Disabled access if notified in advance.

SOUTH OF SCOTLAND

GALLOWAY GOATSMILK GEMS
Bogue Farm
St. Johns Town of Dalry
CASTLE DOUGLAS
DG7 3XF
TEL: **01644 430257**
CONTACT: **Mrs S Little**
PRODUCE: **Goat's milk products, including pressed cheeses; White Diamond, Smokey Quartz, Emerald, Ruby & Sapphire. Soft cheeses; Opal Peridot Cairngorm, Jet & Cintrine & Pearls. Yoghurt, ice cream, raw & pasteurised milk. Mail Order available for pressed cheeses. Min. order 1kg.**
PRICES/PAYMENT: **Cash, cheques only.**
Hours: **Most days (not Wed pm); 'phone first.**
NOTES: **Galloway Goatsmilk Gems also supply Sunrise (Castle Douglas), The Galloway Smoke House (Newton Stewart), Glenkens Cafe (Castle Douglas) and local hotels and restaurants.
Also throughout Scotland through a local wholesaler.**

CREAM O' GALLOWAY
Rainton
Gatehouse-of-Fleet
Castle Douglas
DG7 2DR
Tel: 01557 814040
Fax: 01557 814040

Email: wilma@creamogalloway.prestel.uk.co
Contact: Wilma Dunbar
Produce: Premium and Super Premium Ice Cream and frozen yogurt, using wholemilk from their Farm Assured herd of Ayrshire cows. Free range eggs, sugar, dried skimmed milk and double cream, plus real food flavours (eg. strawberries, raspberries, bananas, fudge cake etc.), specifically free from chemical additives or gums. Also stock Scottish fruit wines and Scottish Ales.
Prices/Payment: Ice cream £2.70-£3 per half litre. Cash and cheques only.
Hours: April-Oct, 11am-6pm daily.
Notes: Disabled access to shop only. Nature trails, adventure playground, tea shop, tasting, viewing gallery. Cream O'Galloway supply to selected Safeway stores in Scotland and far North of England, selected Tesco stores in Scotland and Peckhams in Glasgow & Edinburgh. They also supply independent hotels and restaurants.

LOCH ARTHUR CREAMERY
Camphill Village Trust
Beeswing
Dumfries
DG2 8JQ
Tel: 01387 760296
Fax: 01387 760296
Contact: Barry Graham
Produce: Organic dairy produce, traditional farmhouse cheddar, cloth bound cheddar produced in 18-20 lb rounds. Crannog, a full fat soft cheese - mild but full flavoured. Produced in 8oz rounds. Criffel, a semi-soft, rind washed cheese with a creamy texture in rounds of approx 3 lb. Fresh curd cheese in 1lb or 4lb containers. Natural live yoghurt. Also stock gift items and pottery and other organic foods. Mail Order available. No min. order charge.
Prices/Payment: Loch Arthur Farmhouse Cheese, £8 per kg. Soft & semi-soft cheeses £9.30 per kg. Cash and cheques only.

Hours: Mon-Fri, 9am-12pm and 2pm-5.30pm.
Notes: Disabled access.
Cheesemaking can be viewed whilst buying. Loch Arthur supply to Iain Mellis Cheesemongers (Edinburgh and Glasgow), Dam Head Farm Shop (Edinburgh), Neals Yard Dairy (London). They are interested in supplying any surplus to the trade.

FLOORS CASTLE KITCHENS
Kelso
TD5 7SF
Tel: 01573 223333
Fax: 01573 226056
Contact: Philip Massey
Produce: A wide range of preserves, pies, cakes, soups, mayonnaises, Christmas cakes, mince pies, shortbread & biscuits. Also stock speciality foods, condiments and ingredients.
Prices/Payment: All major credit cards. Visa, Mastercard, Amex, Switch.
Hours: 10am-4.30pm year round.
Notes: Disabled access. Castle tour, gift shop & self-service restaurant.

THE TEVIOT GAME FARE SMOKERY LTD
Kirkbank House
Kelso
TD5 8LE
Tel: 01835 850253
Fax: 01835 850293
Contact: Keith Rothwell
Produce: Smoked eel from the River Tweed, smoked wild pheasant shot locally. Smoked salmon and trout, also smoked wild salmon for Tweed anglers. All smoked in the traditional way. Also stock chutney and sauces. Honey and shortbread etc. Mail Order service country wide by next day delivery. Also special Mail Order selections for Christmas and Easter. No min. order.
Prices/Payment: Smoked trout pâté £2.25 per quarter pound pot, Smoked Tweed eel (whole) £8.35 per lb. All major credit cards and Switch.

Hours: 10am-5pm every day Apr-Sept. 10am-4.30pm except Sunday Oct-Mar.
Notes: Disabled access. Teviot Watergardens are nearby. Teviot Game Fare supply J.R.Mitchell & Son.

DUNLOP DAIRY
West Clerkland Farm, Stewarton
Kilmarnock
KA3 5LP
Tel: 01560 482494
Contact: Ann Dorward
Produce: Hard cheeses made from goat's, sheep's and cow's milk. Traditional Dunlop cheese made with Ayrshire cow's milk.
Prices/Payment: Cash and cheques only.
Hours: Dawn till dusk.
Notes: Disabled access. Dunlop Dairy also supply Iain Mellis, Cheesemonger.

FENCEBAY FISHERIES
Fencefoot, Fairlie
Largs
KA29 0EG
Tel: 01475 568918
Fax: 01475 568921
Email: fencebay@aol.com
Contact: Bernard Thain
Produce: Smoked salmon, kippers, pâtés, smoked trout and smoked haddock. Range of herring marinades. Fruits de mer. Smoked venison, duck and chicken. Homemade ice creams. Also stock chutneys, jams, soups, honey and oils. Mail Order service available. No min. order.
Prices/Payment: All major credit cards. Amex and Switch.
Hours: Mon-Sat, 8.30am-5.30pm. Closed Sun.
Notes: Disabled access and disabled toilet. Seafood restaurant, cookshop and local crafts. Fencebay Fisheries supply to Murchies, Mis en Plas, Cairns and Barratts of Cookridge. They are interested in supplying more to the trade.

E. BLACKLOCK (MOFFAT) LTD
Moffat Toffee Shop
High Street
Moffat
DG10 9DL
Tel: 01683 220032
Fax: 01683 221650
Contact: J. Blair Blacklock
Produce: Moffat Toffee with no artificial colourings or flavours used. Tablet, walnut, ginger, vanilla. Fudge and truffles in numerous flavours. Also stock probably the largest selection of sweets in Scotland, with over 200 jars of loose sweets.
Prices/Payment: Large tins of Moffat Toffee, £3.50, small tins £2.20. Barclaycard, Bank of Scotland, Visa.
Hours: 9am-6pm seven days a week.
Notes: No disabled access. Tastings. Moffat's Toffee Shop supply to Allsorts Toffee Shop (Castle Douglas), Rock Shop (Lanark), House of Bruar (Perthshire) and Sweet Shop (Peebles).

GALLOWAY SMOKEHOUSE
Carsluith
Newton Stewart
DG8 7DN
Tel: 01671 820334
Fax: 01671 820545
Contact: A.E. Watson
Produce: Smoked fish, game, poultry, dairy products and meat. Fresh fish, game, shellfish. Also stock a full range of local jams, honey, pickles etc. Write or 'phone for Mail Order service.
Prices/Payment: Cash, cheques, Access, Mastercard etc.
Hours: 9am-5.30pm every day.
Notes: No disabled access. Tastings are held on a regular basis.

COLFIN SMOKEHOUSE
Port Patrick
Stranraer
DG9 9BN
Tel: 01776 820622
Fax: 01776 820622
Contact: Scott Baillie
Produce: Smoked salmon, trout, kippers, mackerel, cheeses etc. All brined in spring water and smoked over oak shavings from old whisky & sherry casks. Also stock home-made jams and marmalades. Scottish ales made to old recipes. Local honey. Mail Order service operates all year; also local delivery service. No min. order.
Prices/Payment: Packs of smoked salmon from £2.80. All major credit cards taken plus Switch, Delta.
Hours: Mon-Sat, 9am-5pm. Sun, 10am-3pm. 1st Jan-31st Mar: Sun, 10am-12pm.
Notes: Disabled access. Demonstrations on how the salmon are smoked. Colfin Smokehouse are interested in supplying to the trade.

WEST HIGHLANDS & ISLANDS, LOCH LOMOND AND TROSSACHS

SCOTTISH MILK PRODUCTS LTD
Witchburn Road
Campbeltown
PA28 6JU
Tel: 01586 552244
Fax: 01586 554330
Contact: Angela McMillan
Produce: Cheeses; Highland extra mature, available in 2.5kg pre-packs and presentation packs. Mull of Kintyre Truckle (black waxed) and Mull of Kintyre white mature prepacked. Also stock white and coloured, mild & mature cheese packed under the Scottish Pride label. Mail Order available at £5.50 including postage & packing.
Prices/Payment: Truckles 567g – £3.90, 380g – £2.70, 250g – £2.21. Cash and cheques only.
Hours: Mon-Thur, 9am-5pm; Fri, 9am-4pm. Closed Sat and Sun.
Notes: No disabled access. Scottish Milk Products supply to H. McIlchere & Son (Campbeltown), Tesco, Sainsbury and Harrods.

BLACK OF DUNOON (BAKERS) LTD
113 George Street
Dunoon
PA23 8BS
Tel: 01369 702311
Fax: 01369 703778
Contact: Mr Charles D.C. Black
Produce: Traditional Scottish and continental bakers and confectioners. Scottish shortbread and oatcakes. Traditional and modern wedding cakes, novelty cakes etc. Rolls, buns, pies, scones. Large and small loaves etc
Prices/Payment: Retail prices displayed in shops - wholesale prices on request.
Hours: Mon-Sat, 7.30am-6pm. Tearoom closes at 5pm.
Notes: Disabled access. Argyll Street shop has a coffee shop. Black of Dunoon supply other shops over a sixty mile radius. Also suppliers to local hotels etc.

ISLE OF COLONSAY, APIARIES AND OYSTERS
Poll Gorm
Isle of Colonsay
PA61 7YR
Tel: 01951 200365
Fax: 01951 200365
Email: pollgorm@compuserve.com
Internet: www.colonsay.org.uk
Contact: Andrew Abrahams
Produce: Wildflower honey. A very rare honey of extremely high quality. Oysters. Pacific oysters grown in Grade A unpolluted waters. Mail Order on both honey and oysters. Min order 5 doz oysters.
Prices/Payment: Cash and cheques only
Hours: Not open to the public.
Notes: Isle of Colonsay Apiaries and Oysters are interested in supplying to the trade.

THE ISLAND BAKERY
Main Street
Tobermory
Isle of Mull
PA75 6PY
Tel: 01688 302223
Fax: 01688 302478
Email: islandbakery@mull.com
Contact: Joseph/Dawn Reade
Produce: Freshly baked handmade breads. Confectionery and bakery goods. Also stock deli goods, British Farmhouse cheeses, wines and whiskies, meats and charcuterie.
Prices/Payment: All major cards taken.
Hours: 9am-9pm.
Notes: Disabled access. Regular tastings.

ISLE OF MULL CHEESE
Sgriob Ruadh Farm
Tobermory
ISLE OF MULL
PA75 6QD
TEL: 01688 302235
FAX: 01688 302546
CONTACT: Chris & Jeff Reade
PRODUCE: Handmade, traditional farmhouse cheese made using only unpasteurised milk produced on the farm. Tobermory Flavella, selected mature Isle of Mull to which either mixed herbs, cracked black pepper, Mull mustard or caraway seeds has been added. Mail Order available.
PRICES/PAYMENT: Please 'phone for price list.
HOURS: Easter-Sept: Mon-Fri, 10am-4p. Mail order available at all times.
Notes: Disabled access. Farm visit allowing visitors to view milking, cheesemaking, tasting and farm produced light meals in the 'Garden Barn'. Isle of Mull Cheese supply to Neals Yard Dairy (London), Lidgates (London), Chatsworth Farm Shop (Bakewell) and The Cheesemonger (Edinburgh/Glasgow). They are interested in supplying new trade customers.

Editors Note: The first thoughts on compiling this book were collected while visiting this delightful dairy.

TOBERMORY FISH FARM LTD
Main Street
Tobermory
Isle of Mull
PA75 6NU
Tel: 01688 302120
Fax: 01688 302622
Contact: Susie Carmichael
Produce: Fresh rainbow trout, fresh salmon; whisky cured smoked salmon, smoked trout, smoked salmon, trout gravadlax, hot smoked trout (whole or fillets), hot smoked salmon (fillets and steaks), smoked haddock. Also stock Loch Fyne kippers, groceries. Worldwide delivery service. No min. order charge.
Prices/Payment: Smoked trout 114g from £3.15 to smoked salmon 228g @ £8.05. All major credit cards, Switch.
Hours: Mon-Fri, 9am-5p. Sat, 9am-3pm.
Notes: Disabled access. Tobermory Fish Farm supply Dandie Smoked Foods, J. Forteith & Son, Gordon Grants (Iona) and Ferry Shop and to the trade.

ALBA SMOKEHOUSE
13B Kilmory
Lochgilphead
PA31 8RR
Tel: 01546 606400
Fax: 01546 606400
Contact: Mike Leng
Produce: Smokers of salmon, trout, mussels, queen scallops & king scallops. "Hot-smoked" (cooked and smoked) products include Cajun salmon and honey glazed salmon. Also supply kippers. Mail Order service available.
Prices/Payment: Visa, Mastercard accepted
Hours: Mon-Fri, 9.00am-5.00pm. Answerphone and fax service.
Notes: Disabled access to smokehouse only. Scottish food company of the year 1995, 1996, 1997. Alba supply hotels and restaurants.

COCKLES
11 Argyll Street
Lochgilphead
PA31 8LZ
Tel: 01546 606292
Fax: 01546 606292
Contact: Elizabeth Cockhill
Produce: Langoustine, flat fish, lobster, crab. Also stock health foods and delicatessen items, herbs, spices, cheeses, smoked salmon, all fish and shellfish.
Prices/Payment: Cash and cheques only.
Hours: Mon-Sat, 9.30am-5.30pm.
Notes: Disabled access.

RITCHIES OF ROTHESAY
37 Watergate
Rothesay
Isle of Bute
PA20 9AD
Tel: 01700 505414
Fax: 01700 505414
Contact: Mr N. Richie
Produce: Non-dyed Loch Fyne kippers. Smoked Scottish salmon, smoked haddock, trout and mackerel fillets. Mail order service for all smoked fish products.
Prices/Payment: Cash and cheques (with orders) only.
Hours: 7.30am- 5pm.
Notes: Ritchies not only supply hotels and restaurants but also private customers.

INVERAWE SMOKEHOUSES
Inverawe
Taynuilt
PA35 1HU
Tel: 01866 822446
Fax: 01866 822274
Email: info@inverawe.co.uk
Contact: Diana Baird
Produce: Traditionally smoked salmon, trout, caviars, haddock, halibut, eels, kippers, pâté and smoked cheese. Also stock jams, sauces, home baking, smoked meats and herring. World wide Mail Order. No min. order.

Prices/Payment: 8oz smoked Inverawe salmon-sliced pack £9.95 inc. p&p. Credit cards plus Amex, Switch, Connect.
Hours: Shop open every day from March-October.
Notes: Disabled access. Tearoom, nature trail and fisheries. Inverawe Smokehouses supply Jenners (Edinburgh), Chatsworth Farm Shop (Bakewell) and eighty hotels and restaurants but are willing to expand.

ROCKLEY SEAFOODS
Ichrachan
Taynuilt
PA35 1HP
Tel: 01866 822305
Fax: 01866 822305
Contact: Alison or Dave Rockley
Produce: Fresh wild diver-gathered scallops, fresh oysters. Creel caught langoustines (very large). Smoked Scottish salmon. Mail Order only.
Prices/Payment: Fresh scallops, £13.50 per 10. Fresh oysters, £14.50 per doz. All major credit cards. Delta, Switch, Solo and J.C.B.
Hours: Mail Order available 24 hrs.
Notes: Rockley Seafoods are interested in supplying to the trade.

The following are SHOPS within this region which do not produce but do sell quality or organic foods.

GEORGE STRACHAN
Station Square
Aboyne
AB34 5HX
Tel: 01339 886121
Produce: Grocery store, with a wide range of mustards and jams. Also a wide range of whiskies.
Hours: Mon-Fri, 8.30am-5pm.

GRIERSON BROTHERS
148 King Street
Castle Douglas
DG7 1LU

Tel: 01556 502637
Produce: Butchers who stock meat from their own farm. Beef is Galloway Cross, hung for about two weeks. Lamb, fresh pork. Also home cured bacon and gammon. Beef ham with mixed spices. Black, white and fruit pudding and haggis.
Hours: Mon-Sat, 8am-5pm.

THE ORGANIC FOOD SHOP
45 Broughton Street
Edinburgh
EH1 3JU
Tel: 0131 556 1772
Fax: 0131 558 3530
Produce: Shop is based on an organic deli. Fresh fruit and vegetables, 100% organic, from home and abroad. Fresh and frozen: beef, lamb, pork, poultry, organic fish. Beer and wines. Grains, pulses, nuts, dried fruit, organic bread, ice cream, sorbets, yoghurts. Home Shopper scheme. Box scheme. Min. order £15.
Hours: Mon-Fri, 9.30am-6pm. Sat, 9.30am-5.30pm.
Notes: Disability access. The Organic Food Shop is interested in supplying to the trade.

EVERGREEN WHOLEFOODS
18 Nithsdale Road
Pollokshields
Glasgow
G41 2AN
Tel: 0141 422 1303
Produce: Organic and unprocessed foods. Wheat, gluten free, sugar free, where possible. A vegetarian shop with a wide range of vegan products. Twice weekly delivery of fresh fruit and vegetables; usually over thirty different items. Dried goods.
Hours: Mon-Sat, 9am-6pm.
Notes: Disabled access.

MacCALLUMS OF TROON
944 Argyle Street
Glasgow
G3 8YJ

Tel: 0141 204 4456
Fax: 0141 423 9294
Produce: Wide range of wet fish,
shellfish, lobsters. Fish parfaits and
terrines. Also in season a good
selection of wild mushrooms.
Hours: Mon-Fri, 9am-5pm. Sat, 9am-
3pm.

THE OLIVE TREE
7 High Street
Peebles
EH45 8AG
Tel: 01721 723461
Produce: A good selection of Scottish
produce. Smoked salmon, Galloway
oatcakes, preserves and wines.
Cheeses, bread and shortbread.
Hours: Mon-Sat, 9am-5.30pm.

NORTH WALES

ALWYN THOMAS BAKERS & CONFECTIONERS
124 Vale Street
Denbigh
LL16 3BS
Tel: 01745 812068
Contact: Alwyn Thomas
Produce: Organic wholemeal bread. Full range of traditional breads and confectionery – rye, sunflower, multigrain, soda, oatie, granary, onion, cheese & onion, focacccia, ciabatta, croissants to name but a few.
Prices/Payment: Organic wholemeal bread, 60p per 400g, 92p per 800g. Cash and cheques only.
Hours: 9am-5pm. Thurs, close 1.30pm
Notes: Disabled access.

ORGANIC FOOD
Ty Newydd
Denbigh
LL16 5DD
Tel: 01745 812882
Contact: Ms D.S. Jones or C.J.Dear
Produce: Vegetables and fruit. Meat, fruit, fish, fruit juices, dried fruit, milk, butter, bread and honey. Also stock cheese and wholefoods, oils and spreads. Home delivery by telephone orders. No min. order charge.
Prices/Payment: Carrots, 35p per lb. Sprouts 48p per lb, spring onions, 48p All major credit cards.
Hours: Fri, 10am-5pm. Sat, 10am-1pm
Notes: Disabled access. Victorian farmyard with cobbled frontage. Organic Food supply to Country Kitchen. They are interested in supplying to the trade.

POPTY'R DREF BAKERY AND DELICATESSEN
Porthmarchnad (Upper Smithfield Street)
Dolgellau
LL40 1ET
Tel: 01341 422507

Contact: Evan & Maggie Roberts
Produce: Traditionally made bread, including locally milled stoneground wholemeal flour and cakes, pastries and morning goods using all vegetarian products. Also stock over 80 types of Welsh, Irish, Scotch, English and Continental cheeses. Welsh oak smoked salmon, own lean roasted hams, home-made Christmas puddings and mincemeat. Also stock wholefoods, continental salamis, teas, tisanes, coffee beans ground to customers' requirements. Mail Order on some goods.
Prices/Payment: Cash, cheques only.
Hours: Mon-Sat, 8am-5pm; closed Sundays and Bank Holidays,
Notes: Disabled access via one wide step. Popty'r Dref are always willing to offer tastings of cheese plus advice. Interested in supplying to hotels & restaurants.

FOREST HILL TROUT FARM & FISHERY
Downing, Whitford
Holywell
CH8 9EQ
Tel: 01745 560151
Fax: 01745 560151
Contact: Ms Von Gibson
Produce: Rainbow trout grown and reared from fry in running constant spring water in large natural pools for the table. Also large fish up to 8 lbs for stocking fishing lakes. Also stock jams, mustards, garden produce, seafoods and seafish and flowers in season.
Prices/Payment: Rainbow Trout £1.60 per lb. Fishing £9 for a four-hour session. Cash, cheques only.
Hours: Shop: Summer, 10am-6pm. Winter, 10am-4pm. Fishery: Winter, 8am-4pm. Summer, 8am-9pm.
Notes: Disabled access. Feed the trout from the observation platform, poolside terrace where tea, coffee and home-made cakes are served in summer season. Fishing on four lakes. Forest Hill already supply to the trade.

MEGAN'S KITCHEN
The Bishop Trevor, Abbey Road
Llangollen
LL20 8SN
Tel: 01978 860063
Fax: 01978 860063
Contact: Patricia Bugler
Produce: This restaurant produces
'bake at home mixes'; they include
mixes for Welsh cakes, date & walnut
scones, fruit scones, apricot &
hazelnut scones. Also sell baked
Welsh cakes to local outlets.
Prices/Payment: From £2.50 for
Welsh cake gift boxes 400g & from
£2.50 for scone mixes 800g. Cash,
cheques only.
Hours: 10am-5pm. Closed Wed.
Notes: Limited disabled access.
Customers can see Welsh cakes being
cooked in the restaurant/dining room.
Suppliers to outlets, Megan's Kitchen
is interested in supplying to the trade.

BLAS AR FWYD
25 Heol yr Orsaf
Llanrwst
Conway
LL26 0BT
Tel: 01492 640215
Fax: 01492 642215
Contact: Deiniol ap Dafydd
Produce: Delicatessen foods, freshly
craft made - no mixes, powders or
preservatives. Pâtés, veg. pâtés,
pastries, cakes, desserts, jams, salads,
meats, pickles, chutneys and cheese.
Also stock Farol dairy cheeses, small
production foods and wines. Full
home delivery throughout North
Wales. Mail Order beyond. No min.
order - just reasonable amounts.
Prices/Payment: All major cards
taken and Delta, Switch.
Hours: Mon-Sat, 8a.m-6pm. Closed
Sun. Brasserie open Wednesday to
Sunday, 10am -10pm.
Notes: Disabled access; disabled
toilet in brasserie. "Best Deli in
Wales", "Best Brasserie in Wales" -
Real Food magazine. Interested in
supplying to the trade throughout
North Wales.

FELIN CREWI WATERMILL
Penegoes
Machynlleth
SY20 8NH
Tel: 01654 703113
Fax: 01654 703113
Contact: Winnie & Tony Morris
Produce: Traditional stoneground
(mill stones powered by water wheel)
flour; wholemeal, plain, self raising,
breadmix. Also muesli - own recipe
"Old Mill", bran, wheatbran, rolled
oats, wheatgerm, oatbran, country
malt. 500g, 1kg, 1.5kg, 16kg and
25kg bags or made to order. Mail
Order available. No min. order but
charge postage and packing.
Prices/Payment: Cash and cheques only
Hours: 'Phone in advance, open most
days 10am-4pm (April-October).
Notes: Disabled access to 16th
century watermill and the shop. Felin
Crewi supply shops and wholesale to
bakers and restaurants.

BACHELDRE WATERMILL
Church Stoke
Montgomery
SY15 6TE
Tel: 01588 620489
Fax: 01588 620489
Contact: Tony & Helen Jay
Produce: A range of stoneground
organic and non-organic flours. All
are strong and suitable for baking
bread and other baked products.
Producers of wheat, rye and malted
products. Available by Mail Order.
No min. order charge.
Prices/Payment: £1 per 1.5 kg, £9
per 16kg, £16 per 32kg for organic
stoneground flour. Cash and cheques
only.
Hours: Shop, most days 8.30am - 5.30pm
Notes: Also self catering apartments,
touring caravan/camping park on site.
Bacheldre Watermill supply numerous outlets including Aardvark
(Carmarthen), Sherwood Wholefoods
(Market Drayton), Harvest Wholefoods
(Bishops Castle) and The Bran Tub
(Gt. Malvern). They are interested in
supplying more to the trade.

SOUTH WALES

PARK FARM MEATS
Park Farm, Llantilio Crossenny
Abergavenny
NP7 8TD
Tel: 01600 780218
Fax: 01600 780218
Contact: A.V. Watkins
Produce: Home produced beef, lamb and pork. Fed on animal feed grown and prepared on the farm, no routine antibiotics, artificial hormones and no growth promoters. Also meat products such as sausages and beefburgers made on the premises. Hams and tenderloin purchased for specific orders.
Prices/Payment: Cash and cheques only
Hours: By arrangement, please phone for details.
Notes: Disabled access. Shop is in farmyard with free access to livestock etc. Park Farm Meats supply to trade.

VAUXHIRE CO
Bryan-y-Pant Cottage, Upper Llanover
Abergavenny
NP7 9ES
Tel: 01873 880625
Contact: L Chirnside
Produce: Honey from the bees. Candles and wax products. Mail Order available. No min order charge.
Prices/Payment: Cash and cheques only
Hours: Please 'phone for details.
Notes: No disabled access. Vauxhire Co. are interested in supplying to trade

BARON JACKSON WELSH MUSHROOMS
Mushroom Farm, Bryn Road
Coychurch
Bridgend
CF35 6AE
Tel: 01656 766436
Fax: 01656 766436
Contact: I.J. and R.L. Hanmer
Produce: Quality farm fresh Welsh mushrooms, grown and packed.
Prices/Payment: Cash and cheques only
Hours: Mon-Fri, 8am-4pm. Sunday, 8am-12pm.
Notes: Disabled access. Group visits arranged by appointment; farm, garden and animals. The Mushroom Farm supply Filco Foods at Llantwit Major, Cowbridge, Caerau, Sarn, North Cornelly, Tai Bach, Brintirion and Talbot Green. Wholesale supplies are direct from farm or F Ley and Sons Ltd. in Swansea.

PENCOED ORGANIC GROWERS
Felindre Nurseries, Felindre
Pencoed
Bridgend
CF35 5HU
Tel: 01656 861956
Contact: Yvonne Leslie and John Roberts.
Produce: Seasonal vegetables grown by the nursery. Customers order their vegetables to collect next day.
Prices/Payment: Please 'phone for price list. Cash and cheques only.
Hours: Collection advised when order placed.
Notes: Disabled access.

GORNO'S SPECIALITY FOODS LTD
Unit 4, Fairfield Industrial Estate
Taffs Well
Cardiff
CF4 8LA
Tel: 01222 811225
Fax: 01222 811299
Contact: Andrew or Franco Gorno
Produce: Gorno's manufacture pepperoni for pizzas. Traditional Italian sausage, merguez, Toulouse sausages and a variety of matured salami. They import and stock prosciutto crudo, parmesan grana padano (wheels, blocks or grated). Also a variety of pizza toppings, pizza sauces etc. All products guaranteed 100% meat. Also stock a variety of continental cheese, Italian pasta and a variety of Italian groceries.
Prices/Payment: Please 'phone for price list. Cash and cheques only.

Hours: Mon-Fri, 8.30am-5pm. Sat, 9am-3pm.
Notes: Disabled access. Wholesale orders sent by road. Min order open for discussion. Gorno's Speciality Foods supply to Valvona & Crolla (Edinburgh), Shelley Deli (Cardiff), Wally's Deli (Cardiff) and Casa Marchini (Aberdeen). They are interested in supplying to the trade.

THE FRUIT GARDEN/ ICES FROM THE FRUIT GARDEN

Groes Faen Road, Peterson-super-Ely
Cardiff
CF5 6NE
Tel: 01446 760358
Contact: Linda George (ice cream); Charles George (fruit).
Produce: PYO (June-Aug) strawberries, raspberries, black and red currant, gooseberries, tayberries, etc. Specialists in early protected strawberries, raspberries and blueberries for shops and restaurants. Also produced at the Fruit Garden are luxury quality ice creams and sorbets using their own fruit. No artificial colourings or flavours.
Prices/Payment: Cash, cheques only.
Hours: Jun-Aug, seven days a week 9.30am-7.30pm.
Notes: Disabled access. The Fruit Garden supply Shelleys Delicatessen (Cardiff), Jenkins (Cowbridge) and La Patisserie (Cardiff) with ice cream. They supply Fruit Bowl (Pontcanna) and Huw Jones (Porthcawl) with fruit. Interested in supplying more to trade.

MEDHOPE ORGANIC GROWERS

Tintern
Chepstow
NP6 7NX
Tel: 01291 689797
Contact: Sandra Scott/Sally Field
Produce: Organically grown fruit and vegetables; home-made chutneys, jams and cakes. Also stock organic dried goods & tins, e.g. rice, pasta, sauces, etc. Also organic bread and dairy products. Box

schemes to Newport and home delivery to Monmouth and Chepstow. Min order £10.00.
Prices/Payment: Cash and cheques only
Hours: 9am-5pm seven days a week.
Notes: Disabled access. Gardens, tea room, pets corner, plant sales area.

WHITEBROOK ORGANIC GROWERS

The Old Rectory
Llanvaches
Newport
NP6 3AY
Tel: 01633 400406
Contact: Paul Cooper
Produce: An extensive range of home grown and imported organic vegetables, fruit and salads; also herbs. Also stock organic dried foods (nuts, rice, cereals etc.). Juices, wines and household cleaning products. Home delivery service and box scheme. Min order £5.
Prices/Payment: Cash and cheques only.
Hours: 24 hrs a day answering machine.
Notes: Whitebrook Organic Growers, supply to Pulse Wholefoods and are interested in supplying to the trade.

SELWYN'S PENCLAWDD SEAFOODS

Lynch Factory, Marsh Road
lLanmorlais
Swansea
SA4 3TN
Tel: 01792 850033
Fax: 01792 850033
Contact: Mrs Alyson Jones
Produce: Fresh cockles picked on the Burry inlet and processed in factory. 100% vegetarian laverbread. Also stock frozen prawns, crabsticks, whelks, mussels. Mail Order Sep-Jun. No min. order.

Prices/Payment: Cockles wholesale at £3.50 per kg, Laverbread wholesale at £2.50 per kg. Seasonal variations. Cash, cheques only.
Hours: 9am-4pm each day except Sat.
Notes: Disabled access. Production can be viewed in the scenic setting on marshland. Selwyn's do supply to the trade,/are interested in doing more.

WEST AND MID WALES

FISH ON THE QUAY
Cadwgan Place
Aberaeron
SA46 0BT
Tel: 01545 571294 **Fax:** 01545 570160
Contact: Peter Bottoms
Produce: Live and cooked shellfish from Cardigan Bay. Fresh fish. Also stock Loch Fyne products. Mail order, home delivery service available. Min order £40.00
Prices/Payment: Cash and cheques only
Hours: 9.30am-5pm.
Notes: Disabled access. Fish restaurant – Hive on the Quay – adjoining. Fish on the Quay are possibly interested in supplying to the trade, depending on location.

WENDY BRANDON HANDMADE PRESERVES
Felin Wen
Boncath
SA37 0JR
Tel: 01239 841568 **Fax:** 01239 841746
Contact: Ian /Wendy Brandon
Produce: Wide range of preserves and pickles including marmalade sweetened with cane sugar and concentrated apple juice. Chutneys and jams, jellies, vinegars, vanilla fudge, chocolate fudge sauce, tomato jam. Also stock Brogdale apple juice, Newquay honey and Tregroes waffles. Mail Order service available, U.K. and Worldwide. No min. order.
Prices/Payment: Apricot chutney 200g, £2.85. Strawberry jam 340g, £3.50. All major credit cards taken.

Hours: Mon-Fri, 9am-5pm. Sat, 9am-1pm. Other times by appointment.
Notes: Disabled access possible to shop. They hold tastings. They supply Iain Mellis, Moorelands Foods, Conran Shop and Ramsbottom Victuallers.

ALBERT REES
H515, Market Precinct
Carmarthen
SA32 8DX
Tel: 01267 237687/231204
Contact: Albert, Chris, Ann Rees
Produce: Cured bacon and ham, e.g. Carmarthen ham. Home cooked meats, faggots and sausages. Also stock dairy produce; cheese, butter, eggs and gammon bacon. Mail Order for Carmarthen ham, Welsh cured bacon and ham. No min. order.
Prices/Payment: Carmarthen ham £2.50 per quarter lb, sausages £1.89 per lb. Cash and cheques only.
Hours: 9am-4.30pm six days a week at Carmarthen. Thurs-Sat at Cardigan market and Friday at Pembroke Dock.
Notes: Disabled access at three sites.

PENCRUGIAU ORGANIC FARM SHOP
Pencrugiau
Felindre Farchog
CRYMYCH
SA41 3XH
TEL: 01239 881265
CONTACT: Mike Ray
PRODUCE: Wide range of field, market garden and glasshouse crops, e.g. peas to pumpkins, lettuces, tomatoes, cucumber, peppers, carrots, potatoes, cauliflower, calebrese, herbs, onions, etc.
PRICES/PAYMENT: Prices are competitive, but seasonal. Cash and cheques only.
Hours: 9am-6pm seven days a week
NOTES: Disabled access. Pencrugiau Organic are interested in more wholesale trade.

COTTAGE CATERERS
Min-yr-Afon
Jordanston Bridge
Castle Morris
Haverfordwest
SA62 5UP
Tel: 01348 891296
Fax: 01348 891296
Contact: Alan and Olwen Davis
Produce: A wide range of home-made pastries and dishes designed for reheating at home - from a Welsh lamb pasty to Scampi Sicilienne or poulet à l'oriental (Thai curry sauce). Vegetables, rice, mixed salads and desserts also available. Also stock a small selection of wine.
Prices/Payment: From £1.20 for a Pembrokeshire pasty to £7.95 for Scampi Sicilienne. Cash and cheques only.
Hours: Non specific, from very early until any reasonable hour in the evening.
Notes: Wheelchair access without a problem.

LLANGLOFFAN FARMHOUSE CHEESE
Llangloffan Farm
Castle Morris
Haverfordwest
SA62 5ET
Tel: 01348 891241
Fax: 01348 891241
Contact: Miss Joanne Downey
Produce: Traditional farmhouse cheese made by hand on the farm. Chive and garlic also available. The cheese is only produced when the cows eat grass. Also stock several varieties of Welsh cheeses, pre-serves, ice cream, honey, butter and organic butter. Mail order available, next day delivery. Please contact Miss Downey for details. Min order £20.
Prices/Payment: Llangloffan farmhouse cheese £8.60 per kg. Llangloffan chive and garlic £8.71 per kg. Cash and cheques only.
Hours: Mon-Sat, 9am-5.30pm. Closed Sun. Open Bank Holidays.

Notes: Disabled access. Cheese demonstrations, teashop. The Downeys already supply to Blas ar Fwyd (Llanrwst), Neals Yard Dairy, Paxton & Whitfield and Jeroboams Affineur (all London). They are interested in supplying more to the trade.

THE PUMPKIN SHED
(Rhodiad-y-Brenin, St. Davids)
The Walled Garden
Solva
Haverfordwest
SA62 6PJ
Tel: 01437 721949
Contact: Magda Piessens
Produce: Pumpkins, PYO herbs,vegetables and herb plants. Also stock local organic potatoes, vegetables, fruit and cheeses.
Prices/Payment: Cash and cheques only.
Hours: Wed, 1pm- 4pm. Thur, 10am-4pm. Fri, 10am-3pm. Sat, 10am-4pm.
Notes: The Pumpkin Shed is a 1.75 acre walled garden situated on the A487 just outside Solva.

WELSH HAVEN PRODUCTS
Whitegates
Little Haven
Haverfordwest
SA62 3LA
Tel: 01437 781552
Fax: 01437 781386
Contact: Richard Llewellin
Produce: Organic chicken and duck. Also vacuum packed portions of ostrich steaks, sausages and burgers. Available by Mail Order, next day carrier in mainland Britain, or by road on M4 corridor weekly. Min order 10kg.
Prices/Payment: Fresh chickens for £1.48 per lb. Ostrich steaks £5.50 per lb. Visa, Mastercard taken.
Hours: 9am-6pm.
Notes: Disabled access. Tastings, coffee shop. Welsh Haven Products are interested in supplying to the trade.

GREENMEADOW MUSHROOMS
Bush Lane
Kilgetty
SA68 0RB
Tel: 01834 813190
Contact: Chris Beasley
Produce: Mushrooms; closed cup, open cup and flat.
Prices/Payment: £1 per lb. Cash and cheques only.
Hours: Mon-Fri, 10am-4pm.
Notes: Disabled access. Customers welcome to view the process. Greenmeadow Mushrooms are interested in supplying to the trade.

GRAIG FARM ORGANICS
Dolau
LLANDRINDOD WELLS
LD1 5TL
TEL: **01597 851655**
FAX: **01597 851991**
EMAIL: **sales@graigfarm.co.uk**
INTERNET: **www.graigfarm.co.uk**
CONTACT: **Bob & Carolyn Kennard**
PRODUCE: **A wide range of award-winning organic & additive-free meats & meat products, including beef, lamb, mutton, pork, poultry, fish, pies, etc. Overall winner 1997/8 Organic Food Awards. Also stock a range of groceries. Nationwide Mail Order. No min order charge but free delivery over £40.**
PRICES/PAYMENT: **Visa, Mastercard. Switch.**
HOURS: **Farm Shop, Mon-Sat, 9am-5.30pm.**
NOTES: **Disabled access. Visitor Centre planned for future. Graig Farm supply numerous outlets and are interested in supplying to the trade.**

YAN TAN TETHERA
Llugwy Farm
Llanbister Road
Llandrindod Wells
LD1 5UT
Tel: 01547 550641

Internet: www.ruralwales.org.uk/powysfayre
Contact: Belinda Scadding
Produce: Organic greek-style sheep milk yogurt made from milk produced on the farm. Also available seasonally a mature organic unpasteurised sheep milk cheese, Ba'a Brigit, in 2 sizes of approx 1.5 and 4 lbs. All Soil Assoc. approved G2291. Cheese available by Mail Order. Min order 1 small cheese.
Prices/Payment: Cash and cheques only.
Hours: Please 'phone ahead for farmgate sales.
Notes: Yan Tan Tethera supply to Georges (Kington), Presteigne Wholefood Co-Op, Organic Options (Leominster) and Green Link (Malvern).

PENBRYN CHEESE
Ty Hen
Sarnau
Llandysul
SA44 6RD
Tel: 01239 810347
Contact: Mrs A. Degen
Produce: Organic Gouda-type cheese made by hand in the traditional way from unpasteurised milk from their own Friesian-M.R.I. herd. Natural rind, made with vegetarian rennet. Available in mild and mature. 1kg or 3kg rounds.
Prices/Payment: Mild £2.80 per lb, mature £3.50 per lb (retail). Cash and cheques only.
Hours: Mon-Sat, 12pm-5pm.
Notes: Disabled access. Penbryn Cheese supply Llwynhelyg Farmshop (Sarnau), Wilson (Cardigan), Blas ar Fwyd (Llanrwst) and Vivian's (Richmond).

TEIFI VALLEY FISH
Ty Mawr
Llanybydder
SA40 9RE
Tel: 01570 480789
Contact: Peter Jarrams
Produce: Fresh trout from the farm,

frozen fish, fresh and frozen salmon, steaks and cutlets. Frozen cod, plaice and prawns. Local sea trout sometimes available. Dressed crab. Free range eggs.

Prices/Payment: Fresh trout, £1.85 per lb, Scottish Salmon whole £2.30 per lb. Cash and cheques only.

Hours: 8am-8pm every day.

Notes: Disabled access. Trout fishing lake, coarse fishing lake. Farm shop and Trout Farm. Teifi Valley Fish supply to the trade.

ORGANIC FARM FOODS
Lampeter Industrial Estate

LAMPETER

Swansea
SA48 8LT
TEL: **01570 423099**
FAX: **01570 423280**
EMAIL: **organicfarmfoods.co.uk**
INTERNET:
www.organicfarmfoods.co.uk
CONTACT: **Fiona**
PRODUCE: **Full range of fresh fruit and vegetables, all organic. Range of dairy products available. "Grade-out" products available at discounted prices.**
PRICES/PAYMENT: **Cash and cheques only.**
HOURS: **Shop times: Mon, Tues, Thurs, Fri, 9am-5pm. Wed, Sat, 9am-1pm. Factory times: Mon-Fri, 9-5pm.**
NOTES: **Entrance is flat, no steps involved.**

LLANBOIDY CHEESEMAKERS
Cilowen Uchaf
Login
Whitland
SA34 0TJ
Tel: 01994 448303
Fax: 01994 448303
Contact: Sue Jones
Produce: Llanboidy and laverbread

cheese. Farmhouse cheese made from unpasteurised Red Poll cow's milk. A full fat hard cheese with a firm creamy texture. Plain or with laverbread. Suitable for vegetarians. Mail Order, 10lb or 5lb cheeses or 2lb wedges upwards will be sent by first class post.

Prices/Payment: Cash, cheques only.

Hours: Farm can be viewed by prior appointment only.

Notes: Llanboidy supply Howells (Cardiff), Vivians (Richmond), Wells Stores and Blas ar Fwyd and also restaurants and hotels and are happy to supply more.

MERLIN CHEESES
Tyn-y-Llwyn
Pontrhydygroes
Ystrad Meurig
SY25 6DP
Tel: 01974 282636
Contact: Gill Pateman
Produce: Merlin goat's milk cheddar cheeses made in two sizes; 900g and 200g mini. Made in 15 varieties; mild, mature, garlic & chive, celery, pineapple, apricot, peach, herb, olive, walnut, smoked, pear & cinnamon, apple and ginger. Mail Order available anywhere in U.K., sent by courier; leaflet available. Min. order, 4 minis for £15 or 8 minis for £25.

Prices/Payment: Cash and cheques only.

Hours: By appointment only; please 'phone to arrange.

Notes: No disabled access, farm is on a mountain. Views over the Ystwyth valley and lots of animals. Merlin cheese is sold to wholesalers nationwide and is widely available in delis and cheese specialist shops. Merlin are interested in selling more to the trade.

The following are SHOPS within this region which do not produce but do sell quality or organic foods.

Hours: Mon, Sat, 8.30am-1pm. Tues, Thurs, Fri, 8.30am-5pm. Wed, 8.30am-4.30pm.

DIMENSIONS
15 Holyhead Road
Bangor
Gwynedd
LL57 2EG
Tel: 01248 351562
Fax: 01248 351562
Produce: Organic herbs and spices, dried fruit, nuts and seeds, beans and pulses, sweet and savoury snacks. Organic bread, fruit and vegetables, chilled and frozen, take-aways. Remedies, gifts, natural body care and cleaning products. Box scheme. Min. order £5.
Hours: Mon-Sat, 9.30am-5.30pm.
Notes: Disabled access.

SPICE OF LIFE
1 Inverness Place
Roath
Cardiff
CF2 4RU
Tel: 01222 467146
Fax: 01222 467146
Produce: Wholefoods, nuts, dried fruit, beans & pulses, cereals, grains, rice, pasta, herbs & spices. Organic vegetables and bread, olive oils, honey, free range eggs. Organic vegetable box scheme.
Hours: 10am-5.30pm.
Notes: Spice of Life are interested in supplying to the trade.

THE FISH SHOP
Unit 4
The Old Abattoir
Builder Street
Llandudno
LL30 1DR
Tel: 01492 870430
Fax: 01492 870327
Produce: Locally caught fresh fish. Oak smoked fish, poultry, meat and game. Fresh local game.

THE BETTER FOOD CO
1 Hobbs Lane, Barrow Gurney
Bristol
North Somerset
BS48 3SU
Tel: 01275 474545
Fax: 01275 474783
Email: betterfood@compuserve.com
Contact: Philip Haughton
Produce: Home delivery and hamper company. Full grocery service including meats, wines, specialist sausages and kebabs. Box scheme available. Min order charge £10.
Hours: Mon-Fri, office hours.

BUXTON FOODS LTD
12 Harley Street
London
W1N 1AA
Tel: 0171 637 5505
Fax: 0171 436 0979
Email: buxton@compuserve.com
Contact: Elizabeth Buxton
Produce: Organic wheat-free flour, organic dairy-free chocolates. Vegetable chips, sweet potato chips. No min. order.
Payment: Visa, Mastercard & Switch.
Notes: Buxton Foods Ltd supply to good food shops nationwide and selected Sainsburys, Waitrose and Safeway and are interested in supplying to the trade.

THE CHOCOLATE CLUB
Unit 11
St Pancras Commercial Centre
63 Pratt Street
NW1 0BY
Tel: 0171 267 5375
Fax: 0171 267 5357
Email: 100533.
2406@compuserve.com
Contact: Carolyn de la Force
Produce: Handmade chocolate delux.
Prices/Payment: Amex, Switch, Visa, Mastercard taken.
Hours: 8am-5pm.

CROSSE FARM BAKERY
Unit 4, Cranmere Road
Exeter Road Industrial Estate
Okehampton, Devon
EX20 1QA
Tel: 01837 55457
Fax: 01837 53874
Contact: Harriet Helliwell
Produce: Handmade cakes, puddings and speciality breads; using butter, free range eggs and local fruit. A speciality is Dartmoor gingerbread made with stem ginger, raw cane sugar and marmalade. Mail Order service available for Christmas cakes, puddings and gingerbreads. £15 min. order; please give three days advance notice.
Prices/Payment: From £6 upwards for cakes and puddings. £1.50 upwards for breads. Cash and cheques only.
Hours: Telephone orders only.
Notes: Crosse Farm Bakery also supply Country Cheeses (Tavistock and Exeter), Red Lion Deli (Okehampton), Bon Gout Deli (Exeter), Watermans Food Hall (Bristol) and always welcome new enquiries.

CURRANT AFFAIRS
Riverview Cottage
Grange Road
Brompton-on-Swale
Richmond
North Yorks
DL10 7HJ
Tel: 01748 811770
Contact: Gillian or Alex Ives
Produce: Producers of luxury fruitcakes which are mixed and decorated by hand. Their luxury cakes are baked to recipes which have been adapted by Currant Affairs See main entry – Richmond, Yorkshire
Prices/Payment: Please 'phone for a price list. Cash and cheques only.
Notes: Currant Affairs sell to Lewis & Coopers (Northallerton) and Philberts of Darlington. They are interested in supplying more to the trade.

THE FISH SOCIETY
Freepost Gl 2485
Haslemere, Surrey
GU27 2BR
Tel: **01428 644382**
Fax: **01428 642513**
Email: **thefishsoc@aol.com**
Contact: **Mrs Carole King**
Produce: **High quality frozen fish for home eating. Orders are packed with dry ice and delivered by overnight courier. The range goes from cod fillets (around £10 per 1200 g pack) to rock lobster tails (around £28 per 600g), by way of a hundred other types of fish including boquerones, king prawns in garlic butter, pike and wild Indian Ocean prawns. New price list sent out every two months. No min order, but delivery charge is £12 for orders under £40 and £6 for orders over £40.**
Payment: **All major cards taken except Amex**
Contact Hours: **24 hour answer phone service.**
Notes: **To receive next mailing - phone, fax or email your name and address.**

THE FRESH FOOD COMPANY
326 Portobello Road
London
W10 5RU
Tel: 0181 969 0351
Fax: 0181 964 8050
Email: organic@freshfood.co.uk
Internet: www.freshfood.co.uk
Contact: Thoby Young
Produce: Fresh organic foods (fruit, veg, meat, bakery, dairy etc). Fresh British fish and shellfish. Organic drinks and water. Organic dry goods and low toxicity cleaning products. Organic veg boxes from £12.50. No min. order charge but service charges apply.
Payment: All major credit cards taken.
Contact Hours: Mon-Fri, 9am-6pm.
Notes: The Fresh Food Company are interested in wholesale enquiries.

GOOD FOOD DIRECT LIMITED
11 Harby Lane
Plungar
Notts
NG13 0JH
Tel: 01949 861592
Fax: 01949 861592
Contact: Anna Higgins
Produce: Speciality food. Oils, dressings, preserves, condiments, chutneys, herbs, spices and sauces. 70 products. No min. order. Please 'phone for further details.
Payment: Cheques only.
Notes: Good Food Direct are happy to consider supplying to the trade.

GRAMMA'S
P.O. Box 218, London
E6 4BG
Tel: **0181 470 8751**
Fax: **0181 548 8755**
Contact: **Ms Dounne Alexander**
Produce: **Traditional Caribbean Herbal Foods. A range of four concentrated herbal pepper sauces (mild, hot, extra-hot & super hot) and four concentrated herbal seasonings (original, hot & spicy, curry, creole) available individually or in gift boxes. Mail Order service; no minimum order.**
Prices: **Herbal pepper sauces £3.50, herbal seasonings £3.95, gift sets £12.50.**
Hours: **Orders sent by post Mon-Sat; allow 14 days delivery. Cash, cheques only.**
Notes: **Tasting demonstration can be arranged for groups/clubs; ring in advance. Suppliers to Fortnum & Mason. Ms Alexander is interested in supplying to restaurants, hotels and airlines.**

GRIMBISTER FARM CHEESE
Grimbister Farm, By Kirkwall
Orkney
KW15 1TT
Tel: 01856 761318
Fax: 01856 761318
Contact: Hilda Seator

Produce: Handmade traditional Orkney farmhouse cheese. Varieties consist of plain, smoked, chive, garlic, caraway and walnut. Mail Order available. Min. order 1 whole round.
Prices/Payment: Plain £4.40 per kg. Flavoured £4.50 per kg. Smoked £5.50 per kg. Cash and cheques only.
Hours: Mail Order only.
Notes: Grimbister Farm Cheese supply to Neals Yard Dairy (London), The Big Cheese (Aberdeen) and they also already supply to the trade.

HAMBLEDEN HERBS
Court Farm, Milverton
Taunton
Somerset
TA4 1NF
Tel: 01823 401205
Fax: 01823 401001
Contact: Gaye Donaldson
Produce: Organic top quality dried herbs and spices. Organic herbal teas, infusions, cocoa, flower waters, tinctures. 500 herbs and spices from around the world. Mail Order available. Please 'phone for catalogue. No min. order charge.
Prices/Payment: All major credit cards. Switch and Delta.
Hours: Mail Order only.
Notes: Hambleden Herbs supply to Planet Organic, Bluebird and Selfridges (all London).

JACK SCAIFE BUTCHER LTD
The Factory, Mill Lane
Oakworth, Keighley
West Yorks
BD22 7QH
Tel: 01535 647772
Fax: 01535 646305
Email: sales@jackscaife.co.uk
Internet: www.classicengland.co.uk/scaife.html
Contact: Angela Battle
Produce: Traditional dry cured bacon and hams. Dry cured ox-tongues. Honey roast pork sausage, Cumberland sausage and beef

sausages. Also stock British competition winning black and white puddings. All available by Mail Order, overnight delivery service to home or work address.
Prices/Payment: Please 'phone for price brochure. Mastercard, Visa, Delta and Switch taken.
Hours: Not open to the public.
Notes: Jack Scaife also supply to Fortnum and Mason (London), Hannells of Mayfair (London), House of Lords (London) and Lewis and Cooper.

LUNN-LINKS
Greenbrier, Victoria Road
Brixham
Devon TQ5 9AR
Tel: 01803 853579
Fax: 01803 853579
Email: llorganic@aol.com
Contact: Stephen Lunn
Produce: Kitchen Garden organic range of herbs and spices, soya flour, soya beans, soya tvp, pasta sauce, peanut butter and condiments. Fairtrade Foundation organic black tea. Min order £35.
Payment: Cheques only.
Contact Hours: Please 'phone for details.
Notes: Lunn-Links are interested in supplying to the trade.

MEAT MATTERS
2 Blandys Farm Cottage
Letcombe Regis, Wantage
Oxon
OX12 9LJ
Tel: 01235 762461
Fax: 01235 772526
Contact: Diane Glass
Produce: Organic pork, beef, lamb, chicken, pies, beefburgers, sausages, organic fruit and vegetables, organic dairy products, juices and dry goods. No min order charge. Home delivery free of charge in London & Oxon.
Payment: Visa & Mastercard.
Contact Hours: 24 hour telephone line.

Notes: Meat Matters supply to El Piano (York) and Organic Shop (Jersey). They are interested in supplying other health/organic retail outlets.

NATURAL DELIVERY WHOLEFOODS
Unit 1, The Vincent Works
Brough, Bradwell,
Hope Valley, Derbyshire
S33 9HG
Tel: 01433 620383
Fax: 01433 621961
Contact: Andrew Greaves
Produce: Fresh organic fruit and vegetables. A wide range of wholefoods; please 'phone for booklet. Also veg box scheme. Min order £10 plus £1 delivery charge.
Payment: Cash and cheques only.
Contact Hours: Mon, 9am-3pm. Tues-Fri, 9am-5pm. Sat, 9.30am-1pm.
Notes: Natural Delivery supply a number of local restaurants and hotels.

ORGANICS DIRECT
1-7 Willow Street, London
EC2A 4BH
Tel: 0171 729 2828
Fax: 0171 613 5800
Email: info@organicsdirect.co.uk
Internet: www.organicsdirect.com
Contact: Ysanne Spevack
Produce: Organic vegetarian foods. Fresh fruit and vegetables, hand-baked breads and cakes, ready made soups, baby foods, groceries, beers and wines.
No min. order. Free home delivery.
Payment: All major credit cards. Switch. Delta.
Contact Hours: Mon-Fri, 9.30am-6pm. Sat & Sun, 10am-5pm.
Notes: Organics Direct are interested in supplying to the trade.

ORGANIC ROUNDABOUT
28 Hamstead Road, Hockley
Birmingham
B19 1DB
Tel: 0121 551 1679

Fax: 0121 515 3524
Produce: Fresh organic fruit and vegetables - standard 4.5 kg bags available or customers can make their own selection from around 40 items every week with no maximum or minimum order. Delivery to local pick-up points, please ' phone for details.
Prices/Payment: Cash and cheques only.
Hours: Not open to the public.
Notes: Organic Roundabout are interested in supplying to the trade.

THE ORIGINAL SAUSAGE CO.
6 Cardigan Street
Ipswich
Suffolk
IP1 3PF
Tel: 01473 217563
Contact: Chris Finnerhan
Produce: Traditional sausages including; original breakfast (award winning and made to a traditional 1930's recipe), pork & leek, pork and stilton, pork, lemon & ginger, pork and wild garlic, hot 'n' spicy cajun, lamb & mint, wild boar and venison. Gluten free include chorizo, toulouse, Italian, chicken & apricot and original farmhouse. Available by Mail Order, overnight delivery. No min order charge but orders up to £10, p&p is £5.45, 11 lb -15 lb £3.50, 16 lb-20 lb £2.00, over 20 lb free delivery. Also sold at shows.
Prices/Payment: From £2.50 per lb to £3.95 per lb. Major credit cards. Visa, Debit and Switch.
Hours: 24 hours for Mail Order.
Notes: The Original Sausage Co is interested in supplying to the trade.

PORTER FOODS CO LTD
24 Hockerill Court
London Road, Bishop's Stortford
Herts
CM23 5SB
Tel: 01279 501711
Fax: 01279 501727
Email: porter-foods@bt.internet.com

Internet: www.porter-foods.co.uk
Contact: Clive Smith or Claire Saunders.
Produce: Specialist sauces, purées and pastes of an exotic nature as well as other specialist ingredients. Largely selling direct to the trade. Min order charge £180 carriage free. Please 'phone for price list.
Notes: Porter Foods Co Ltd supply to Harrods, Fortnum & Mason and Harvey Nichols (all London). They are interested in supplying more to trade.

PURE ORGANIC FOODS LTD
The Dower House
Leiston, Suffolk
IP16 4UB
Tel: 01728 830575
Fax: 01728 833660
Email: pureorg@aol.com
Internet: www.pureorganic
foods.co.uk
Contact: Lisa Meades
Produce: Organic meat and poultry, specialising in portion-size items packed in sealed trays. Soil Association and Demeter Standard. No min order.
Payment: Please 'phone for price list. All major credit cards taken.
Contact Hours: Place order on Mon. for delivery Tues-Fri same week.
Notes: Pure Organic Foods Ltd supply to D. Lidgate, Planet Organic and Harrods (all London), The Old Dairy Farm Shop (Lady Rose) and are interested in supplying to the trade.

THE SCOTTISH GOURMET
Thistle Mill
Biggar, Lanarkshire
ML12 6LP
Tel: 01899 221001
Fax: 01899 220456
Contact: Joy Douglas
Produce: Authentic Scottish foods from natural sources. Supplied as pre-prepared and cooked dishes, or as ready to cook ingredients. Sea-fish, beef, lamb, game etc. Bakery goods and farmhouse cheeses. Sweets. Malt

whiskies, unusual coffees. No min. order. Club format with 10,000 members.
Payment: See club programme for prices. All credit cards and Switch.
Contact Hours: 24 hour answerphone service.
Notes: Coffee shop. Light lunches, teas etc. Disabled access.

SKY SPROUTS ORGANIC GARDEN
Gosworthy Cottage
Harberton, Totnes
Devon
TQ9 7LP
Tel: 01364 72404
Fax: 01364 72404
Email: skysprouts@thenet.co.uk.
Contact: Brett Kellett
Produce: Certified organic sprouted beans and seeds. Sunflower, alfalfa, hemp sprouts, also mixed bean and Mung bean sprouts. Mail Order service available.
Prices/Payment: Cheques only
Notes: Sprouting beans are a rich source of vitamins. Sky Sprouts already supply other outlets and are willing to supply to the trade in bulk.

THE STRAIGHT FORWARD TRADING COMPANY
12A Kenyon Mansions
London W14 9RN
Tel: 0171 381 4378
Fax: 0171 381 6869
Contact: Charles Barnes
Produce: A wide range of high quality food. Ham, goose, partridge, hare, duck, quail or guinea fowl, each stuffed with foie gras. Sauces, flavoured oils, terrines, truffles, olive oils, gormande baskets, Basalmic vinegar, etc.
Notes: Please ring for details of prices and ordering details.

THE SWALEDALE CHEESE COMPANY
Mercury Road, Gallowfields
Richmond
North Yorks
DL10 4TQ

Tel: 01748 824932
Fax: 01748 822219
Contact: David Reed
Produce: A range of Swaledale cheeses, handmade to the original, traditional Swaledale recipe. Swaledale is a full fat, crumbly yet moist cheese lightly pressed with an open texture, mild but distinctive. Mail order service available; please 'phone for an order form.
Prices/Payment: No min. order for mail order service. Cash & cheques only.
Notes: Already suppliers to local shops in the area, company is interested in supplying to restaurants, hotels and other outlets. It is not open to the public.

TIDEFORD FOODS
Higher Tideford
Cornworthy
Totnes
Devon
TQ9 7HZ
Tel: 01803 712276
Fax: 01803 712388
Contact: Diana Cooper
Produce: Fresh, chilled organic soups, pestos and sauces sold in returnable kilner jars available by Mail Order. Also prepared meals. No min order charge, but P&P £6.
Prices/Payment: Cheques only.
Notes: No disabled access. Tideford Foods supply to Waitrose and Ticklemore Cheese but they are interested in supplying more to the trade.

TRADITIONAL NORFOLK POULTRY
33 Thetford Road
Watton
Thetford
Norfolk
IP25 6BX
Tel: 01953 885404
Fax: 01953 889262
Contact: Mark Gorton
Produce: Organic chicken and organic turkey. Chickens all year round. Turkeys at Christmas. Available by Mail Order. Min order 8 chickens or 1 turkey.
Prices/Payment: Chicken £2-£3 per lb. Turkey £2.50 - £3.50 per lb. Cash & cheques only – credit cards taken shortly.
Hours: Mail Order only.
Notes: Traditional Norfolk Poultry are interested in supplying to the trade.

TREGANNICK FARM
Drakewalls, Gunnislake
Cornwall
PL18 9ED
Tel: 01822 833969
Fax: 01822 834285
Contact: Richard & Jo Carlisle
Produce: A traditional slow maturing breed of table chicken. Organically produced (Soil Assoc. producer No P0036). Free ranging on organic grass. Reared traditionally to give a special flavour. Delivery via their own van in Devon & Cornwall and by carrier elsewhere. No min. order.
Notes: No credit cards. Also supplies to Riverford Farm Foods West Country Organic Foods. The Carlisles are interested in supplying to the trade. Farm not open to the public for direct sales.

TREVERVAN HOUSE QUALITY PRESERVES & PICKLES
Trevervan House
Trewarmett
Tintagel
Cornwall
PL34 0ES
Tel: 01840 770486
Fax: 01840 770486
Contact: Jo Smith
Produce: Handmade luxury quality jams and marmalades with a high fruit content. Sugar-free 100% fruit spreads. Chutneys and pickles. Mail Order available. Orders taken by letter, telephone or fax. No min. order. 'Phone for a mail order leaflet.
Prices/Payment: Grapefruit marmalade with brandy, £1.07 per 227g jar.

Apple chutney £1.04 per 227g jar.
Raspberry & peach spread sweetened
with apple juice, £1.25 per 198g jar.
All major credit cards taken.
Hours: Not open to the public.
Notes: Trevervan House supply
Londis (Tintagel), Merlins Gifts
(Tintagel), Country Goodness (East
Looe) and Paraphernalia (St.Ives).
Trevervan supply to some trade
outlets and are interested in supplying
to more.

VIVIAN'S HONEY FARM
Hatherleigh, Okehampton
Devon
EX20 3LJ
Tel: 01837 810437
Fax: 01837 810437
Contact: George & Margaret Tonkin
Produce: Honey from their own bees.
Clover honey from hedgerows and
clover pastures. Six sizes of glass jars
from 1.5oz to 1lb. Over 30 filled
pottery containers from bone china to
stoneware. Also Heather honey from
Dartmoor in 8oz & 1lb glass. Mail
order price list on request. No min.
order.
Prices/Payment: Clover, 1lb glass
£2.50. Heather, 1lb glass £2.98.
(retail). No min. order. Cash and
cheques only.
Notes: Suppliers to The National
Trust in Devon & Cornwall and
approx 100 other outlets. Interested
in selling to catering trade, especially
7lb pails and individual portions. Not
open to the public for direct sales.

**THE WILTSHIRE
TRACKLEMENT CO**
**The Dairy Farm
Pinkney Park
Sherston, Malmesbury
SN16 0NX**
TEL: 01666 840851
FAX: 01666 840022
**CONTACT: Guy Tullberg/Shirley
Bailey**
**PRODUCE: Mustards: Chilli, Cider,
Black, Tarragon, Herb, Garlic &
Chive, Green Peppercorn, Spiced
Honey, Beer, Strong English,
Horseradish. Chutneys: Tomato,
Country Garden, Apple, Salsa ,
Piccalilli. Sauces: Horseradish &,
Horseradish & Dill, Dill Tarragon,
Tartare, Apple, Cranberry, Mint,
Cumberland, Barbecue, Brown, Red
& Yellow Devill Sauce. Jellies:
Apple & Mint, Sage & Thyme,
Rosemary, apple/cdr Brandy,
Spiced Redcurrant, Redcurrant,
Red Pepper/Chilli, Thai, Basil &
Tarragon Vinaigrette. Available by
Mail Order. Min order 6 jars in any
combination.**
**PRICES/PAYMENT: From £1.70 for
cider mustard to £2.70 for vinaig-
rettes. Access and Visa cards taken.**
**HOURS: 9am-5pm telephone
enquiries only.**
**NOTES: Local stockist: Skidmores
(Sherston). Others - Partridges
(London), Kendals (Manchester)
and Watty's Delicatessen (Exeter).**

**Please note that many other firms in the main regional listings also sell by mail
order as well as direct to the public – see the heading "mail order" on page 196 in
the "Index of Food by Type" to access contact information on those firms**

The idea of farmers taking their produce to market and selling it direct is of course not a new one but the concept has recently undergone a revival if not rebirth following the success of such markets in the USA. There are now a number of urban centres where, usually on a weekly basis, not only farmers but organic growers, cheese makers and food makers of all types gather to sell their wares directly to the consumer. This is, like the box scheme, part of a mood among discerning food buyers for buying direct – not only for reasons of economy but also for freshness and quality. The following are brief details of the markets currently under way. We have given contact numbers in every case so please be sure to check with them that the market is taking place on the days and in the place given before starting out.

ASHFORD FARMERS' MARKET
is held each Thursday in Ashford Town Centre, Kent between 9am and 4pm. It is however small and seasonal so be sure to check it is on before leaving.
Contact: David Lloyd at Ashford Borough Council on 01233 33030.

BATH FARMERS' MARKET
is normally held on the 1st and 3rd Saturday of the month at Green Park Station, Bath. Usually 35 stalls.
Contact: Richard on 0117 942 1850.

BRIDPORT FARMERS' MARKET
Contact: Janet Osbourne or Tim Crabtree on 01308 459050.

BRISTOL FARMERS' MARKET
is held fortnightly on a Wednesday in the city centre between 9.30am and 3.00pm with 25 or 30 stalls.
Contact: Grace Davis at Bristol City Council on 0117 992 4476.

CULLUMPTON FARMERS' MARKET
is held with about 25 stalls on the 2nd Saturday of the month at Station Road car park Cullumpton from 10am-1pm.
Contact: Tracy Frankpitt, Market Organiser, Coley Croft, c/o Peverstone, Cullumpton, Devon EX15 1RW.

FROME FARMERS' MARKET
is held on the 2nd Saturday of the month at The Cheese & Grain Building, Market Yard, Justice Lane, Frome.
Contact: Denise Finch at the above address or 'phone 01373 455420. Fax: 01373 453704.

GLASTONBURY FARMERS' MARKET
is held on the 4th Saturday of the month at St. John's Car Park, behind the High Street, Glastonbury – 9.30am to 1.30pm.
Contact: Kate Hall, Local Agenda 21 Officer at Mendip Council on 01749 343399.

HOLMFIRTH FARMERS' MARKET
is held on 2nd and 4th Sunday of the month.
Contact: Gerald Riley on 01484 223474 or Mira Kubala on 01484 223572

LOSTWITHIEL FARMERS' MARKET
is held in the community centre Lostwithiel, usually every 2 weeks from 10am-3pm.
Contact: Mrs Joy Cheeseman, Market Controller on 01840 250586 or on their website at
www.cliffcheeseman.purplenet.co.uk
Email: cliffcheeseman@purplenet.co.uk

WOLVERHAMPTON FARMERS' MARKET
is held every Wednesday in School Street, town centre, from 10am-3pm.
Contact: Karen Crosby, Divisional Manager Markets at Wolverhampton Borough Council on 01902 555210. Fax: 01902 554329.

NOTES: We have received reports for some months of a proposed market in **Loughborough.** However our contact with the Charnwood Borough Council on 01509 263151 has revealed that nothing has yet been finalised.

One widespread and excellent source of quality and handmade foods are the Women's Institute Markets. Members of local WIs will assemble, usually on a weekly basis, to sell the produce of their own kitchens and gardens to the general public. As well as having to comply with all the relevant food and trading legislation the produce, by its very nature, is fresh and reasonably priced. If you have never partaken of the delights of a WI Market, have a browse through the following list and make a visit. The venues below are active on a weekly basis unless otherwise stated. However, please 'phone **01189 394646** to double-check that a market is taking place if you are travelling a long distance.

They also operate a parcel scheme which enables customers to send parcels of WI produce to friends or relatives (minimum value £10). To send a parcel, ring the number above and they will give you a contact 'phone number for the area where your parcel is to go. You can then place your order. Those places marked * in the list below are the only ones that **do not** participate in this scheme.

AVON

Backwell
Fri 1.45 - 3.15
WI Hall, Station Road

Bath
Fri 10.00 - 11.30
St. Stephen's Centre
St. Stephen's Church,
Lansdowne Road

Bath (Green Park)
Tue 9.30 - 2.00
Green Park Station Market
Sainsburys Car Park)

Chew Valley
Fri 10.00 - 11.00
The Old School Room, The Parade,
Chew Magna

Clevedon
Fri 2.30 - 3.45
1st Clevedon Scout Hall
off Great Western Road,
(opposite
entrance to Safeway car park)

Doynton
1st & 3rd Sat 10.30-11.30
Village Hall, Doynton

Freshford
Tues 10.30 - 11.30
[1st & 3rd Tues of every month]
Village Memorial Hall,
Freshford Lane

Keynsham & District
Fri 10.30 - 11.30
Main Hall, Fear Institute, High Street

Marshfield
Fri 10.30 - 11.30
Church Hall, Tormarton Lane

Nailsea & District
Fri 10.00 - 11.15
The Methodist Church, Silver Street

Portishead
Fri 10.15- 11.15
Folk Hall, High Street

Thornbury
Wed 9.30 - 11.00
Cossham Hall

Westbury on Trym & District
Fri 10.30 - 11.30
Methodist Church Hall,
Westbury Hill

Weston-Super-Mare
Wed 10.15 - 11.15
Corpus Christi Hall,
Walliscote Road

Wrington Vale
Fri 10.30 - 11.30
Scout Hall, Wrington

BEDFORDSHIRE

Ampthill
Thurs 8.00 - 12.00 [April-Sept]
[8.15-12.00 Oct-March]
Market Place, Bedford Street

Bedford
Wed 7.30 - 1.00
Horne Lane (open Market)

Dunstable
Wed 8.30 - 12.30
Methodist Church Hall,
Ashton Square

Leighton Buzzard
Tues 8.30 - 12.30
[8.30 - 3.00 in Summer]
Market Square

Shefford
Fri 8.30 - 11.00
St. Michael's Church Hall,
Ampthill Road

BERKSHIRE

Cookham
Fri 9.00 - 10.45 [March-Oct]
Fri 9.15 - 10.45 [Nov-Feb]
Pinder Hall, Lower Road

Earley
Fri 8.00 - 10.30
Silverdale Centre,
Maiden Erlegh School
Campus, Silverdale Road

Pangbourne
Fri 9.30 - 11.00
Parish Hall

Reading
Thurs 9.30 - 12.30
St. Mary's Church House,
Chain St

Tadley
Wed 8.30 - 10.15
Community Centre,
Newchurch Rd

Windsor & District
Thurs 10.00 - 11.30
WI Hall, The Green, Datchet

Wokingham
Fri 12.00 - 1.00
Wokingham District Council
Offices Sat 10.00 - 12.00
[1st Sat in the month]
Rose Street Methodist Hall

Yateley
Fri 10.00 - 11.00
Monteagle Community Hall &
Yateley WI Hall, Reading
Road [alternates between the two]

BUCKINGHAMSHIRE

Amersham
Fri 8.00 - 11.15
Free Church Hall, Sycamore Corner

Buckingham
Sat 8.00 - 12.00. Bull Ring

Milton Keynes
Fri 8.00 - 1.00
Madcap Centre, corner of Creed St/Church St, Wolverton

Olney & District
Thurs 7.30 - 12.30
The Market Square

Princes Risborough
Thurs 9.15 - 12.00 [March-Dec] Market Square

Thame
Tues 8.00 - 12.00
Thame Market Square, Upper High St

CAMBRIDGESHIRE - CAMBRIDGE

Cambridge
Thurs 8.00 - 12.00
Market Square

Great Shelford
Wed 8.30 - 11.00
Memorial Hall

CAMBRIDGESHIRE - HUNTINGDON & PETERBOROUGH

Huntingdon
Fri 8.30 - 11.00
WI Centre, 6A Walden Road (off Ring Road)

St. Ives
Fri 8.15 - 12.00
Corn Exchange

St. Neots
Thurs 8.30 - 12.00
Church Rooms, Church Walk

Wansford
Thurs 9.30-10.30 [fortnightly]
The Community Hall

CAMBRIDGESHIRE - ISLE OF ELY

Ely & District
Fri 8.30 - 11.30
The Old Dispensary, St Mary's Street

March
Wed 9.15 - 12.00
Scout Hall, Mill View Car Park, Creek Road

Wisbech
Thurs 8.30- 11.30
St. Peter's Church Hall

CHESHIRE

Farndon
Wed 9.00 - 11.30
Chapel House, Church Street

Frodsham
Thurs 9.00 - 12.00
Wellspring Centre, Church St

Macclesfield
Fri 9.30 - 11.30
Senior Citizens Hall, Duke Street Car Park

Nantwich
Thurs 8.00 - 12.00
Market Hall

Neston
Fri 8.00 - 12.00
Market Hall (underneath Town Hall)

Tattenhall
Fri 9.15 - 11.15
Barbour Institute, High Street

Willaston (Wirral)
Fri 9.00 - 11.30
Memorial Hall

CLEVELAND

Guisborough
Thurs 12.30 - 2.30
St. Nicholas Church Hall, Bow Street

Stockton
Fri 9.25 - 11.00
Stockton Parish Church Hall High Street

Yarm
Fri 1.00 - 3.00
Methodist Church Hall (Catholic Church Hall June-Oct)

CORNWALL

Callington
Wed 10.15 - 11.45
WI Hall, Haye Road

Falmouth & District
Fri 9.30 - 11.30
The Athenaeum Club, Kimberley Place

Helston
Fri 7.45 - 12.00
Corn Exchange Coinagehall Street

Illogan & District
Tues 9.15 - 11.00
Harris Memorial Hall,

Launceston & District
Tues 8.30 - 12.00
Town Hall

Liskeard
Fri 8.30 - 11.15 [April-Sept]
Fri 8.30 - 11.00 [Oct -March]
Longroom, Public Hall, West Street

Penzance
Thurs 8.30-11.45
St John's Hall

Perranporth
Fri 10.00 - 11.30
Memorial Hall

Roseland & District [Portscatho]
Fri 2.00 - 3.15 [March-Oct]
Portscatho Memorial Hall

Torpoint
Tues 9.30 - 11.30
Silver Band Hut, Antony Road

Truro & District
Tues 9.15 - 2.00
Trelawney Bar Hall for Cornwall

Veryan
Fri 10.30 - 11.30
Royal British Legion Hall

Wadebridge
Thurs 08.45-12.00
Town Hall

CUMBRIA-CUMBERLAND

Brampton
Wed 8.00 - 11.30
The Moot Hall

Cockermouth
Fri 9.30 - 12.00 [Apr-Dec]
Christ Church Rooms, South Street

Whitehaven
Thurs 10.30 - 12.00
YMCA, Irish Street

Wigton
Tues 8.00 - 1.30
Market Hall

CUMBRIA-WESTMORLAND

Ambleside
Fri 10.00 - 11.30 [March-Dec]
St. John's Ambulance Hall, Stockghyl Lane

Eden Valley (Appleby)
Fri 8.30 - 11.00
Appleby Public Hall

Kendal
Fri 10.30 - 11.30 [end Feb-Dec]
YWCA Hall, Stricklandgate

Kirkby Lonsdale
Thurs 10.15-11.30 [Feb-Dec]
The Reading Room, Institute

Kirkby Stephen
Fri 2.00 - 3.00 [March-Dec]
Methodist Sunday School

Milnthorpe & District
Fri 10.00 - 11.15 [March-Dec] Memorial Hall,
(ex British Legion Hall)

Ulverston & District
Thurs 9.30 - 11.30 [March-Dec] Coronation Hall, County Square

DERBYSHIRE

Bakewell
Sat 9.45 - 12.30
Bakewell Town Hall

Belper & District
Fri 9.45 - 12.00
Masonic Hall, Campbell Street

Buxton
Sat 10.00 - 4.00 [May-mid Oct]
Pavilion Gardens

Chesterfield
Sat 8.00 - 4.30
Open Market, New Square

Derby
Fri 10.00 - 12.00
Community Centre,
Uttoxeter Road, Mickleover Village

Glossop & District
Sat 9.30 - 11.30
Labour Club, Chapel Street

* Hope Valley
Fri 9.45 - 11.30
Hathersage Methodist School Room, Hathersage

Matlock & District
Fri 9.45 -12.05
Imperial Rooms, Imperial Road

DEVON

Axminster
Thurs 9.30 - 11.30 [Winter]
9.00 - 12.00 [Summer]
Masonic Hall, South Street

Barnstaple & District
Fri 7.00 - 1.00
Pannier Market, Butcher's Row

Bideford
Sat 7.00 - 12.00
Tues 8.00 - 12.30 [Mar - Dec]
13/14 Butcher's Row, Pannier Market

Exeter
Fri 8.15- 10.30
St Sidwell's Methodist Church Hall, Sidwell Street
Methodist Church

Exmouth & District
Fri 8.30 - 11.15
Wesley Hall, Tower Street

Holsworthy
Wed 10.00 - 12.30
The Crown and Sceptre

Honiton
Fri 10.00 - 11.15
Red Cross Hall, King Street

Ivybridge & District
Fri 8.45 - 11.30
Dartmoor Leisure Centre

Kingsbridge
Wed 8.30 - 12.00
Foyer of Town Hall

South Molton
Thurs 7.00 - 1.00
Pannier Market

Newton Abbot
Wed 8.00 - 3.00
Newton Abbot Indoor Market

Tavistock
Fri 7.00 - 12.00
Pannier Market

Tiverton & District
Fri 7.30 - 11.00
Memorial Hall, Angel Hill

DORSET

Bridport (West Dorset)
Sat 9.00 - 11.30
WI Hall, North Street

Christchurch & District
Mon 9.30 - 11.30
United Reformed Church Hall, Millams Street

Dorchester
Fri 8.30 - 11.00
Magistrates Room - Corn Exchange

Gillingham & District
Fri 9.30 - 11.00 [Jan/Feb/March) Fri 9.30 - 11.30 [Apr-Dec] Methodist Church Hall, High Street

Isle of Portland
Fri 9.00 - 11.30
Jubilee Hall, Easton

Kinson & District
Thurs 10.00 - 12.00
Pelhams Community Centre, Kinson, Bournemouth

Shaftsbury
Thurs 10.00 - 12.00
Shaftsbury Town Hall

Sherborne
Thurs 8.45 - 11.30
Church Hall, Digby Road

Sturminster Newton
Mon 9.30 - 11.30
Royal British Legion Club, Bath Road

Swanage
Fri 10.00 - 11.30
Catholic Hall, Remstone Road

Verwood
Fri 10.00 - 11.30
Memorial Hall

Wimborne
Fri 10.00 - 12.00
Allendale Community Centre, Hanham Road

* Wool
Thurs 10.00 - 11.00
The D'urberville Centre, Colliers Lane

Wyke Regis
Fri 9.00 - 10.15
WI Hall, Gallwey Road

DURHAM

Barnard Castle
Wed 10.30 - 12.00
St. Mary's Parish Hall

Consett
Fri 10.00 -11.30 [March-Dec]
St John Ambulance Hall, John Street

Darlington
Tues 10.00 - 11.30
Friends Meeting House, Skinnergate

Durham City
Fri 10.00 - 11.00
Shakespeare Hall, North Road

Sedgefield
Fri 9.30 - 11.00 [closed Aug & Jan] Parish Hall

ESSEX

Bishop's Stortford
Thurs 7.00 - 12.00
Fri 8.00 - 12.00
Watson's Poultry Market, Hadham Road
Sat 8.00 - 12.00
Apton Road Day Centre

Danbury
Thurs 9.00 - 10.45
Danbury Sports & Social
Centre, Eves Corner

* Epping
Mon 8.00 - 1.00
[Nov-April] Centre Point, St.
Johns Rd,
[May-Oct] High Street, Epping

Great Dunmow
Thurs 9.30 - 12.15
Catholic Church Hall, Mill
Lane

Hadleigh
Tues 8.15-1.15[Feb-mid Dec]
United Reformed Church,
Church Road

Halstead
Fri 8.30 - 11.00
Bull Hotel, Bridge Street

Hatfield Peverel
Thurs 9.00 - 10.30
The Village Hall

Maldon
Thurs 9.00 - 1.00
Friary, Maldon

Rayleigh
Wed 9.00- 12.00
Mill Hall Foyer, Bellingham
Lane

Saffron Walden
Tues & Fri 8.30 - 11.30
Rear of Town Hall

Shenfield & District
Fri 9.00 - 11.30
Shenfield Parish Hall, Hutton
Road

Stanway
Fri 1.45 - 3.45
Stanway Village Hall, Villa
Road

Walton & District
Fri 10.00 - 12.00
Red Triangle Club, Portobello
Road

GLOUCESTERSHIRE

Cheltenham
Thurs 10.30 - 12.00
The Foyer
Everyman Theatre, Regent St.

Cheltenham (Warden Hill)
Fri 9.30 - 10.30
Warden Hill United Reformed
Church Hall, Salisbury
Avenue

Chipping Campden & District
Fri 9.00 - 11.00
Lower Room, Town Hall

Cinderford
Fri 9.45 - 11.15
Belle View Community
Centre,
Belle View Road

Cirencester
Fri 8.00 - 10.30
Bingham House, Dyer St

Coleford & District
Fri 10.15 - 11.45
[closed Jan & Feb]
Community Centre,
Bank Street

Fairford
Wed 9.30 - 11.00
Palmer Hall, Fairford

Gloucester
Thurs 9.00 - 2.30
Fri 8.30 - 12.30
Wheatstone Hall,
(City Museum Building),
Brunswick Rd

Greet & District
Thurs 9.45 - 10.45
The Parish Hall, Cowl Lane,
Winchcombe

Lechlade & District
Thurs 9.00 - 11.00 Winter
9.00 -11.30 Summer
The Methodist Church Hall
High Street

Minchinhampton
Thurs 9.00 - 11.00
Market House, The Porch
Room

Moreton-in-Marsh & District
Thurs 10.00 - 11.30
WI Hall, New Road

Nailsworth
Fri 9.15 - 10.45
Parish Room, St. George's
Church

Newent & District
Fri 10.00 - 11.00
Newent Memorial Hall

Northleach & District
Thurs 9.45 - 10.30
Cotswold Hall

Painswick
Fri 10.00 - 11.00
Painswick Town Hall

Stroud
Fri 8.00 - 11.30
The Shambles, Stroud

Tetbury
Fri 9.30 - 11.00
Market Hall, Town Hall

Tewkesbury
Fri 9.45 - 11.30
Town Hall, High Street

HAMPSHIRE

Alresford
Thurs 9.00 - 11.30
Community Hall, West Street

Alton
Fri 9.15-11.00
Alton Community Centre

Andover
Fri 8.00 - 11.45
The Guildhall, High Street

Bishop's Waltham
Fri 9.30 - 11.00
Jubilee Hall, Little Shore Lane

Chandlers Ford
Tues 9.30 - 11.00 [except
those that follow a Bank
Holiday]
Age Concern Hall, Brownhill
Road

Fordingbridge
Fri 10.00 - 11.30
Avonway Community Centre

Hartley-Wintney
Fri 10.00 - 11.00
WI Hut, Green Lane

Hythe & Waterside
Thurs 10.00 - 12.00
Hythe Community Centre

Lymington
Fri 9.45 - 11.30
Lymington Community
Centre, Cannon Street

New Milton
Thurs 10.45 - 11.45
The New Milton Scout
Centre, Caird Avenue

Ocean Village (Southampton)
Wed 10.30 - 3.00
Ocean Way Canute Pavilion,
Ocean Village

Petersfield
Fri 9.00 - 10.30
St. Peter's Hall

Portchester
Sat 10.00 - 11.00
Portchester Methodist Church
Hall, Castle Street

Ringwood
Wed 10.00 - 11.30
The Activities Centre,
Greyfriars
(behind the Public Library)

Romsey
Fri 10.00 - 11.00
United Reform Hall

Stubbington
Fri 9.45 - 10.45
Methodist Church Hall, Mays
Lane

Titchfield
Fri 10.00 - 11.15
Parish Rooms, High Street

Waterlooville & District
Thurs 9.30 - 11.30
St. George's Church Hall,
St. George's Walk

Whitchurch
Fri 10.00 - 11.30
Parish Hall, London Road

Winchester
Fri 8.30 - 11.30
Badger Farm Community
Centre, Olivers Battery

HEREFORDSHIRE

Bromyard
Thurs 9.00 - 12.00
Public Hall, New Rd

Hereford
Fri 8.00 - 11.30
Market Place, St. Peter's
Church House, St. Peter's Sq.

Kington & District
Fri 10.00 - 11.30
Baptist School Room, Bridge
Street

Ledbury
Fri 10.00 - 12.00
St. Catherine's Hall, High St.

Leominster & District
Fri 8.30 - 12.00
Grafton House Market,
Saverite Car Park

Ross-on-Wye
Sat 8.30 - 12.00
Merton House Annexe, Edde
Cross St

South Wye (Hereford)
Fri 1.00 - 2.30
St. Martins Church Hall, Ross
Road

HERTFORDSHIRE

Baldock & District
Fri 9.30 - 11.00
Baldock Community Centre

Berkhampsted
Sat 7.30 - 11.30
Berkhampsted Market,
High Street

Bovingdon & District
Sat 10.00 - 11.30
Memorial Hall, High Street

Cuffley & District
Thurs 10.00 - 12.00
Cuffley Hall (Back),
Maynard Place

Harpenden
Fri 9.00 - 11.30
Methodist Church Hall
High Street

Hatfield & District
Sat 8.00 - 1.00
Hatfield Market Place

Hertford
Fri 9.30 - 11.30
Castle Hall, Hertford

Kings Langley
Thurs 10.00 - 12.00
Oddfellows Hall, High Street

Little Hadham & District
Thurs 12.30 - 3.00
[1st Thurs of each month]
Little Hadham Village Hall

Marshalswick
Fri 2.00 - 4.00
St. Mary's Church Hall,
Sherwood Av

Redbourn
Thurs 9.30 - 11.30
Village Hall, High Street

Royston
Wed 8.00 - 12.30
Sat 7.45 - 12.30
Corn Exchange, Market Hill

St. Albans
8.30-11.00 1st Sat each month
Church Parlour, Trinity
Church, Beaconsfield Road

Sawbridgeworth
Fri 11.00 - 1.00
Church House

Ware & District
Fri 9.30 - 12.00
Place House, Blue Coats
Yard, East Street

ISLE OF WIGHT

Freshwater (West Wight)
Fri 9.30 - 11.00
Wesley Hall, Brookside Road

Newport
Fri 9.30 - 11.00
Hollyrood Hall, High Street

Ryde
Fri 9.30 - 11.30
St. John Ambulance Hall,
Newport St

Shanklin
Fri 10.00 - 11.30
Falcon Cross Hall, Falcon
Cross Road

* Yarmouth
Wed 9.45 - 12.00 (May to
Sept)
Yarmouth Town Hall, Town
Hall Square

KENT EAST KENT

Ashford
Fri 8.30 - 11.30
Willesborough WI Hall,
Church Road

Canterbury & District
Fri 9.00 - 10.30
St. Peters Church of England
Hall, St. Peters Lane

Charing & District
Thurs 9.30 - 11.30
1/2 Palace Farm Cottage,
Market Place

Dover
Thurs 9.00 - 11.00
Biggin Hall, High Street

Folkstone & District
Fri 9.30 - 11.00
United Reformed Church
Hall, Castle Hill Avenue

* Hythe
Fri 09.30-12.00 Chapel Street

Romney Marsh
Fri 9.30 - 11.30
Methodist Church Hall, High
Street, New Romney

Sandwich & District
Thurs 8.30 - 12.00
The Cattle Market

Sittingbourne
Fri 9.00 - 11.00
The Masonic Hall, Albany Rd

Thanet Villages
Fri 9.30 - 11.00
Church House,
Kent Gardens Birchington

KENT WEST KENT

Bearsted
Sat 10.00 - 11.00
WI Hall, The Street

Bexley
Thursday 10.30 - 11.30
Freemantle Hall, Bexley High
Street

Borough Green
Thurs 2.00 - 3.15
Borough Green Village Hall

East Peckham & District
Thurs 10.45-11.45 [Feb-Dec]
Methodist Curran Hall

Eynsford District
Fri 2.00 - 3.00
Eynsford Village Hall, High
Street
(Opposite Castle Hotel)

Hawkhurst
Thurs 10.00 - 11.00
Dunks Hall, Rye Road

Ide Hill
Wed 11.00 - 12.00 [March-
Dec]
Ide Hill Village Hall

Longfield
Fri 10.30 - 11.30
Jubilee Hall, Main Road

Maidstone
Thurs 11.00 - 12.30
United Reformed Church
Hall, Week Street

Orpington
Fri 10.00 - 12.00
The Aubrey Mullock Hall,
The Orpington Halls, High
Street

Rochester
Thurs 11.00 - 12.15
Eastgate Adult Education
Centre, High Street

Sevenoaks
Thurs 10.00 - 11.30
The Drill Hall, Argyle Road

Tenterden & District
Fri 10.00 - 11.00
St.Mildred's Church Hall,
Church Road

Tonbridge
Fri 10.00 - 11.00
Scout Hut, Lamberts Yard

Tunbridge Wells
Thurs 10.30 - 11.30
Toc H Hall, Little Mount Sion

LANCASHIRE

Carnforth & District
Fri 10.30 - 11.30 [March-
Dec]
Civic Hall, North Road

* Clitheroe
Tues 10.30 - 11.45 [March-
Dec]
Lower St. Mary's Parish Hall,
off York Street

Garstang & District
Thurs 10.00 - 11.30 [March-
Dec] St. Thomas's Hall,
Church Street

Kirkham & District
Thurs 10.30 - 11.30 [March-
Dec]
United Reformed Church,
Poulton Street

Longton
Fri 10.30 - 11.45 [March-
Dec] WI Hall, School Lane

LEICESTERSHIRE

Ashby
Thurs 8.00 - 12.00
Town Hall, Ashby-de-la-
Zouch

Ashby-de-la-Zouch & District
Fri 9.30 - 11.30
Memorial Hall, North Street

Birstall
Fri 10.00 - 11.15 [Feb-Dec]
Methodist Church Hall,
Wanlip Lane

Blaby & District
Fri 10.15 - 11.30 [Feb-Dec]
The Social Centre, Leicester
Road

Glenfield & District
Fri 10.00 - 11.15
St Peters Church Centre,
Church Road

Lutterworth & District
Thurs 10.00 - 11.30 [March-
Dec]
Methodist Hall, Bitteswell
Road

Market Harborough
Tues 8.00 - 4.00
Stall G1, Market Hall,
Northampton Rd

Melton Mowbray
Tues 9.30-11.30 [March-Dec]
Gloucester House, Norman
Way

Oadby & Wigston
Fri 10.00-11.00[mid Feb-Dec]
Trinity Methodist Church
Hall, Harborough Road

Oakham
Fri 09.30 - 11.15 [Feb-Dec]
Congregational Church Hall,
High Street

Syston & District
Fri 10.00 - 11.15 [Feb-Dec]
Methodist Church Hall, High
Street

LINCOLNSHIRE – NORTH

Alford
Tues 9.30 - 12.00
St. Wilfrid's Church Hall,
Church Street

Chapel-St-Leonards
Thurs 9.45 - 11.45
Village Hall, Sea Road

Gainsborough & District
Tues 9.00 - 11.45
Rechabites Hall, Lord Street

Lincoln
Fri 8.30 - 12.30
Bailgate Methodist Church
Hall

Market Rasen
Fri 8.15 - 11.15
The Church Room, Market
Place

Wainfleet & District
Fri 10.00 - 11.30
OAP Hall, Rumbold Lane

LINCOLNSHIRE – SOUTH

Grantham
Fri 9.00 - 11.00
United Reform Church Hall,
Castlegate

Sleaford
Fri 12.00 - 3.00
United Reformed Church,
Southgate

Stamford
Friday 8.30 - 10.30
Blue Room, Stamford Arts
Centre

LONDON BOROUGHS

* Barnes
Fri 10.00 - 12.00
Barnes Community
Association,
Rose House, High Street

MIDDLESEX

Ashford
Fri 1.00 - 2.00
Methodist Church Hall,
Clarendon Road

Ruislip
Fri 10.00 - 11.30
The Stables (rear of Library),
Manor Farm Complex, Bury
Street

* Stanwell
Tues 11.00 - 12.00
Village Hall, High Street

NORFOLK

Attleborough
Thurs 8.45 - 11.00
Youth & Community Centre,
Church Road

Aylsham
Fri 8.50 - 12.00
Aylsham Town Hall, Market
Place

Brooke & District
Fri 9.15 - 10.30 [closed Jan]
Brooke Methodist Hall,
Bungay Road

Cromer
Tues 9.30 - 11.30
WI Hall, Garden Street

E. Dereham
Fri 9.45 - 11.15
The Club Room, Barwells
Court

Diss
Wed 8.30 - 11.30
United Reformed Church
Hall, Mere Street

Downham Market
Sat 7.45 - 11.30
Downham Square Market
Place

Drayton & District
Fri 9.00 - 11.00
Bob Carter Centre, School
Road

Fakenham & District
Thurs 8.30 - 11.45
Old Cattle Market, Bridge
Street

Harleston & District
Wed 9.30 - 11.15
WI Hall, Chandler's Lane

Heacham & District
Fri 10.00 - 11.30
[British Winter time]
10.00 - 12.00 [Summer time]
Church Hall, High Street

Holt
Fri 9.30 - 11.30
Parish Church Hall, Church
Street

King's Lynn
Fri 7.45 - 2.00
Tuesday Market Place

Loddon & District
Tues 9.15 - 10.45
The Hollies, High Street

Long Stratton & District
Fri 8.30 - 10.30
Chip Inn car park

North Walsham
Fri 9.30 - 12.00
[9.30 - 11.30 Jan-March 31st]
St. Benet's Hall

* Norwich
Thurs 7.30 - 12.00
Norwich Provision Market

Reepham
Wed 8.00 - 11.00
Bircham Centre, Market Place

Sheringham
Thurs 10.00 - 11.30
Sheringham Little Theatre

Swaffham & District
Fri 8.45 - 11.45
[not first 2 weeks of Jan]
Assembly Rooms, Market
Place

Watton
Wed 8.30- 11.45
Watton Community Christian
Centre

Wymondham
Fri 9.00 - 11.30
The Damgate Rooms, Chain
Entry

NORTHAMPTONSHIRE

Brackley & District
Fri 8.30 - 11.00
WI Hall, Manor Road

Daventry
Tues 8.30 - 11.30
United Reformed Church Hall

Kettering & District
Fri 8.45 - 11.00
Corn Market Hall, Kettering

Oundle & District
Thurs 9.30 - 10.30 [March-
Dec] Victoria Hall

Towcester
Thurs 9.00 - 12.00 [Feb-Dec]
Chantry House, Market Sq

Wellingborough
Wed 8.30 - 11.30
Tithe Barn

NORTHUMBERLAND

Hexham
Tues 10.00-11.30 [April-Dec]
St Aidens Church Hall,
Beaumont Street

Ponteland
Fri 10.00 - 11.15
Merton Hall, Ponteland

NOTTINGHAMSHIRE

Bingham & District
Thurs 7.30 - 12.00
WI Hall, Station Street

Newark
Wed 8.00 - 1.00
Butter Market, Town Hall

Nottingham
Fri 8.00 - 12.30
YMCA Hall, Shakespeare
Street

Retford
Sat 8.00 - 12.00
Ebsworth Halll

Southwell & District
Sat 8.30 - 11.30
WI Hall, Queen Street

Worksop Area
Fri 9.45 - 11.30
St. Anne's Scout HQ, Slack
Walk

OXFORDSHIRE

Abingdon
Fri 9.30 - 11.30
Roysse Room, The Guildhall

Banbury
Sat 8.00 - 12.30
Market Place

Bicester
Fri 8.30 - 11.00
Methodist Hall, Sheep Street

Bloxham
Fri 10.00 - 11.30
Ex-Serviceman's Hall, High
Street

Burford
Fri 8.15 - 11.45 [Feb-Dec]
The Tolsey, High Street

Chipping Norton
Fri 9.15 - 10.30
The Lower Town Hall

Eynsham & District
Thurs 9.00 - 10.30 [closed
January]
St. Leonards Church Hall,
Thames Street

Faringdon & District
Fri 9.30 - 11.00
Faringdon Corn Exchange

Henley on Thames
Fri 10.00 - 11.30
Town Hall, Market Place

Wallingford & District
Fri 9.45 - 11.15
Regal Centre

Wantage
Fri 9.45 - 10.45
The Vale & Downland
Museum, Church Street

Witney
Fri 8.30 - 10.30[closed
January]
Masonic Hall, Church Green

Woodstock
Fri 8.45 - 10.30
St. Hugh's Hall, Hensington
Road

SHROPSHIRE

Bridgnorth
Sat 8.15 - 12.00
Shakespeare Inn, Skittle Alley,
West Castle Street

Church Stretton
Fri 9.15 - 10.45
Scout Hut, Church Street

* Ludlow
Sat 8.30 - 11.30
The Womens Centre, Church
Street

Market Drayton
Wed 8.00 - 1.00
The Coach House,
Corbet Arms Hotel, High
Street

Much Wenlock
Thurs 7.30 - 12.00
Corn Exchange, High Street

Newport
Fri 7.30 - 12.00
Parish Rooms, New Street

Oswestry
Wed 7.00 - 2.00
Sat   7.30 - 1.00
Powys Hall, Bailey Head

Shrewsbury
Sat 8.00 - 1.00
Shrewsbury Indoor Market
Hall

Wellington
Thurs 8.00 - 1.00
Wellington Market

Whitchurch
Fri 7.30 - 12.30
New Market Hall

SOMERSET

Bridgwater
Fri 8.00 - 11.30
Charter Hall, Town Hall

Burnham-on-Sea
Fri 10.30 - 12.00
Community Centre, Burrow
Road

Chard & District
Thur 8.30 - 12.00
Guildhall Extension

Cheddar Valley
Tues 10.30 - 11.30
Church House, Church Street

Crewkerne
Fri 9.00 - 11.00
Speedwell Club, Abbey Street

Frome
Thurs 8.00 - 12.30
Market Hall

Huish Episcopi & District
Fri 8.30 - 11.15
All Saints Hall, North Street,
Langport

Minehead
Fri 10.00-11.00
Friends Meeting House,
Bancks Street

Street
Thurs 10.00 - 11.00
Crispin Hall,
High Street

Taunton
Wed & Fri 8.00 - 2.00
2 & 3 Bath Place

Wells
Fri 10.00 - 11.00
Seagger Hall,
Union Street

Wessex (Somerton)
Sat 9.30 - 11.30
Wessex Rooms
Broad Street, Somerton

Williton
Fri 10.00 - 11.15
Red Cross Centre,
Killick Way

Wincanton & District
Fri 9.30 - 12.00
Ash House, (next to
Weatherhead's shop), High
Street

Yeovil
Fri 8.00 - 2.00
Wessex Room, Princes Street

STAFFORDSHIRE

Burton & District
Thurs 7.00 - 11.00
Open market place at
entrance to Market Hall

Eccleshall
Fri 9.00 - 11.00
The Methodist Church Room,
Stone Road

Leek Moorlands
Wed 8.30 - 3.30
Butter Market, Leek

Lichfield
Fri 7.30 - 2.00
Lichfield Market Square

Newcastle-under-Lyme
Fri 9.15 -12.00
St. Giles Church Hall

Ringhills
Alternate Thursdays 10.30 -
12.00. Forget-me-Not Room,
Codsall
Alternate Fridays 10.00 -
11.30 The Jubilee Hall,
Brewood

Rugeley
Thurs 8.00 - 12.00
Market Square
[all year except for 2/3 wks
Dec/Jan]

Stone
Sat 10.00 - 12.30
The Crown Hotel, High Street

Tamworth
Fri 10.00-12.00
Supper Rooms , adjoining
Assembly Rooms,
Corporation St. Town Centre

Uttoxeter
Wed 8.30- 12.00
Wilfrid House, Carter Street

Whittington
Thurs 2.00 - 3.30 [closed
August] Village Hall

SUFFOLK EAST

Beccles & District
Fri 9.45 - 11.30
Public Hall

Bungay & District
Thurs 9.30 - 11.00
The Community Centre,
Upper Olland St

* Eye & District
Wed 10.00 - 11.00[Feb-Dec]
Eye Town Hall

Felixstowe & District
Fri 10.00 - 11.00
Trades & Labour Club, High
Street

*Framlingham
Tue 9.00 - 11.00
Framlingham United Free
Church

Halesworth
Fri 10.00 - 11.30
St. Mary's Church Hall

Ipswich
Thurs 10.15 - 11.30
St. Christopher's Church Hall,
Renfrew Road

Lowestoft & District
Fri 8.45 - 11.30
British Telecom Hall,
Clapham Road

Saxmundham & District
Wed 10.00 - 11.00
Gannon Rooms, Station
Appproach

Southwold
Fri 10.15 - 11.30 [March-Dec]
United Reform Church Hall,
High Street

Stowmarket & District
Thurs 9.00 - 11.30
St. Peter's Church Hall,
Church Walk

Woodbridge
Thurs 10.00 - 11.15
Woodbridge Community
Centre

SUFFOLK WEST

Bury St. Edmunds
Wed & Fri 8.30 - 12.00
Oddfellows Hall, 19 Whiting
Street

Clare & District
Fri 10.00 - 11.45
The Baptist Chapel, Clare

Hadleigh
Fri 8.30 - 11.45
United Reformed Church
Hall, Market Place

Long Melford & District
Fri 9.30 - 12.00 [closed Jan]
Old School

Newmarket
Tues 9.30 - 12.00 [Feb-Dec]
The Stable, High Street,
(above Gateway Supermarket)

SURREY

Banstead
Thurs 10.30 - 11.45
Banstead Community Hall,
Park Road

Bookham & District
Fri 10.15 - 11.30
The Main Hall, Old Barn
Hall,
Church Road, Great Bookham

Chiddingfold
Fri 9.00-10.30
Ex-Servicemen's Club,
Woodside Road

Chobham
Thurs 9.30 - 11.00
Chobham Village Hall

Cranleigh
Fri 9.30 - 11.0
The Bandroom, Village Way

Dorking
Fri 9.45 - 11.00
The Mulberry Centre,
Junction Road

* East Surrey Hospital
Fri 10.30 - 3.00 (2nd or 3rd
Fri ea month)
Canada Avenue, Redhill

Elmbridge
Fri 11.00 - 12.00
Hersham Village Hall,
Queens Road, Hersham,
Walton-on-Thames

Farnham
Fri 9.45 - 11.30
United Reformed Church
Hall, South Street

Godalming
Fri 8.30 - 10.30
[closed for 2 weeks after
Christmas]
Milford Village Hall

Horley
Fri 10.30 - 12.00
St. John's Ambulance Hall,
Victoria Road

Jacobs Well
Fri 10.00 - 11.30
Village Hall, Jacobs Well
Road

Leatherhead & District
Fri 10.30 - 11.30
Leatherhead Parish Church
Hall, Church Road

Oxted
Thurs 10.30 - 11.30
Red Cross Centre, Hoskins
Road

Pirbright
Thurs 10.45 - 11.45
Lord Pirbright Hall

Reigate
Fri 9.30 - 11.30
Methodist Church Hall, High
Street

Richmond
Friday 10.15 - 12.00
Council for Voluntary
Services,
1 Princes Street, Richmond
(town centre)

SUSSEX EAST

Battle
Fri 9.45 - 11.30
Langton Hall, High Street

Crowborough
Fri 8.30 - 11.00
Community Association Hall,
Pine Grove

Hastings
Fri 10.30 - 11.30 [March-Dec]
All Saints Church Hall, All
Saints Street

Lewes
Fri 10.00 - 11.00
St Thomas' Church Hall,
Cliffe Street

Lindfield
Thurs 10.00 - 11.15
The King Edward Hall

Mayfield
Fri 10.00 - 11.00
[not open 1st Friday of the
month]
London House, High Street

Newhaven
Thursday 10.00 - 11.00
Hillcrest Centre
Hillcrest Road

Newick & District
Fri 10.00 - 11.00
Village Hall

Pevensey Bay
Fri 10.30 - 11.30 [March-Dec]
St. Wilfrid's Hall

Ringmer
Tues 10.00 - 11.00
Ringmer Old Village Hall

Rottingdean
Fri 10.00 - 11.30
Whiteways Centre,
Whiteways Lane

Rye
Fri 10.00 - 10.45 [March-Dec]
Rye Community Centre,
Conduit Hill

Waldron
Wed 10.30 - 11.00
Lucas Hall

SUSSEX WEST

Ardingly
Thur 10.00-11.00
Ardingly Village Hall
(Hapstead Hall) High Street

Billingshurst & District
Tues 10.00 - 10.45
Village Hall, Roman Way

Burgess Hill
Thurs 10.00 - 11.30
Burgess Hill Theatre Club,
Church Walk

Chichester
Tues, Wed & Fri 8.00 - 3.30
Thurs & Sat 8.00 - 1.00
Butter Market, North Street

Durrington & District
Thurs 10.00 - 11.00
Church Hall, New Road

Emsworth
Thurs 10.00 - 11.30
Baptist Church Hall, North St

Felpham Rife
Fri 10.00 - 11.00
Memorial Village Hall,
Vicarage Lane

Ferring & District
Wed 10.00 - 11.00
Ferring Village Hall

Havant
Fri 9.30 - 12.00
United Reformed Church
Hall, Elm Lane

Horsham
Thurs 8.30 - 11.00
The Old Town Hall, Market
Square

Lancing
Fri 9.30 - 11.00
Roman Catholic Church Hall,
North Road

Petworth & District
Fri 10.00 - 11.45
Leconfield Hall

Rustington & District
Thurs 10.00 - 11.00
Parish Church Hall, The Street

Selsey
Fri 10.00 - 11.30 [May-Sept]
Scout Headquarters, School
Lane

Southwick & Shoreham
Fri 10.00 - 11.00
Southwick Community Centre

Steyning
Fri 8.00- 12.00 [mid April-end
Oct]
Penfold Church Hall, Church
Street

Storrington & District
Fri 9.30 - 11.00, Village Hall

West Worthing
Tues 10.30 - 12.00
Heene Community Centre

TYNESIDE

Gosforth
Fri 10.00 - 11.30 [Feb-Dec]
South Northumberland
Cricket Club, High Street

Whitley Bay
Fri 10.00 - 11.00
St. Edwards Parish Centre,
Roxburgh Terrace

TYNE & WEAR SOUTH

Biddick Farm (Washington)
Sat 10.00 - 2.00
[1st Sat each month, except
Jan]
Washington Arts Centre Craft
Market, Fatfield Road,
Fatfield, Washington

Ryton & District
Fri 10.30 - 12.30
Ryton Social Club, Main Road

WARWICKSHIRE

Alcester
Fri 8.30 - 12.00
Behind "Transformers", 37
High Street

Coleshill
Fri 8.30 - 11.00
Parish Rooms, High Street

* Kenilworth
Thurs 9.30 - 11.00
The Youth Club, Bertie Road

Leamington & District
Fri 9.30 - 10.45
St. Peter's Church Hall,
Dormer Place

Rugby
Thurs 10.00 - 11.30
John Lees Hall, Regent Street

Shipston-on-Stour
Sat 8.00 - 10.45
Townsend Hall, Sheep Street

Stratford-upon-Avon
Fri 10.30 - 11.30
Shottery Memorial Hall,
Hathaway Lane

Wellesbourne
Fri 10.00 - 11.30
Methodist School Room,
Bridge Street

WEST MIDLANDS

Allesley
Wed 9.45 - 11.00
Village Hall, Birmingham
Road

Balsall Common
Sat 10.00 - 11.00
Village Hall, Station Road

Dorridge
Fri 10.00 - 11.30
Bentley Heath Community
Centre,
Widney Road, Bentley Heath

Hall Green
Thurs 9.30- 11.00
Friends Meeting House,
Hamlet Road

Sutton Coldfield
Fri 1.30 - 3.00 [closed
August]
United Reformed Church
Hall, Gracechurch Centre

WILTSHIRE

Bradford-on-Avon
Thurs 10.30 - 12.00[1st & 3rd
Thurs each month] Trinity
Church Hall, Church Street

Chippenham
Fri 7.15 - 11.00
St. Andrews Church Hall,
just off Market Place

Corsham
Fri 9.30 - 11.00
St. Aldhelms Church Hall,
Pickwick Road

Cricklade
Fri 9.30 - 11.00
[last Friday of month)], Town
Hall

Devizes
Thurs. 10.00-11.30
The Library, Sheep Street

Downton & District
Fri 10.00 - 11.30
Downton Memorial Hall

Salisbury
Sat 7.00 - 2.00
The Guildhall Square,The
Market Place

Swindon & District
Fri 9.30 - 11.30
St. Adhelms Hall, off Regent St.

Tisbury
Sat 10.00 - 11.00
[1st & 3rd Sat of every month]
Victoria Hall

Trowbridge
Sat 8.45 - 12.00 [Fortnightly]
Salvation Army Room, Castle
Street

Vale of Pewsey
Tues 9.30 - 11.00
Bouverie Hall, Pewsey

Warminster & District
Fri 10.00 - 12.00
The Library, Three
Horseshoes Mall

Westbury
Fri 10.00 - 12.00
Parish Church Hall, Church
Lane

Wilton & District
Fri 10.00 - 11.00
Wilton Community Centre,
West Street

Wroughton
Fri 9.45 - 11.00
Ellendune Hall, Barretts Way

WORCESTERSHIRE

Droitwich
Fri 9.00 - 11.00
The Old Library

Evesham
Fri 8.30 - 11.15
Wallace House, Oat Street

Hagley & District
Fri 9.00 - 11.00
Hagley Community
Centre,Worcester Road

Malvern
Fri 8.45 - 11.15
Lyttleton Rooms, Church
Street

Pershore & District
Sat 9.00 - 11.00
The Pershore Men's Club,
45a High Street

Redditch & District
Fri 8.00-12.00
St. Stephens Church, Church
Green

Tenbury Wells
Tues 9.30 - 12.00
The Scout Hut, Palmers
Meadow

Upton-on-Severn
Sat 9.00 - 11.30
Winter 9.30-11.30
The Church Room, Old Street

Worcester
Fri 9.00 - 11.00 (Summer)
Fri 9.20 - 11.00 (Winter)
St. Clement's Church Hall,
Henwick Rd

EAST YORKSHIRE

Beverley
Fri 10.00 - 11.30
Memorial Hall, Lairgate

NORTH YORKSHIRE – EAST

Easingwold
Fri 9.30 - 11.30 [Feb-end of
Dec]
The Parish Room, Tanpit Lane
(past the Library)

Northallerton & District
Fri 11.00 - 1.00
Town Hall, High Street

Pickering
Thurs 9.45 - 11.45
WRVS Hall
(Over 60's Club), Hungate

Selby & District
Thurs 10.00 - 11.30
Hawdon Institute, off Market
Place

Stokesley & District
Fri 12.00 - 2.00 [Fortnightly]
Methodist Hall, High Street

NORTH YORKSHIRE – WEST

Skipton
Wed 8.30-11.45 [April-Dec]
The Craven Site, The
Devonshire Hotel

Wensleydale
Thurs 10.00 - 11.15
The Community Centre,
Leyburn

SOUTH YORKSHIRE

Doncaster
Fri 10.00 - 12.30
Women's Centre, Cleveland
Street

Penistone
Thurs 10.00 - 12.00
St. John's Community Centre,
Church Street

Sheffield
Sat 9.00 - 12.00
Scout Hut, Spooner Road,
Broomhill

Thorne
Fri 9.15 - 11.15
Old Folks Centre, Church
Street

Tickhill
Fri 10.00 - 11.45
Parish Room, Tickhill

WEST YORKSHIRE

Otley & District
Fri 10.00 - 11.45
[closed Jan & August Good
Friday]
Otley Civic Centre,
Boroughgate

WALES

CLWYD-DENBIGH
Denbigh
Fri 10.00 - 12.00 [March-
Dec] The Church Institute

Glan Conwy
Sat 10.00 - 11.30
Church House

Llangollen
Fri 10.00 - 12.00 [March-
Dec]
Town Hall, Castle Street

Ruthin
Fri 9.45 - 12.15 [Feb-Dec]
Market Hall, Market Street

Wrexham
Fri 10.00 - 12.00
Memorial Hall

CLWYD-FLINT

Hawarden & District
Thurs 10.00 - 12.00
[Fortnightly]
Community Rooms, 7 Glyn
Way

Mold & District
Fri 8.30 - 12.00 (Produce &
Crafts) [end Jan-mid Dec]
T.A Drill Hall, High Street
Fri 8.00-1.00 (Plants) [March-
end Oct] St. David's Walk,
High Street

DYFED-CAERFYRDDIN

Carmarthen
Wed 8.00 - 4.00
Sat 8.00 - 2.00
Carmarthen Market

Llandeilo
Fri 8.00 - 12.45
Llandeilo Civic Hall, Crescent
Road

* Llandovery
Fri 10.00 - 12.00
The Castle Hotel, King's Road

Llanelli
Thurs 9.00 - 12.00
Llanelli Outside Market

Newcastle Emlyn
Fri 9.45 - 12.15
Church Hall, Church Road

DYFED-CEREDIGION

Aberporth
Tues 9.30 - 12.00
Festival Room, Village Hall

Aberystwyth
Thurs 8.30 - 12.00
Market Hall, Great Darkgate
Street

Cardigan
Fri 9.30 - 1.00
Guildhall, Cardigan

Lampeter
Tues (every other) 8.30 -
12.00 AFC Social Club,
Drovers Road

New Quay & District
Fri 11.00 - 12.30
New Quay Memorial Hall

Tregaron
Tues 10.00-1.00 [Fortnightly]
Tregaron Memorial Hall

DYFED-PEMBROKESHIRE

Fishguard & District
Tues 9.00 - 12.00 [May-Sept]
Unity Hall, Rope Walk

Haverfordwest
Fri 10.00 - 12.00
Albany Church Hall

Manorbier & District
Wed 10.30 - 12.00 [April-mid
Sept]
Village Hall

* Narberth & District
Thurs 8.30 - 12.00
Queens Hall

Pembroke
Thurs 9.30 - 1.00
Town Hall

Pembroke Dock
Fri 8.45 - 1.00
Pater Hall, Pembroke Dock

Penally
Wed 10.00 - 12.00 [April-end
Sept]Village Hall

Saundersfoot
Thurs 9.45-12.30
The Captain's Table, The
Harbour

* St. Davids & District
Thurs 10.00 - 12.00 [March-
Oct]
St. Davids Memorial Hall

Tenby
Fri 9.30- 11.30
St. John's Hall, Warren Street

GLAMORGAN

Barry
Thurs 2.30 - 3.30 [March-
Dec]
St. Paul's Hall, St. Paul's
Avenue

Cowbridge
Fri 10.00 - 11.30 [March-
Dec]
(9.45 on 1st Fri of month for
disabled and prams)
Lesser Hall

Llantwit Major & District
Fri 10.30 - 11.45 [March-
Dec]
The Pensioners Centre,
Llantwit Major

Oystermouth & District
Thurs 10.30 - 12.00 [April-
Oct] [Xmas Markets 7, 14 &
21 Dec] Victoria Hall, Dunns
Lane, Mumbles, Swansea

Porthcawl
Wed 10.30-12 noon
Ground Floor Room YMCA
25 John Street

GWENT

Abergavenny
Tues 8.30 - 1.00
Market Hall

Chepstow
Fri 8.00 - 12.00
Forecourt of Peacocks Store,
High Street

Monmouth
Fri 8.00 - 1.00 Shire Hall

Newport
Wed 11.00 - 1.00 [Feb-mid
Dec] St. Basil's Church Hall,
Caerphilly Road, Bassaleg

Usk
Thurs 9.15 - 11.15
Catholic Hall, Abergavenny
Road

GWYNEDD CAERNARFON

Pwllheli
Fri 9.00-12.00
The Old Library, Frondeg

Trefriw
Fri 10.00 - 12.00 [March-
Dec] Village Hall
1st Tuesday 10.00 - 12.00
St Mary Hall, Conwy

GWYNEDD-MEIRIONYDD

Bala
Thurs 9.45 - 11.45 [March-
Dec] Canolfan Bro Tegid,
High Street

Dolgellau
Thurs 9.30 - 12.00
Nevadd Idris Hall, Eldon
Square

POWYS-BRECKNOCK

Builth Wells
Fri 9.00 - 12.00
Builth Wells Post Office

Hay-on-Wye
Thurs 8.30 - 12.30
The Butter Market

POWYS-MONTGOMERY

Llanfyllin
Sat 9.00 - 11.00
Llanfyllin Public Institute

Newtown
Fri & Sat 9.00 - 2.00
Last Tues of each month 9.00
- 2.00
Newtown Market Hall

Welshpool
Sat 8.00 - 12.30
Food Hall, Welshpool Town
Hall

POWYS-RADNOR

Knighton & District
Sat 9.30 - 11.00
Knighton Farm Supplies,
Brookside

Llandrindod Wells & District
Fri 8.00 - 11.30
Gateway Arcade

CHANNEL ISLANDS

GUERNSEY

St. Peter's
Wed 10.00 - 11.30
Community Hall,
St. Peter's

Guernsey-Vale
Fri 9.30 - 10.30
Vale Douzaine Room

JERSEY

Georgetown
Tues 10.00 - 11.00
Georgetown Methodist
Church Hall,
St. Saviour

St. Peter's
Wed 2.00 - 3.00
Philadelphie Church Hall

I N D E X   B Y   F O O D   T Y P E

To avoid unhelpful repetition (for both the compiler and the reader of this index) we have not included every reference to staples such as biscuits, bread, cakes, cheese, eggs, fruit and vegetables, meat, milk, pies, sausages or wholefoods etc. for such items appear so regularly that they will be found on nearly every spread in the book. **We have however largely concentrated on specialist items**. In respect of the staples this means that for example eggs are included where they are free range, bread, say, where it is organic, sausages where they are from venison or game and meat where it is perhaps from a rare breed source.

INDEX BY BUSINESS NAME

I N D E X   O F   P L A C E   N A M E S

D I R E C T O R Y   O F   S H O P S

In the main listings of firms who produce and sell from their premises we have also mentioned shops where these products may also be purchased. The following is a directory of those shops with their telephone numbers. We have checked these numbers but should you experience difficulty in getting through we suggest you return to the original listings and ask the firm there to provide you with an alternative number.

Aardvark	01267 232497	Casa Marchini	01224 314981
Alana Wholefoods	0171 837 1172	Caseus	0171 720 7200
Alldays	01983 872627	Caterite	017687 73518
Alligator Wholefoods	01904 654525	Chalmer Bakery	013397 55474
Allon Meale & Son	01692 580226	Charles McHardy Butchers	
Allsorts Toffee Shop			01569 762693
Castle Douglas	01556 502903	Chatsworth Farm Shop	01246 583392
Arcadia	01232 381779	Cheese Box	01252 735758
Archiriboldos	01423 508760	Cheese Shop Chester	01244 346240
Arundell Arms	01566 784244	Cheeseboard	01684 891900
Ashfield Farm	0151 336 8788	Cheeseman	01603 768211
Bailey's Delicatessen	01978 860617	Cherry Gardens - Groombridge	
Bailey's Delicatessen	01502 710609		01892 863658
Balmoral Estate Shop	013397 42334	Chesterton Farm Shop	01285 653003
Barber and Manuel	01568 613381	Chiddingstone Causeway P.O. Stores	
Barratts of Cookridge	01132 674 414		01892 870327
Bath Cooked Meats	01225 425640	Chocolate Shop	01732 742350
Bawtry Delicatessen	01302 711114	Christys Farm Shop	01636 816472
Belsay Blacksmiths Coffee Shop		Clive Ramsay	01786 833903
	01661 881024	Clives Fruit Farm	01684 592664
Bluebird Store	0171 559 1000	Clovelly Fish	01237 470470
Boathouse Farm Shop	01825 750302	Cooks Pantry	01636 703313
Bon Gout Delicatessen	01392 435521	Corbins	01825 766670
Bradshaws Farm Shop	01902 844064	Corbridge Larder	01434 632948
Bran Tub	01684 891191	Corncraft	01449 740456
Brendan Anderton Butchers		Coufisserie Verdonh	01722 327422
	01772 783321	Country Bumpkins	01926 425571
Bristol Guild of Applied Arts		Country Cheeses	01822 615035
	01179 265 548	Country Foods, Exeter	01392 494049
Brodie Country Fayre	01309 641555	Country Kitchen	01986 872000
Brough Butcher	01704 574069	Country Kitchen	01896 822586
Bruce's Fishmongers	01608 661207	Country Produce, Horsham	
Buckwells of Southsea	01705 827753		01403 274136
Bumble Bee	0171 607 1936	Country Store, Helston	01326 564226
Burford Garden Co	01993 823117	Country Store, Falmouth	01326 311507
Burwash Manor Shop	01223 264674	County Stores	01823 272235
C.L. Lewis	01344 620481	Coxeter's	01367 252202
C.L. Lewis Ascot	01344 620141	Cubbons Fish Mongers	01624 822914
Cairns	01563 521639	Cumming & Spence	01856 872034
Cambs Farm Shop	01623 882036	Currant Affairs	0116 251 0887
Camelot Fruit Farm	01963 440280	D.W. Wall & Son, Ludlow	
Canterbury's Delicatessen	0115 981 2365		01584 872060

DANDIE SMOKED FOODS	01403 790454
DENIS BREWIN QUALITY FOODS	
	01509 215260
DERBYSHIRE LARDER	01629 584373
DODDINGTON POST OFFICE STORES	
	01795 886261
DOVECOTE DELICATESSEN	01963 351118
E H BOOTHS, KNUTSFORD	01565 652525
E. ALLAN & SON	01969 667219
E.W. KING	01787 372105
EDWARDS BUTCHERS	01492 592443
ELLERYS	01738 633362
EVERTONS OF OMBERSLEY	01905 620282
FAIRFIELD	01225 333129
FARMHOUSE	01452 521784
FENTON BARNS FARM SHOP	01620 850294
FENWICK'S OF NEWCASTLE	0191 232 5100
FERRY SHOP	01681 700470
FIELDS DELI	01493 332467
FINAGHY QUALITY FRUIT CENTRE	
	01232 612444
FINE CHEESE CO BATH	01225 463499
FINE CHEESE CO CHELTENHAM	
	01242 255022
FISH AND FOWL	0171 284 4184
FISHER & DONALDSON,	
DUNDEE	01382 223488
FISHER & DONALDSON,	
ST ANDREWS	01334 472201
FLORES HOUSE DELICATESSEN	01572 755601
FOOD FOR ALL SEASONS	01728 604414
FOOD FOR THOUGHT	01952 728038
FOOD FOR THOUGHT,	
GUILDFORD	01483 33841
FOOD FOR THOUGHT,	
KINGSTON	0181 546 7806
FOOD LIFE	0161 446 1123
FORTNUM & MASON	0171 734 8040
FRANKLIN HOUSE BAKERY	01790 753486
FRANKLINS CIDER	01584 810488
FRESH FRUITS	0131 6247057
FRESHLANDS	0171 250 1708
FRUIT BOWL	01222 383697
FULL OF BEANS	01273 472627
G WILLAM'S FARMSHOP	01905 756490
G.H. MACARTHUR & SON	01334 473339
GAIA	01926 338805
GARDEN FARM BLOFIELD	01603 715034
GARLANDS FARM	01491 671556
GARRISON CRAFTS	01475 530536
GARSON FARM SHOP	01372 464778
GEORGE BALL,	
CHORLEY MARKET	012572 66058
GEORGES, KINGTON	01544 231400
GLUTTONS	01865 553748
GOOD NATURE	01726 832110
GOOSE GREEN DELICATESSEN	0161 926 9895
GORDON GRANTS	01681 700382
GOURMETS LAIR	01463 225151
GOWANS	01983 873951
GRASSROOTS	0141 353 3278
GREEN CITY WHOLEFOODS	0141 556 7283
GREENAWAYS GARAGES	01566 775140
GREENMOUNT MEATS	01762 871393
GREENWHEEL	01179 559264
GROUSE INN, CABRACH	01466 702200
GROVELANDS FARM SHOP	01189 884822
GUY'S	01392 259338
H. MC ILCHERE & SON	01586 552309
HARRODS	0171 730 1234
HARROWAY ORGANIC	
GARDENS FARM SHOP	01256 895346
HARVEST WHOLEFOODS	01588 638990
HARVEST WHOLEFOODS	01225 465519
HARVESTORE, HEREFORD	01432 268209
HARVEY NICHOLS	0171 235 5000
HAYS CATERERS	01748 824052
HENDERSONS FARM SHOP	0131 225 6694
HERBIES DELI	0131 332 9888
HINTON STORES	01225 722401
HOCKERTON FARM SHOP	01636 816472
HOLE IN THE WALL	01584 811429
HOME FARM	0161 224 8884
HORNERS	01728 668336
HOUSE OF BRUAR	01796 483236
HOUSE OF CRAFTS	01929 422431
HOWARD & SON	01603 624928
HUDSON COFFEE HOUSE	0121 643 1001
HUDSONS	01323 724546
HULMES FISH SHOP	01335 342141
HUMES BUTCHERS	01379 852235
HUNTERS OF HELMSLEY	01439 771307
HUSSEYS, KINGTON	01544 230381
HUW JONES	01656 782862
I MCINTOSH	01346 516913
I R MELLIS	0131 447 7414 /8889
IAIN MELLIS	0131 2266215
ICE QUEEN	01736 795761
INFINITY FOODS	01273 603563
INTERNATIONAL CHEESE SHOP	
	0171 628 6637/0171 631 4191
J & J GRAHAMS	01768 862281
J. FORTEITH & SON	01631 569100
J.R. MITCHELL & SON	01573 224109
JACOBS	01326 315070
JED FOREST DEER FARM PARK	01835 840266
JEFF PEARCE	0121 643 3929
JENKINS COWBRIDGE	01446 773545

Jenners	0131 225 2442	Mycock Butchers	01433 630376
Jennings Butchers	0118 934 1447	No 27 Kensington Church Street	
Jeroboams Affineur	0171 924 4200		0171 937 9574
John Stockwell	0171 538 8711	Nadder Food Co	01722 744707
Kelly of Cults	01224 867596	Nancassick Farm Shop	01872 862224
Kelsey Brothers Farm Shop		Narraway's	01905 424488
	0181 300 9382	National Trust, Devon & Cornwall	
Kelso Home Bakery	01573 226782		01392 881912 / 01208 74099
Kendalls of Manchester	0161 832 3414	National Trust, Stourhead	
Kingfisher Farm	01306 730703		01747 840161
La Fromagerie	0171 359 7440	Natural Choice	01455 635254
La Patisserie	01222 843969	Natural Choice	01335 346096
Lairds Larder	01899 220639	Natural Food Store	01379 651832
Lane's Bakery	01638 741249	Natural Path	01460 62593
Lea's Farm Shop	01788 832640	Naughty But Nice	01326 573747
Ledgates	0171 727 8243	New Leaf	0131 228 8840
Lewis & Cooper	01609 772880	Newton Dee Village Store	01224 868609
Lidgates	0171 727 8243	Nickies Delicatessen	01142 665178
Limoncello	0171 713 1678	No 4 Chepstow Road	0171 229 5285
Loaves & Fishes	01394 385650	No 80 Queensway	0171 229 4459
Logans	01736 331520	Old Leake Post Office	01205 870201
Londis in Pewsey	01672 562270	Orford Supply Stores	01394 450219
Lou Hart	0171 515 2495	Organic & Options	01568 612154
Lowes Country Store	0131 660 2128	Oscars West Malling	01732 874377
Ludlow Larder	01584 877353	Oxford Cheese	01865 735703
Lurcocks of Lenham	01622 858345	Oxford Cheese Co	01865 721420
M & H Price	0121 427 2514	P. Bowditch Fish Shop	01823 253500
M Black	019755 62400	Palmers M.I. Filling Station	
M Balls	01603 755452		01846 662439
Mackintosh's of Marlborough		Park Farm, Snettisham	01485 542425
	01672 514069	Partridges	0171 730 0651
Macknade Farmshop	01795 534497	Pawson	01756 749260
Maddrell's Fish Mongers	01624 842643	Paxton & Whitfield	01225 466403
Main Stores Horning	01692 630236	Paxton & Whitfield	0171 930 0259
Marshford Organic Nursery		Peacocks	0117 974 1852
	01237 477160	Peckham & Rye	0141 445 4555
Martins Delicatessen	01963 350208	Peppers Whole Foods	0116 270 2974
Mayby's Delicatessen	01451 870071	Perry Court Farmshop	01233 812408
McIntosh of Marlborough		Peter M'Lennan	01397 702116
	01672 514069	Philberts of Darlington	01325 464479
Memorable Cheeses	01473 257315	Philip Warren & Son	01566 772089
Millhouse Delicatessen	0117 973 4440	Piggins Seafoods	01692 581763
Mis en Plas	0141 424 4600	Provender	01460 240681
Mooreland Foods	01625 548499	Provender Wholesales	01953 498639
Mousetrap Cheeseshop Hereford		Puddings & Pie	01626 834047
	01432 353423	Quintessence	01386 553689
Mousetrap Cheeseshop Leominster		R & J Davis	01263 512727
	01568 615512	R A Byford & Sons	01268 742021
Mr Christians Delicatessen		Rackman's	0121 236 3333
	0171 229 0501	Ramus Seafoods	01423 563271
Mrs Bumbles	01993 822209	Ray Harvey	01473 740221
Muker Village Store	01748 886409	Reahs	01765 689208
Mundesley Stores	01263 720391	Real Cheese & Wine	0117 962 8788
Murchies	0141 639 1269	Real Foods	0131 557 1911

Red Lion Delicatessen	01837 54234
Retail Outlet K.D.I.	01343 860321
Rileys Fruit & Veg	0151 608 6208
Rococo	0171 352 5857
Roots	0115 960 9014
Roy Dykes Butcher	01535 605808
Ryan's Stores	01858 880373
Ryans Wholefoods	0131 538 7295
Sacks	01803 863263
Salmons Farm Shop	01608 737371
Scotlands Larder	01333 360414
Seasons	01392 436125
Seasons, Forest Row	01342 824673
Selfridges & Co	0171 629 1234
Shelleys Delicatessen	01222 227180
Sherwood Wholefoods	01630 655155
Simply Sausages	0171 329 3227
Simply Scottish	01835 864696
Simpole Clarke	01780 480646
Skidmores	01666 840268
Smiths Greengrocers	01502 722149
Smithy Farm Shop	01765 640676
Snowdens & Co	01222 489948
Soyfoods	01664 560572
Spar Shop	01579 382912
Sparrows	01986 798207
Spice of Life	01225 864351
Spitalfields Organics	0171 377 8909
St. Augustines Fish	01227 771245
Stones Restaurant	01672 539514
Stovies Healthfoods	01303 851233
Sunnyfields	01703 871408
Super 'M' Blevan	01227 471243
Sutherland Brothers	01955 605070
T Robinson	01768 371388
Taste of Moray	01667 462340
Taylors of Tickhill	01302 742355
Terry's Fish	01273 487268
The Bath Sweet Shop	01225 428040
The Big Cheese	01224 637763
The Bran Tub	01208 76625
The Butterchurn	01383 830169
The Cheese & Wine Shop	01823 662899
The Cheese Shop	0141 337 6606
The Fruit Basket	01584 874838
The Health Food Shop	01203 346200
The Healthy Delicatessen	01349 866177
The Honeypot	015394 36267
The Organic Shop	01451 831004
The Ploughman	01142 812187
The Sausage Shop	01225 318300
The Scottish Deer Centre, Fife	
	01337 810391
The Seasons	01342 824673

The Stables Coffee Shop	01978 780704
The Treehouse	01970 615791
Thomas The Grocer	01986 894754
Throwers Ludham	01692 678248
Tony's Natural Foods	0171 837 5223
Top Notch Company	01730 813900
Total Organic	01224 593959
Traditional Foods	0115 981 3491
Tulleys Farm Shop	01342 718471/2
Valona & Crolla	0131 556 6066
Village Fayre	01225 752670
Villaudry	0171 631 3131
Vivians of Richmond	0181 940 3600
W Lobban & Son	01856 872585
W Martyn	0181 883 5642
Wainhouse Country Store	
	01840 230554
Wally's Delicatessen	01222 229265
Waterman's Food Hall	0117 973 2846
Watty's Delicatessen	01392 256654
Wavells	01983 760219
Weald P.O. Stores	01732 463201
Wealden Wholefoods	01892 783065
Well's Store	01235 535978
Wells Stores	01235 553748
Wensleydale Dairy Products	
	01969 667664
Westwoods	01969 623140
Whitwell's Delicatessen	01572 822588
Wholefoods, Paddington Street	
	0171 935 3924
Wild Oats	01179 731967
Wild Oats, Westbourne Grove	
	0171 229 1063
Wild Thymes	01672 516373
Williams of Wem	01939 232552
Windmill Farm Equestrian Centre	
	01423 503930
Windmill Hill City Farm	0117 966 2681
Worth Eating	01273 570172
Yorkshire Co-op	01274 729500

IRISH ORGANIC FARMERS' AND GROWERS' ASSOCIATION
56 Blessingham Street
Dublin 7
Ireland
Tel: 00 353 1830 7996

LONDON BETH DIN
Head Office, Kashrut Division
735 High Road
London
N12 0US
Tel: 0181 343 6253

ORGANIC FARMERS AND GROWERS LTD
30 High Street
Soham, Ely
Cambridgeshire
CB7 5HF
Tel: 01353 722398

ORGANIC FOOD FEDERATION
The Tithe House, Peaseland Green
Elsing
East Dereham
Norfolk
NR20 3DY
Tel: 01362 637314

ORGANIC LIVESTOCK MARKETING COOPERATIVE
c/o Mary Weston
Carpenters House, Tur Langton
Kibworth
Leicestershire
LE8 0PJ
Tel: 01858 545564

SCOTTISH ORGANIC PRODUCERS ASSOCIATION
Milton of Cambus Farm
Doune
Perthshire
FK16 6HG
Tel: 01786 841657

THE BIO-DYNAMIC AGRICULTURAL ASSOCIATION
Rudolf Steiner House
35 Park Road
London
NW1 6XT
Tel: 01562 884933

THE SOIL ASSOCIATION
Bristol House
Victoria Street, Bristol
BS1 6DF
Tel: 0117 929 0061

THE VEGETARIAN SOCIETY
Parkdale
Durham Road
Altrincham
Cheshire
WA14 4QG
Tel: 0161 928 0793

TRADITIONAL FARMFRESH TURKEY ASSOCIATION
5 Beacon Drive
Seaford
East Sussex
BN25 2JX
Tel: 01323 899802

UKROFS
Room 320C
c/o **Ministry of Agriculture, Fisheries and Food (MAFF)**
Nobel House
17 Smith Square
London
SW1P 3JR
Tel: 0171 238 5915

WAITROSE
Southern Industrial Area
Bracknell
Berkshire
RG12 8YA
Tel: 01344 424680

Also from The Write Angle Press

The Craftworker's Year Book
ISBN 0 9520737 9 X
Nineteenth year in print

an annual directory of craft fairs and craft event organisers.
The most comprehensive guide to the craft circuit available with
dates and venues for thousands of events and markets.

Details for event organisers, including full contact information,
exhibiting costs, selection policy and admission prices.

An essential guide for both exhibitor and visitor on the craft fair circuit.

CraftFinder
ISBN 0 9520737 4 9
in cooperation with the Rural Development Commission

a guide to UK Craft Shops, Galleries and craftworkers who
sell direct from their premises.

both books available from book shops priced £9.95

and from The Write Angle Press on
0181 770 7087 and 0181 298 0929